Hideyuki Takeda Komaki

THE MAKING
OF SCOTLAND

An Illustrated Ethnographical
Account of Scotland
Leading to its Establishment
as the United Kingdom of Scotland

K., M. & C. Publishers

The covers show the Five Sisters of Kintail which flank
the northern side of Glen Shiel (front) and Dawn
on Loch Fyne (back, see page 245)

ISBN 0-9526476-0-5

This edition published in Scotland by K., M. & C. Publishers,
Inverness, U.K.

Sales Agent in Japan: Japan-Scotland Society, 5-25-6, Hiroo,
Sibuyaku, Tokyo 150 Japan. Tel. 03 (3473) 1891.

Complete origination by Hiscan, Inverness.
Printed in Great Britain by Highland Printers, Inverness.

CONTENTS

ACKNOWLEDGMENTS

Time goes swift like an arrow and my travels in Scotland had been undertaken thirty-six times by March 1995 when I retired as Professor of English Literature at Tamagawa University, Tokyo, an institution I had served for twenty-four years.

I have a great fondness for the country of Scotland, taking great delight in its picturesque rural landscapes in which hills, rivers, lochs, dwelling houses, wild and domestic animals, and so on, are as if in harmony with Nature, once a similar situation in old Japan. However, what has been and is a source of great trouble for me is a foreign language and culture which have ethnic identities quite distinct from my own.

In this book, I deal with the historical and ethnographical affairs of pre-Scotland days and for me it was a task of extreme difficulty to translate the text and accurately express such matters in English. Fortunately, Mr Duncan MacLennan, formerly a teacher of English in Inverness, was able to assist me with this formidable undertaking, intermittently, over a period of three years. My thanks are due to him, without whose help and generosity the publication of this book would not have been possible.

Also, I must gratefully acknowledge the help of Mr Walter Cumming, a former teacher of Art, who kindly took the trouble to draw the illustrations for my book. Additional thanks are due to my old friends, Mr Geoff and Mrs Barbara Kirby of Winton, Bournemouth, and to my various friends who frequent The Corriegarth Hotel, Inverness, all of whom have given me sound advice and warm-hearted encouragement over the years.

Finally, I respectfully dedicate this book to the fond memory of three of my erstwhile professors: the late Toyoaki Takahashi and Toshio Nanba, founder-members of our Japan Caledonia Society; and the late Mr Shigenobu Segawa who was my influential professor in my student days. They were all learned men, well acquainted with Scottish affairs, and gave me the benefit of their cordial counsel, tuition, inspiration and support over a considerable number of years.

H. T. Komaki

NOTE ON TRANSLATION

This is an English language version of a book originally published in Japanese and aimed at Japanese readers, particularly students and others with a specialised interest in the subject.

The main intention was – and is now – to present information gleaned from a variety of sources, supplemented by an extensive photographic record, with a conscious restraint in drawing interpretative conclusions.

The translation is essentially that of Mr Komaki but was primarily expressed in his personally unique form of English. Thereafter, alterations have been made only when the intended meaning might be obscured.

Of necessity, there have had to be many corrections and amendments with relation to grammar, spelling, punctuation, etc. but changes in word usage, forms of expression, idiosyncratic syntax and general mode of address have been kept to a minimum in order that the distinctive "voice" of the author be maintained.

Any temptation to re-cast thoughts and ideas has been studiously avoided, even to the extent of retaining archaic expressions and obsolescent or obsolete words. Thus, what the reader receives is what the author says and in the manner of his saying it.

PREFACE

The word "Scotia," the etymological source of "Scotland," meant "Ireland" in Old Celtic and the term "Scotland," which we now use daily, is the shortened nomenclature for "The United Kingdom of Scotland" which was established in 1034 with the enthronement of King Duncan I (1034 – 40), a descendant of the royal family of Scots who came from Northern Ireland (in 498 or 500 A.D.) to Kintyre or Epidum and there founded "Dalriada" or "the Kingdom of the Men of Britain." The present name "Scotland" arose from the establishment of this kingdom.

However, it is difficult to define precisely whose land this was and who were "the Scots," in light of the fact that Neolithic and Bronze Age settlers had flowed in there following the Mesolithic Age. In addition, the Vikings and the Pictish, (whose origins are uncertain), later intermingled with established inhabitants, though the settlers who arrived in the Iron Age were Celts and of the same race as "the Scots," for the Romans called the country "Caledonia" or "the land of the Celts."

After its establishment, the territory of Scotland was, roughly speaking, the domain north of the line linking Berwick-upon-Tweed, the north of Northumbria, and the Solway Firth. The Inner and Outer Hebrides, Orkney and Shetland were the territories of the Vikings, mainly of Norwegian jarls, from about the beginning of the 7th century to the 15th century. In 1266 under the reign of Alexander III (1249 – 86), the Inner and Outer Hebrides were ceded to Scotland in return for 4,000 marks and an annual leasehold charge of 100 marks. This became effective with the Treaty of Perth which followed the "Battle of Largs." The historical background to this was the decline of the national power of Norway and, especially, the death of Magnus, the ruler of the Isle of Man. Orkney and Shetland became part of Scotland in 1470 and 1473 respectively as deposit for the unpaid dowry of Margaret of Norway who had married James III, king of Scotland (1451 – 88). This was agreed by Christian I, father of Margaret and the king of Norway (1450 – 81) and Denmark (1448 – 81).

The sovereignty of established Scotland had temporarily transferred to Maelbaeth or Macbeth (1040 – 57), and then passed to the Canmore Dynasty, the progenitor of which was Malcolm III (1057 – 93), son of Duncan. [1] The line continued through Donald Bane, Duncan II, Donald Bane, Edgar, Alexander I, David I, Malcolm IV, William I (the Lion), Alexander II, and on to Alexander III.

The kingdom prospered throughout the Dynasty, especially under the reigns of the three Alexanders. However, the last Alexander, who had a great deal of influence over Norway after he had acquired the Hebrides, had no successor and he was succeeded by Margaret (1286 – 90), his grand-daughter and the daughter of Erick Magnusson II (1280 – 99) of Norway who had married Margaret, daughter of

Alexander III in 1281 This Margaret (or "the Maid of Norway") was the person with whom Edward I of England (1272 – 1307) had arranged the betrothal of his son (afterwards Edward II) to the queen of Scotland. Her sudden death in 1290 was followed by a succession dispute between the two families of Bruce and Balliol with the interference of Edward I into Scotland's affairs. Scotland was thus confronted with a critical situation with regard to its independence.

In the contest between Bruce and Balliol, in which Edward was virtually the arbitrator, Balliol was chosen as king in 1292 Balliol, who had once paid homage to Edward, afterwards renounced his allegiance to him and a war followed which was a struggle on Edward's part for sovereignty and on Scotland's part for independence. Scotland was invaded by Edward in 1296 The Scots under William Wallace won a battle at Stirling in 1297, but in the following year they were defeated at Falkirk. On the death of Wallace in 1305, Robert Bruce succeeded as national leader and acceded to the throne as Robert I (1306 – 29) in the following year. In 1314 the independence of Scotland was secured by the victory of Bannockburn and this was recognized by Edward III in 1328. However, in the period 1296 to 1328 Scotland was only once under England as a dependency.

Robert I was succeeded by his son David I (1329 – 71). Robert II (1371 – 90), who succeeded David I, was the son of Bruce's daughter Margaret, who had married Walter, the sixth highest steward in the court, and this Robert became the first sovereign of the Stuart Dynasty which came to an end with the defeat at the Battle of Culloden in 1746. This dynasty continued with Robert III (1390 – 1406), son of Robert II; James I (1406 – 37), son of Robert III; James II (1437 – 60), son of James I; James III (1460 – 88), son of James II; James IV (1488 – 1513), son of James III; James V (1513 – 42), son of James IV; Mary Queen of Scots (1542 – 67), daughter of James V; and James VI (1567 – 1625), son of Mary. James IV invaded England in 1513 and suffered a disastrous defeat at Flodden. In 1547, under the reign of Mary, Queen of Scots, Scotland was invaded by an English army under the Duke of Somerset and was defeated at Pinkie. Mary introduced the Reformation in 1560, and in 1603 James VI, the great-grandson of James IV who had married Margaret, daughter of Henry VII, acceded to the throne of England on the failure of a direct heir following the death of Elizabeth I of England, the last of Henry VIII's descendants.

Other important historical events were the success of the Covenanters against Charles I (1639 – 40); the persecution of the Covenanters under Charles II and James II; and the legislative union of the two kingdoms of England and Scotland in 1707 The Stuart sovereignty of England and Scotland was inherited by Charles I (1625 – 49), son of James I of England and VI of Scotland; Charles II (1662 – 85), son of Charles I; James II of England and VII of Scotland (1685 – 89), son of Charles I; Mary (of Modena, 1689 – 94), eldest daughter of James II and consort of William III; and Anne (1702 – 14), daughter of James II. However, on the death of Queen Anne in 1714 the sovereignty was transferred to George I (1714 – 27), son of Ernest Augustus, the elector of Hanover, and Sophia, grand-daughter of James I. James Francis Edward Stuart (1688 – 1776, son of James II and his second wife Modens) and his son, Charles Edward Stuart maintained their claims to the throne, but their claims were refuted. James Francis Edward Stuart rose in revolt in 1715 and his son Charles in 1745 and 1746 along with their supporters, the "Jacobites" (from the Latin for "James"), but they were defeated at the "Battle of Culloden" and the Stuarts ended as a royal family.

The ties between Scotland and myself date back to some forty years ago. My professor, Mr Shigenobu Segawa, was a graduate of Edinburgh University before the War and was thus sympathetic to Scotland. The outset of my ties with Scotland began with his recommendation that I specialize in Scottish affairs, the aim being finally to establish what exactly is the ethnographical state of affairs with respect to the Scottish people. I read texts on ethnic customs, folklore, religious faith, legends and so on, but everything I read and came to know was at first too complex to accept and understand and I was troubled by its obscure nature. I also tried to explicate the mythological background and the attributes of deities which often form the corner stone of human beliefs and customs.

However, it was an almost hopeless task. Druidism, which seems to have been the principal religion before the introduction of Christianity, was a word-of-mouth traditon and its mythological system and doctrine have never been left as written documents. What I came to know was only that they were animistic nature-worshippers who had faith in reincarnation and the transmigration of the soul to the world to which they would go after death, according to the fragmentary descriptions which Greek and Roman classical authors have left.

Originally I had no intention to make a pilgrimage to Scotland. However, I thought that field research might not necessarily be ineffective as a means of obtaining something helpful in pursuing my study. I hoped to encounter what was important about the culture, institutions and customs proper to Scotland and my pilgrimage began in 1973, the year when I achieved my position as professor in the university where I had worked to deal with matters Scottish, and thenceforth I was to go back and forth between Japan and Scotland, each spring and summer, twice in a year.

What I encountered and gathered were mostly antiquities of Scotland which were quite different from what I had originally expected and intended to obtain. There were the ancient monuments which, left by the ancient people there by chance, projected their fleeting days into the landscape of immortality: shell-mounds left by the Mesolithic immigrants who drifted ashore with the tide and wind; chambered cairns and settlements, which Neolithic settlers built, and the utensils they used; megalithic henges, cromlech, menhirs, alignments which Bronze Age settlers built as their sites for rituals and astronomical observations, along with their cairns without chambers, cup-and-ring mark and cup-mark stones which are said to be copies of constellations and diagrams of the orbits of the moon; hill-forts, brochs and settlements and utensils of Iron Age immigrants; Roman forts, stone altars, stone images of deities, and tablets offered to favourite gods and goddesses; enigmatic Pictish symbol stones telling of the social phenomena of the Dark Age; Christian crosses of earliest days; settlements of Vikings; and so on.

My father had been a professional photographer (before the War), while I was not, but as a traveller I took over 55,000 photographs of these ancient monuments. Most of what I acquired was far removed from what I had wanted, due to various circumstances. However, I gathered a certain amount of data which seemed to be related to the kernels of wonders and mysteries recurring in folktales and folklore. Thus was born the idea of converting these data into a book, and I wrote *The History and Civilization of Scotland and its Folklore from the Neolithic Age to the Dark Age* in a recent Japanese publication. This I produced for Japanese students to introduce the country, people, and institutions of ancient Scotland before it had been established in its own name.

Strange to say, in my country, Japan, many people have not realized that Scotland has been and is a member country of the United Kingdom of Great Britain, together with the fact that it was originally an independent kingdom. The veritable cause of such a want of comprehension is no doubt in the nomenclature Japan has given to the terms "English" and "Britain" and not in the fact that the English dynasty has existed for a long time with its capital in London. Such a lack of understanding has obstructed the realization of the true significance of the individual nature of Scotland and the "Union Jack," and through my book I wanted to correct the mental inclination whereby in Japan "Britain" became interpreted as "England" and "British" as "English."

However, it is very fortunate that I can now publish it in an English version with the kind support of my friends in Scotland, especially of Mr Duncan MacLennan. I will deal with what the ancient precursors of Scotland left, what they thought and did, and the legacy of their institutions and customs, along with their ancient monuments.

With regard to the religions of the ancients, unrelated to the East or the West, they were all animists and animistic nature worshippers. I will cover this animistic nature-worship, views on reincarnation and the transmigration of the soul, belief in the after-life, all of which occupied the minds of the precursors of Scotland; their outlook on reading omens, good and bad, of colours and bearings; the source of traditions related to aquatic animals; and the traditions which, arisen from remote antiquity, were stored up in the minds of the ancients and still survive. The timespan to be dealt with is from the Neolithic Age to the establishment of the United Kingdom of Scotland, that is, before "Scotland" had existed. I will include photographs of items of interest and fine appearance where appropriate and relevant.

*   *   *   *

In my travels in Scotland over twenty years I have been indebted to so many people for help in research that it is impossible to name all of them individually. I was also obliged to consult a lot of data and documents, written by many great elders, on the archaeology, history, folk customs and so on of Scotland, as shown in the list of reference books at the end of this book. Though the three capitals shown in parentheses in the text indicate the abbreviations of the books which I consulted for advice, with acknowledgments, I must express my heartfelt thanks to those ladies and gentlemen and great senior scholars to whom or from whose writings I was obliged to refer or quote. And again I must acknowledge the generosity of the staff of Hiscan and Highland Printers, Inverness, who gave me kind advice and warm-hearted assistance in publishing this book.

*   *   *   *

In Scotland, a series of winds comes blowing over the country before spring. The wind which blows at the end of winter is the "Wolf tempest," and after it come the gales known as "Feadag" or "Whistle," a three-day wind. Next comes "Gobag", the sharp-billed one which pecks in every corner - a searching, wounding wind lasting for nine days. After the Gobag comes the "Sguabag," the wind of broom or besom which for many days sweeps over land and sea, whirling in wild gusts; then "Gearan" or "Complaint," a dry sighing and moaning wind of the "period of leanness." The death time of Cailleach Bheur or Beira, "daughter of Jack Frost", is near at hand.

Spring 1995 at Inverness

1

Photograph (1) shows "Cnoc Sligeach", one of the Mesolithic shell-mounds on a small islet, Oronsay, in the Southern Hebrides. These were left by Mesolithic settlers who had drifted ashore impelled by unavoidable tide and wind. This one measures about 25 metres in diameter, 2.5 metres in height and lies just above sea-level, though it must have arisen after the falling of the high sea level of the post-glacial epoch.

Excavations in the middens have revealed artefacts such as hammer-stones, stones with ground ends, antlers, bone implements such as fish-hooks, awls, harpoon-heads and a mass of shellfish debris which relates to the economy of the Mesolithic communities who gathered their food entirely from natural sources.

Oronsay is a small islet, its total measure being only three square miles, and the shell mounds are lonely relics which have been exposed by those five winds blowing at the beginning of every spring for these past 8,000 or 9,000 years.

CONTENTS OF ILLUSTRATIONS AND FIGURES

Illustrations

Figures

CHAPTER I

CHAMBERED CAIRNS, ANTIQUITIES OF THE NEOLITHIC AGE

From about 4000 B.C. to 2500 B.C., Neolithic settlers arrived in Scotland in regular succession. They are presumed to have been early peasant farmers who seem to have reared sheep and cattle and eked out their diet with hunting and fishing, according to evidence which has been excavated. Their homelands are supposed to have been somewhere in southern Britain, Ireland and Western Europe, since constructions similar to theirs are widely distributed there.

These new immigrants constructed chambered cairns and community dwellings (see p75) with the foundations half-

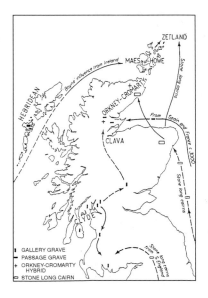

Figure 1 is a distribution map of chambered cairns which were built in Scotland by 2500 B.C., classified by type and surmised places of origin. Differences in individual cairns, (which vary in size, shape, structure of covering, chamber, entrance and facade) seem to stem from race, geometrical habits, scale of immigration, and so on. Chambered cairns have been classified, from the structural point of view, as consisting of two main types - gallery-graves and passage-graves.

buried in the ground and having inside walls built with slabs and blocks of stones. They have left no written record, as was the case with the Egyptians, but they are supposed to have been excellent navigators. Their cairns and settlements are distributed widely throughout the country in the coastal area and its vicinities.

A gallery-grave is a tomb, to the original dolmen of which were appended chambers, one after another, and a series of chambers, serving as a passageway, led to an entrance opening in a forecourt. This type of cairn has been archaeologically presumed to have been brought in by Neolithic people who came from Western Europe. It commonly falls into what is known as the "Clyde-Carlingford group," occurring mainly in Galloway, Arran, Argyle, the Clyde estuary and the Central region. The external appearance of this group is mostly circular or oval with a concave facade.

A passage-grave is a tomb in which an oval chamber or a series of chambers stretches out and connects lengthwise or sideways to the passage leading to the forecourt. At times plural chambers or compartments occupy the centre of the tomb in trefoil or quartrefoil form. The Hebridean, the Orkney-Cromarty, and the Shetland-Clava groups are included in this category. The external appearance is multifarious: some are circular or oval and have a heel-shaped concave facade; others are oblong with a horn pushing out at each corner. Chambered cairns in Japan were mainly built for the interment of successively enthroned emperors and members of the imperial house [2] which began round about 650 B.C., the last period of the Bronze Age. Square in front and round at the back, they were situated in various districts throughout the country, but examples of cairns constructed for the general public are rare. Chambers with paintings on the inside walls have sometimes been found under huge earthern oval mounds from which have been excavated grave-goods such as bell-shaped bronze vessels and swords.

In Scotland, Neolithic Age chambered cairns were also tombs for interment but for whom they were intended is not clear. Though it is uncertain whether they were for the chiefs of the community, as with the Egyptian Pyramids, or for his or her family, or for general community members, most of these chambered cairns became the property of Bronze Age people who observed cremation as their burial mode and thus inhumation burials and cremated bone are sometimes intermingled, together with grave-goods of both the Neolithic and Bronze Ages.

The coverings of the cairns are usually cobbles; their shapes are circular, oval, square or rectangular; and ordinarily a single chamber is set inside and roofed with corbelled vaults or large slabs. The chamber, usually mostly oval or rectangular and at times divided into several compartments by low slab walls, is set in the depths of the cairn like a human womb. The aperture in the middle of a concave facade serves as an entrance through to the passage and usually points to a certain bearing where the sun or the moon repeats its resurrection.

Robert Graves, the author of *The White Goddess*, calls these monuments "Wombs of Earth," and claims that the entrance opening, though it consists of a lintel and upright stones, is a dial to show the passage of the lunar months as the moon appears throughout the year. Mr Graves has a figure which consists of the initial letters of the thirteen tree names which begin with the Gaelic consonants, together with the five Gaelic vowels as shown in Figure (2). Using this he demonstrates that the year begins with the month of "B" at the bottom left-hand side and, revolving clockwise with each month of twenty-eight days, ends with the month of "R." The year begins on the second day after the winter solstice with the next day as a missing day, and he also subscribes to the idea that the five vowels at the bottom symbolize the name of the Creator "Jehovah" or "Iehobhah" in Gaelic. [3]

The pointer of the Plough indicates east in spring, south in summer, west in autumn and north in winter. The sun passes over the solstitial and equinoctial points twice in a year, as it repeats its transmigrations, while the moon completes its tour in a

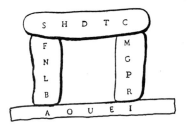

Figure 2

cycle of twenty-eight days, thirteen times in a year. As with the Plough, the sun and the moon are clock dials of the heavens. The aperture of "Womb of Earth" was a "clock" for Neolithic people and a pointer to where the sun and the moon, ejecting an arrow of light, told the time to the "dead" who were waiting for the day of their reincarnation in the "Womb of Earth."

Chambered cairns were therefore places for the observation of rituals allied to the resurrection of the dead. Near the cairns, at times, stands a standing stone or "Phallus" to fulfill the unity of body and soul, though alignment and cromlech were added to some of these structures later in the Bronze Age. This kind of structure was also a means to mensurate the movements of heavenly bodies in addition to being concerned with rituals. Settlers in the primeval ages inevitably felt isolated, exposed and insecure and, being in an immense expanse of primordial forest, thus had a powerful urge to increase their numbers.

1. GALLERY-GRAVES IN SOUTH-WESTERN AND WESTERN SCOTLAND

This type of tomb numbers over fifty, and typical ones are: Cairnholy Chambered Cairns; Mid Gleniron Chambered Cairn in Dumfries and Galloway; Torrylin Chambered Cairn in the Isle of Arran; Nether Largie South Chambered Cairn and Crarae Chambered Cairn in Mid Argyle; and Clach na Tiompan Chambered Cairn in Perthshire.

Cairnholy Chambered Cairns are tombs situated some 150 metres apart on a hillside overlooking the east shore of Wigtown Bay, 4 miles south-east of Creetown. The Southern cairn, Cairnholy Chambered Cairn (I), is 43 metres by 10 metres and the ruined chamber and the crescentic upright stones of the facade make an impressive

2

Photograph (2) shows the entrance and facade of Cairnholy Chambered Cairn (II) and its weird dolmen which stimulates a mysterious, emotional response.

arrangement. The inner chamber and the antechamber (which was appended to the inner one) are probably the earliest parts of the structures set in the cairn. The facade and hearth outside the chamber are presumed to belong to the second phase structure or that which was appended in the Bronze Age. The alignment of nine standing stones, though the original number is unknown, was probably a Bronze Age device to mensurate the movements of heavenly bodies, and the hearth was something connected with a fire-cult in primeval religion. Western Scotland Neolithic pottery sherds, beaker pottery, leaf-shaped arrow-heads, flint knives, food vessel sherds, and so on have been discovered.

The northern cairn, Cairnholy Chambered Cairn (II), is a smaller cairn which measures some 20 metres by 10 metres with its opening between the portal stones, exposing a bipartite chamber. The rear compartment still has its roof, and the portal stones, which still stand to a height of about 3 metres, are very impressive. Objects discovered include beaker pottery, flint tools, and so on.

Mid Gleniron Chambered Cairn, situated 2.5 miles north of Glenluce in Wigtownshire, is a tomb which once possessed a crescentic facade and chamber at the north end with an additional chamber in the middle of the cairn. It is presumed that between the two original chambered cairns another cairn was constructed and the three cairns were united into one long cairn. Thirty-five metres in length, it is 9 metres in width near the south end and 12 metres near the north end. This cairn had almost certainly been used as a burial place in the Bronze Age, considering that nine cremations in cinerary urns have been discovered there.

Torrylin Chambered Cairn has a covering which has been so severely devastated as to make it impossible to determine its original shape, but it is a gallery-grave of the Clyde-Carlingford group which supports the case that chambers were successively appended to the original dolmen. The mound is rectangular and the principal part of the tomb comprises four compartments with pairs of slabs lengthwise to each compartment and with each compartment divided by traverse slabs. The outer section, the entrance and the facade, facing the south-west, are now destroyed. Objects discovered indicate the remains of six adults and a child; a fragmentary Neolithic bowl; a flint knife; and the bones of both domesticated and wild animals such as pig, lamb, ox, otter, bird and fish. These are surmised to have been a dedication to the dead or the remains of a ritual feast.

Nether Largie Chambered Cairn South at Kilmartin, 6.5 miles north of Lochgilphead, is also a tomb which shows most impressively the features of the gallery-grave. The chamber, situated at the centre of a cairn some 40 metres in diameter, is walled by upright slabs and measures 6 metres in length and 1.2 metres in width. Still roofed,

3

Photograph (3) shows the linked chambers of the Torrylin Chambered Cairn where many finds have been excavated.

there are traces that three chambers were added to the original dolmen with traverse slabs and a pair of blocking slabs adjoining the facade. The entrance faces the south-west. The final shape of the cairn is supposed to owe much to a supplementary alteration at the Bronze Age stage when two cists were inserted, one on the north side and the other south-west of the chamber. The original shape of the cairn is thought to have been trapezoidal as the stretch of covering cobbles shows. Neolithic vessels, quartz chips, inhumation burials and other relics have been discovered.

Crarae Chambered Cairn is situated in the premises of Crarae Lodge, one of the most famous Scottish gardens, some 3 miles south-west of Furnace in Mid Argyle. The mound of this tomb is trapezoidal, measuring 35 metres by 18 metres and the drystone walling facade stands some 10 metres in length and in parts to a height of 1 metre.

4

5

Photographs (4) and (5) show the uncovered chamber, the entrance and the segmented compartments of Nether Largie South Chambered Cairn.

The chamber, built of large slabs, is multilateral and its measurements are 5 metres in length by 1.2 metres in width, its forecourt showing traces that it had once been paved. Excavations have not uncovered any important materials.

Clach na Tiompan Chambered Cairn is a ruined tomb with its axis running from north-west to south-east on the north bank of the River Almond, 7 miles south-west of Amulree. It measures 60 metres in length by 11 metres in width, its south-east end being larger. It is a long cairn in which four burial chambers were built, leaving us with a vivid impression that it was once the religious centre of an ancient community which had been there for a long time.

One of the chambers suggests that it was once composed of four large slabs and a capstone with two small segmented compartments in front. It is situated to the north-west, 10 metres from the south-east end, though now it is blocked. There is a second segmented chamber with two compartments 6 metres further west, a third chamber 12 metres east of the north-west end, and a fourth chamber, now destroyed, inserted between the second and third chambers.

6

Photograph (6) shows the chamber of Crarae
Chambered Cairn.

2. PASSAGE-GRAVES OF THE HEBRIDEAN GROUP AND A NOTE ON OSIRIS, THE GOD OF THE EGYPTIAN HELIOPOLIS

The Inner and Outer Hebrides comprise an assembly of yellow sand islands, quite natural but now with few trees, and many chambered cairns survive there. Among the well-preserved are Rubh'an Dunain Chambered Cairn and Ullinish Lodge Chambered Cairn in Skye; Dun Bharpa Chambered Cairn in Barra; Reineaval Chambered Cairn in South Uist; Cletraval Chambered Cairn and Bharpa Langass Chambered Cairn in North Uist; and Callanish Chambered Cairn and Steinacleit Chambered Cairn in Lewis. But chambered cairns in this region are not necessarily the kinds of passage-graves in which a series of chambers stretch out and connect with the entrance through the passage.

Cletraval Chambered Cairn in North Uist belongs to the tombs of the Clyde-Carlingford group, while Callanish Chambered Cairn is a hybrid of gallery and passage tombs. Characteristics common to Hebridean tombs are that the entrance faces mainly the east or the south-east, the plan of the cairn is circular and its chamber is also circular or oval.

Rubh'an Dunain Chambered Cairn at the head of Loch Brittle, 3.5 miles south-west of the Cullin Hills in Skye, measures 20 metres in diameter by 3 metres in height, its entrance facing south-east by east. The passage at its centre is about 3 metres long, quite low and narrow, and it leads to a circular chamber which is now roofless and walled with large slabs, through a bipartite antechamber from a concave forecourt. Though this Cairn was built in the 3rd millenium B.C. and fragments of Neolithic pottery, quartz pebbles, flint, and quartz chips have been found, a beaker used in the later Bronze Age has also been found in a cairn to which access is not easy.

Reineaval Chambered Cairn in South Uist is a circular tomb which measures about 23 metres in diameter and 3.5 metres in height. The cairn itself is encircled by an intermittent peristalith standing to a height of 1 to 2 metres. A cover stone of the chamber is exposed near the east quadrant and traces of the passage can be detected to the east of it.

Bharpa Langass Chambered Cairn, on the western slope of Ben Langass in North Uist, is a circular cairn, the measurement of which is some 25 metres in diameter and 4 metres in height. The passage, measuring 4 metres by 2 metres, is on the east quadrant and, though now partially blocked by fallen stones at the entrance, it is said that it led to an oval chamber which, walled by large slabs and a filling of drystones, lay 4 metres long from east to west and 1.5 metres wide from south to north. The tomb shows traces of use in the later Bronze Age: beaker pottery, barbed arrowheads, pieced talc discs and other artefacts have been excavated.

Callanish Chambered Cairn in Lewis is a Neolithic tomb which Sir James Matheson (1796–1887), the owner of the island, found in 1857 in the course of his excavations for peat supply to the islanders. To the old chambered cairn there was appended in the Bronze Age a new chamber and alignment consisting of thirty-five or more megaliths and a thirteen-megalith cromlech 13 metres in diameter. The chamber is situated in the centre of this cromlech of thirteen megaliths (see p58) and lies 5.4 metres long from east to west and some 4.7 metres wide from south to north. The appended chamber, of a different width, serves as a passage to the original chamber, turning to the passage opening where there is a megalith called "The Callanish Phallus" or "The Epitaph of the Callanish Chambered Cairn" situated in the direction of sunset at the winter solstice (see photo 80).

7

Photograph (7) shows a panoramic view of the Bharpa Langass Chambered Cairn. The loch beyond the cairn is Loch Langass.

This "Callanish Phallus" reminds us of the ancient Egyptian legend of Osiris whose death and resurrection were annually celebrated with alternate sorrow and joy. Seth, the god of Heliopolis in Egypt, killed his brother Osiris, the god of the Nether World (representing one year of 365 days) and, breaking his body into fourteen parts, cast away the remaining fourteenth part, his phallus, into the Nile. Isis, the sister and wife of Osiris, tried to restore Osiris's body to its former state but she could not find the phallus. Therefore, instead of it, she dedicated a statue of the phallus (representing the missing day).

The structure, which consists of one monolith and a cromlech of 13 standing stones, is a symbol of the Under World and signifies a year of the lunar calendar (thirteen months, with each month consisting of twenty-eight days) and a missing day (or the day of the Phallus), and represents a dial which mensurates the year. Sites with a cromlech of 13 megaliths and a monolith, as in the Callanish Chambered Cairn, are imagined to have been places for ritual and for astronomical observation by the community.

[4] Osiris was the offspring of Thoth and his love, Nut, the sky-goddess who, by a curse of the sun-god, Ra, her husband, was

8

Photograph (8) shows a part of the cromlech of the Callanish Chambered Cairn. The tomb has a resemblance to that of the Camster Chambered Cairn in Caithness and South Yarrows Chambered Cairn in Sutherland, in respect of having appended to the main chamber another chamber of different width with a passage and forecourt.

forbidden to give birth to a child in any month of any year. Thoth was the god who, playing at draughts with the Moon, won a seventy-second part of every day and, having compounded five whole days out of these parts, added them to the Egyptian year of three hundred and sixty days. Osiris, Horus, Seth, Isis and Nyphthys were born in these five days which were regarded as being outside the year of twelve months where the curse of the sun-god applied. These five names of gods and goddesses were attached to the five supplementary days which Egyptians needed to insert at the end of every year in order to establish a harmony between lunar and solar time.

Reigning as a king on earth, Osiris reclaimed the Egyptians from savagery, giving them laws and teaching them to worship the gods. To these former cannibalists he introduced the cultivation of grain such as wheat and barley, the gathering of fruits, a corn diet, the brewing of beer from barley and the making of wine from grapes. After being killed by Seth, the broken body of the murdered god, pieced together with the aid of Isis, Nyphthys, Thoth and Horus, was resurrected as a personification of the great yearly vicissitudes of nature and Osiris acquired the title of Lord of the Under World, Lord of Eternity and Ruler of the Dead.

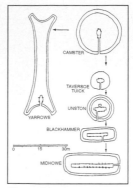

Figure 3

3. PASSAGE-GRAVES OF THE ORKNEY-CROMARTY GROUP

In the Caithness, Sutherland, Orkney and Cromarty regions, which have not been urbanized, there is scattered a great number of well-preserved passage-graves. The tombs in these regions are classified into two types. One is the round cairn and the other is the Pyramid-like long cairn, most of which were built or

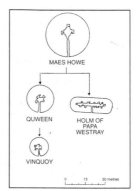

Figure 4

remodelled by settlers coming from Lybia or around there by way of Spain and Southern and Northern France from 2500 B.C. to 2000 B.C.

A characteristic common to both types is that the chamber inside is elongated or circular and the passage is set lengthwise or sideways to the chamber and connected to the facade outside, with some tombs having heel-shaped horns which run as if to embrace the forecourt, while others have no horns. These tombs are further classified into two types according to the structure of chamber inside. The type in which the chamber is stalled by a partition wall or has an antechamber is a tomb of "the Camster type"; and those in which trefoil or quatrefoil chambers are in the wall of the central hall inside the cairn are the "Maes Howe type" as shown in Figures (3) and (4).

Among the chambered cairns of the Camster type is Camster Round Chambered Cairn, which is the prototype and eponym of the type. Examples are Camster Long-Horned Cairn, 6 miles south of Watten; South Yarrows Chambered Cairn, 5.5 miles south-south-west of Wick; Get Chambered Cairn situated 7 miles south of Wick; Coille na Borgie Chambered Cairn, 2 miles south of Bettyhill, Sutherland; The Ord Chambered Cairn at the south end of Loch Shin; Embo Chambered Cairn in Dornoch; Unstan Chambered Cairn in mainland Orkney; and Midhowe Chambered Cairn and Taversoe Tuick Chambered Cairn in Rousay, Orkney.

Among the latter type, the Maes Howe type, are Maes Howe Chambered cairn in mainland Orkney, which is the prototype and eponym of that type, and Cuween Chambered Cairn, also in mainland Orkney.

a. Cairns of the Camster Type

Camster Round Chambered Cairn, similar examples of which are said to be seen in Spain, is situated 70 metres north-north-west of the Camster Long-Horned Cairn. It measures 17 metres in diameter and 3.5 metres in height. The passage entrance is narrow and low and leads in from the south-east. Its passage, 6 metres in length, is composed of four opposed pairs of upright slabs projecting like door-jambs, connecting with two inner chambers which are divided into three compartments, walled by drystones and large vertical slabs and roofed with flat slabs. The remains of several skeletons, burnt bones, artefacts of pottery, flint tools and polished knives are said to have been found there. The cairn was constructed in the 3rd or 4th millennium B.C.

9

Photograph (9) shows the Camster Chambered Cairn.

10

*Photographs (10) and (11) show an overall view of
Camster Long-Horned Cairn and the inside of the
chamber located at the centre of the cairn.*

Camster Long-Horned Cairn, situated near Camster Round
Chambered Cairn, runs its pebbly axis 70 metres long from north-east
to south-west with a short horn at each corner. The distance between
the ends of the horns at the north and east is 20 metres and between
those at the south and the west, 12 metres. This cairn has two
chambers, one near the north end and the other at the centre of the
cairn, their apertures facing the east. The chamber located at the
centre of the cairn is divided
into tripartite compartments
by slabs and its passage is 3
metres long. The other is a
single polygonal chamber 5
metres in diameter, walled by
vertical slabs, and it has a
passage 6 metres long. This
cairn is supposed to have
stemmed from free-standing
round cairns remodelled into
an enormous cairn through
several alterations in the
Bronze Age, presumably as
seen in the Mid Gleniron
Chambered Cairn.

South Yarrows Chambered
Cairn is also a long-horned
cairn of pebbles. While it has
an affinity with the Clyde-
Carlingford gallery-grave, it is

11

12

*Photograph (12) shows a panoramic view of South
Yarrows Chambered Cairn on the top of which
stands a "phallus", and (13) the chamber with its
facade.*

a typical passage-grave which has stalled chambers with a concave
facade and horns. It measures 73 metres in length, 28 metres in width
between the ends of the horns at the east, and 16 metres between
those at the west. There is a short passage set right in the centre of
the east facade and this leads to the chamber, dividing it into three
compartments with upright slabs. On the top of the cairn stands a
menhir which seems once to have symbolized a phallus for the
chambered cairn.

Get Chambered Cairn is a short-horned cairn which was built in
the 4th or 3rd millennium B.C. The mound is trapezoidal and
measures 4.5 metres by 3 metres. The passage, facing the south-
west, is 3 metres long and the antechamber is 2 metres square. The
now roofless innermost chamber, circular with walled upright slabs,

13

14

Photograph (14) shows the facade,
antechamber and innermost chamber
of Get Chambered Cairn.

is 3.5 metres in diameter and the north and south sides of the
cairn are conspicuously concave. Flint arrowheads, pottery and
animal bones have been excavated there.

    Coille na Borgie Chambered Cairn is a huge long-horned cairn of
pebbles with its long axis running from north to south. It measures 70
metres in length and two or three chambers are supposed to have been

therein. One lies in the forecourt between the north horns, the covering of which is widest and highest. It is surmised that its passage was about 4 metres long and its outermost compartment 2 metres long and some 1 metre wide and high. The outer compartment connects with the middle and innermost compartments, the innermost compartment being 3.6 metres by 3 metres, consisting of six huge slabs with drystone walling.

This cairn again suggests that plural free-standing cairns were united into a long cairn. In the middle of the cairn stands a standing stone or "phallus". This cairn was once in the depths of a wood supposedly the home of a dryad or a nymph as its Gaelic name indicates (see p237).

The Ord Chambered Cairn is 27 metres in diameter and some 4 metres high, though its passage was filled up after an excavation in 1967. This cairn had a passage, an antechamber and an inner chamber similar to that of Get Chambered Cairn. Cremation burials, sherds of pottery and flint flakes have been excavated. The site is in an area to which thronged settlers of each epoch from the Neolithic Age. There are the remains of another chambered cairn, consisting of only the large slabs of the chamber and passage,

15

Photograph (15) shows a panoramic view of Coille na Borgie Chambered Cairn, on top of which is a representation of a "phallus".

16

Photograph (16) shows the Ord Chambered Cairn.

17   18

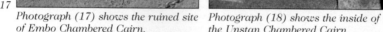

Photograph (17) shows the ruined site   Photograph (18) shows the inside of
of Embo Chambered Cairn.   the Unstan Chambered Cairn.

together with cairns of unknown date and a number of hut circles from the Iron Age.

Embo Chambered Cairn, situated by the seaside at Embo, 2 miles north of Dornoch, is a ruined cairn which once contained two passage tombs. The south chamber, measuring 2.3 metres by 1.7 metres, retains a short entrance passage of about 1.5 metres having upright slabs once used for walling. Several inhumations and sherds of beaker ware have been found there. In the Bronze Age a secondary cist was set in this chamber and inhumation burials, food vessels and beads have been uncovered there.

The north chamber is more ruined and all that remains are its five upright slabs. One cist is inserted between these two chambers and the burial remains of two infants, a food vessel and fragments of a beaker have been found. Presumably it was a cairn formed from two independent chambered cairns joined together. Excavations from this cairn include a number of cremation deposits and the bones of animals and birds, including a squirrel and a guillemot, evidence which might reveal something of the ritual practices of Neolithic and Bronze Age people.

Unstan Chambered Cairn, 2 miles north-west of Stromness, is a derivative of the cairn of the Camster type with the entrance on the south-east quadrant. Its passage is 6 metres long by 1.6 metres wide and connects sideways with the chamber. The chamber, walled by drystones and measuring 6 metres long by 1.8 metres wide, is divided into ten compartments by four large slabs. Four two-shelved compartments are along one side, to which the passage opens, and a cylindrical compartment is innermost. A small additional cell is in the centre of the opposite side. This cairn is supposed to have been built in the 3rd millennium B.C. and a great deal of sherds of Unstan pottery, birds and animal bones, leaf-shaped arrowheads, flint-tools and an inhumed body have been excavated.

19

Photograph (19) shows the inside of Midhowe Chambered Cairn.

Midhowe Chambered Cairn is a long cairn of the Camster type. In the centre of the cairn, measuring 32 metres in length and 13 metres in width, is encased a passage of dry wall which measures 23 metres in length and 2 metres in width with the entrance to the south-west. On both sides of the passage are set twelve compartments, divided by pairs of upright slabs, comprising 24 cells in all. The 12 cells along the east side of the passage are fitted with stone shelves where there have been found the remains of twenty-five people, together with some complete skeletons, the age of which is unknown.

b. Cairns of the Maes Howe Type

Maes Howe Chambered Cairn, the design and workmanship of which is said not to have reached Britain nor any place to the north and west of the Mediterranean region until the Neolithic Age, is thus the prototype and eponym of that type. The cairn, presumed to have been built before 2700 B.C., measures 35 metres in diameter in the foundation and 7 metres in height. The entrance of the passage faces the south-west, its length is about 9 metres and its height and width are 1.3 metres and 0.9 metres respectively. It leads to the main hall where three chambers were fitted on each of three sides of the wall,

20

Photographs (20), (21), (22) and (23) are, respectively, an overall view of Maes Howe Chambered Cairn; its passage; one of the chambers; and the runic graffiti left by the Vikings who broke into it in the 12th century.

21

22

except for the side of the passage. The main hall is 4.5 square metres and the size of the chamber or niche 8 cubic metres. No grave-goods nor burial remains have been found, but on the surface of the walls of the main hall there are graffiti and drawings of dragons or serpents, left by the Vikings who invaded there in the 12th century.

23

24

*Photograph (24) shows a panoramic view of Cuween
Chambered Cairn.*

Ian Grimble, the author of *Highland Man*, deciphered one of the
graffiti, consisting of 24 runic letters, as [5] "Ingibjorg hin fahra a
morhg kona, haefir farit lut in hir mikl oflati." It means "Ingibjorg the
fair widow, many a haughty woman has stooped to walk in here."
"Ingibjorg" is, in this connection, a name identical with that of
Thorfinn the Mighty's wife who was bereaved of her husband in 1064
and remarried with Malcolm III.

Cuween Chambered Cairn is also a tomb classified as belonging to
the Maes Howe type. It is set in a mound some 16 metres in diameter
and 2.5 metres in height and the passage, which runs in from the
south-east, measures 5.5 metres long, 0.8 metres high and 0.7 metres
wide, leading to a rectangular hall. The size of the chambers is
roughly 3 metres long by 1.5 metres wide. There are four cells fitted
into the wall facing the hall, and from the two cells of the west side

there have been excavated eight inhumation burials and five human skulls, together with the skulls of twenty-four dogs which might have been an offering to the dead.

25

Photograph (25) shows the Dwarfie Stane Chambered Cairn.

Dwarfie Stane Chambered Cairn, situated on the east side of the valley between Quoys and Rackwick in Hoy in Orkney, is a variant of the normal chambered cairn. Examples are said to have existed in France, Iberia and the Mediterranean coast region in the Neolithic Age. It has a passage and two chambers which were dug with a hard rock-cut stone on a block of Devonian red sandstone measuring 8.5 metres by 4.5 metres and 2.5 metres high. The passage faces the west and is 2.2 metres long, 0.65 metres high and 0.7 metres wide, and two cells flank either side of the passage. Both cells are 1.5 metres wide, 0.9 metres deep and 0.7 metres high. A square block of stone, presumed once to have closed the entrance, lies just outside the entrance.

4. PASSAGE-GRAVES OF THE SHETLAND-CLAVA GROUP

The characteristic common to the chambered cairns in Shetland is that the tombs are small and oval or circular with curved facades and heel-shaped external facing. Most of them contain a cruciform or trefoil chamber which is approached by a passage leading in from the centre of the facade while the external facing is usually surrounded by kerbstones at the base.

Punds Water Chambered Cairn in mainland Shetland is a typically heel-shaped cairn which was built on a small knoll on moorland some 2 miles north-west of Mavis Grind in the 3rd or 2nd millennium B.C. The nature of the soil of the Shetland Islands is Devonian red sandstone as in the Orkney Islands. In spite of this, the tomb is of white quartzite and its facade is concave, some 15 metres long, looking towards the south-east. The passage, 3.6 metres long and lying in the centre of the cairn, leads to a trefoil-shaped chamber inside. The outer wall of the cairn, with large stones used at places, stands over 1 metre in height.

26

Photograph (26) shows the ruined chamber of Gallow Hill Chambered Cairn.

Gallow Hill Chambered Cairn, also a tomb built in the 3rd or 2nd millenniun B.C., is situated beside the A971, 0.3 miles beyond Bridge of Walls. It is now so destroyed as to make it difficult to determine the original structure, but it is presumed once to have been a huge round cairn with an imposing kerb of boulders. It was some 25 metres in diameter and in the centre can be detected traces of a circular chamber 3 metres by 2 metres, some 8 metres off from the facade. In the neighbourhood were Bronze Age settlements such as Scord of Brouster, Pinhoulland and Ness of Gruting (see p75).

Towie Knowe or Fairy Knowe Chambered Cairn, situated on the narrow strip between Loch of Housetter and Beorgs of Housetter, is also a ruined chambered cairn built in the 3rd or 2nd millennium B.C., once having had a heel-shaped external facing 8 metres in diameter and 1.2 metres high with the chamber about 2 metres by 3 metres opening to the south-east. To the south of this cairn, about 80

27   28

Photographs (27), and (28) show the ruined chamber of Towie Knowe and a view of the Giant's Grave Standing Stones.

metres apart, there is a pair of standing stones, a very impressive late Neolithic monument, known locally as "Giant's Grave." The red and broad stones stand aligned north to south. The stones are 2.4 metres and 1.8 metres high respectively and at their base is a ruined Bronze Age cairn with kerbstones.

Chambered cairns of the Clava type, which are supposed to have originated in the Mediterranean region and been brought over by way of the Iberian Peninsula, are clustered in the outskirts of Inverness and have a characteristic whereby the tomb is circular with a corbelled passage, or annular with no means of access from the outside. The foundations of the tombs, having no heel-shape, are surrounded by circular kerbstones and set within a stone circle or a ring of standing stones. Typical and well-preserved are Corriemony Chambered Cairn, situated beside the Enrick River at the head of Glenurquhart, and the Chambered Cairns at Clava, 5 miles east of Inverness.

Corriemony Chambered Cairn is a circular cairn which was built in the late 3rd millennium B.C. Its diameter is 15 metres and it is 2.5 metres high at its greatest height with a kerb at the base. The cairn is surrounded by a stone ring 22 metres in diameter and consisting of eleven upright stones. The ring seems to have been a set of facilities for ritual and astronomical observation. The passage entrance, looking towards the south-west, is 1 metre high, roofed with the original stone slabs. The length of the passage is 7 metres

29

*Photographs (29), (30), (31), and (32) show the
entrance of the passage of Corriemony Chambered
Cairn; the chamber; the ring of standing stones; and the
stone with massive cup-marks.*

30

31

32

and it leads to the central circular chamber with a drystone walling some 2 metres high. The chamber has no roof and is some 3.6 metres in diameter with traces of corbels on its edge. A massive cup-marked slab, which is said to be a copy of "The Plough", lies on top of the cairn. The flooring of the chamber is of sand, partially paved with flat slabs, and a crouched inhumation burial has been excavated, along with burnt bone, from under the floor.

The chambered cairns of Clava are now three: Clava Chambered Cairns South-east, Central and North-west, all roofless. The South-east cairn has an entrance of a corbelled passage which points south-west by south, the quarter of sunset at the winter solstice, and leads to the central chamber some 3.5 metres in diameter. The passage is 6 metres long, 1 metre high and 0.6 metres wide and the chamber is set within a massive walling of drystones and heavy slabs 6 metres thick and 2 metres high, one of the slabs retaining cup-marks. The external diameter of the cairn is 16 metres with an imposing kerb of boulders at the base, the kerbstone at due north having cup-marks, relics of Bronze Age people. Surrounding the cairn is a stone ring which is some 32 metres in diameter and comprises a twelve upright-stone zodiac (the original number being unknown). Fragments of vessels and a quantity of cremated bone have been excavated from within.

The North-west cairn is similar to this cairn in structure, size, stone ring and location of chamber and passage, and one of the slabs inside the chamber has cup-marks. It might have been a calendar to tell the passage of time to the "dead" awaiting reincarnation. The Central cairn is an annular cairn with a stone ring of nine upright stones as shown in Figure (5). The cairn is roughly circular, 17 metres in diameter with a kerb of boulders 1 metre high, and the chamber is

3.6 metres in diameter set within a walling of slabs 0.9 metres high, though it is not known whether it had been originally roofed or not.

Some of the kerbstones have cup-marks and the diameter of the stone ring is about 30 metres. One stone on the north-west side and two on the east and south-east

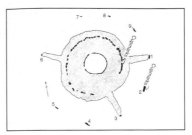

Figure 5

sides are linked to the cairn by a spoke-like cobble-paved causeway 2 metres wide and 0.3 metres above the ground. Stone number (7) is roughly north. The direction extending from the centre of the cairn to stone number (1) is due east and the direction of sunrise at each equinox (azimuth 90) 06:00 GMT; the direction extending from the centre of the cairn to stone number (5) is that of sunrise at midwinter (azimuth 230), 15:20 GMT; stone number (9) is roughly the direction of sunrise at midsummer (azimuth 310), 20:40 GMT. At Clava, roughly speaking, the movement of the sun at midwinter is from azimuth 130 to 230 and that at midsummer from azimuth 50 to 310.

33

Photographs (33), (34), (35) and (36) show an overall view of Clava cairns; a view of the Central cairn; the passage and chamber; and the cup-marks remaining on a kerbstone of the North-east cairn.

34

35

36

5. TOMBS IN THE GRAMPIAN, CENTRAL, EASTERN AND LOWLAND REGIONS

Grampian, Central Eastern and Lowland regions were assembly places of the settlers who flowed in during the late Neolithic and Bronze Ages. In Grampian district there remain Cairn Catto Long Cairn; Midmill Long Cairn built in the 4th or 3rd millennium B.C.; and Raedykes Ring Cairns on the crest of Campstone Hill, 190 metres above sea-level near Stonehaven, built in the 3rd millennium B.C. In

Perthshire there is Fowlis Wester Cairn, Standing Stones and Stone Circle; and in Lothian district there is Mutiny Stone Long Cairn.

Cairn Catto Long Cairn is a great wedge-shaped long cairn situated 4 miles south-west of Peterhead and, though the cairn itself is so destroyed as to defy detection of the position of its chamber, it is a similar type of cairn to the Camster Long-Horned Cairn. It is now bare and made of a great number of pebbles, just as with Coille na Borgie Chambered Cairn and South Yarrows Chambered Cairn. Its axis running from north-west to south-east, it measures some 50 metres long, 20 metres across and 2

37

Photographs (37) and (38) show overall views of Cairn Catto Long Cairn and Midmill Long Cairn.

metres high with the south-eastern end slightly higher. Midmill Long Cairn is a turf-covered cairn situated on a low ridge, 0.8 miles south of Kintore, although the presence of the actual chamber has not been confirmed. It is 70 metres long, 25 metres wide and 3 metres high with its axis running from east to west.

38

39

Photograph (39) shows a cairn and stone ring of Raedykes Ring Cairns (the first and best-preserved one).

Raedykes Ring Cairns constitute an assembly of four ring cairns. Each is an annular cairn similar to the Central Cairn at Clava, originally having a stone ring in its circumference. The first and best-preserved one is 9.5 metres in diameter and its mound is 0.5 metres high with a kerbed open area in the centre. The stone ring or stone circle surrounding the mound is 17 metres in diameter and consists of eight stones up to 1 metre high with a recumbent stone and two flankers on the south-west arc (the western flanker is 1.7 metres and the eastern one 1 metre high). The second cairn is some 20 metres to the north-west of the first one and is oval, measuring 9 metres by 8 metres and 0.5 metres high, with some standing stones left.

The third one is 20 metres further to the north-west and the size and scale is approximate to the second one. The fourth, some 100 metres north-west of the first one, is 10 metres in diameter and 0.5 metres high, and the stone circle consists of five stones (originally 13 stones), some 14 metres in diameter, surrounding the cairn.

Fowlis Wester Cairn, Standing Stones and Stone Circle, situated on the Moor of Ardoch, is so severely damaged a complex as to leave only two standing stones and a cairn with a ruined stone circle. The upright stones are some 2 metres high and one stone has a single cup-mark. The cairn, allied to a kerb cairn, is some 5 metres in diameter, and from it quartz and cremated bone have been excavated. The stone circle retains four stones with traces of the stone-holes of another seven stones. Judging from the size and array of the stone-holes, it might once have been a gigantic-scale site for ritual and astronomical observation.

40

Photograph (40) shows an overall view of Fowlis Wester Cairn, Standing Stones and Stone Circle.

Mutiny Stone Long Cairn, the former name of which was "Mittenfull of Stones," is on Byrecleugh Ridge, 5 miles north-west of Longformacus. It lies 85 metres long with its axis running from the north-east to the south-west of the ridge. Its width is between 8 metres and 2 metres and it rises to 2.5 metres at the highest point. In this cairn the presence of a chamber has not been ascertained.

CHAPTER II

MONUMENTS OF THE BRONZE AGE

As seen in the chambered cairns in Corriemony, Cairnholy, Clava and Callanish, some groups of the early Bronze Age settlers used chambered cairns of the Neolithic Age as graves, appending to them facilities called "standing stones" or "stone circles," but some groups built their own cairns. These new cairns usually had no appendix but, at times, had the traditional aspect of a "concave facade" proper to the chambered cairns in the Neolithic Age. Although the cairns were often built within existing facilities of stone circles and standing stones, they were on the whole built separately from facilities for ritual and astronomical observation and the burial mode in those days gradually shifted from interment to cremation.

In the early Bronze Age interment took place using a kind of stone cist, the capstone of which at times had stone-axe marks, as shown in Figure (6), and cup-marks, and the stone cist was inserted somewhere under the covering of the cairn. However, with the arrival of the Beaker Folk, whose formal burial mode was cremation, cinerary urns and beakers began to be popular for dealing with cremated bone. Thus, at times, insertions of burials by different burial modes such as stone cists and cinerary urns can be found under the covering in the same cairn.

Cremation very often took place when pestilences were prevalent, even when the formal burial mode was interment. However, the shift from interment to cremation in the Bronze Age seems due to the fact that people

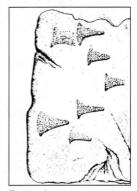

Figure 6

had probably deified the power of fire, as the Zoroastrians had done in later days. Though it remains no more than speculation, they might have thought of fire as a God of light, purification and energy, a god who could give new life to clay and metallic objects and even resurrect the dead.

1. BRONZE AGE CAIRNS

Bronze Age cairns were widely scattered in places once populated by Bronze Age settlers. There are cairns built in flatlands, such as: Nether Largie Mid and North Cairns; Dunchraigaig Cairn; Ri Cruin Cairn, some 7 miles north of Lochgilphead, Mid Argyle; Huly Hill Round Cairn; and Newbridge in Edinburgh. However, many of them were built on the tops of high hills nearer to the Heavens. Such are Tinto Hill Cairn in Clydesdale; Eildon Mid Hill Round Cairn, 1 mile south-east of Melrose; the cairns on Dreva Craig Fort in Peebles-shire (see p91) and Black Hill Lesmahagow Fort (see p99) in Clydesdale; Cat Cairn and Crab's Cairn on Tullos Hill, Loirston Park near Aberdeen; Memsie Round Cairn, Rathen in Banff and Buchan; Nether Cairn and Upper Cairn, in North Muir in Tweedsdale; Fairy Knowe Cairn, Arthrey Hill in Stirling; Judge's Cairn near Kilbride; Cairnpapple Round Cairn in the outskirts of

41

Photograph (41) shows Nether Largie Mid Cairn and the cist in the south quadrant, the capstone of which has a cup-mark and an axe-mark.

Edinburgh (see p43); and
Auchagallon Cairn in the Isle of
Arran. An elevated ground had
something in common with
"sith" or "Tom na h-Iubraich"
(see p260) in later days, just as in
Wales "Snowdon" was "the Tomb"
(Yr Wyddfa < Gwyddfa) (see photo
303).

Tinto Hill Cairn is on the
summit of Tinto Hill, 712 metres
above sea-level, and is one of the
largest Bronze Age round cairns
in Scotland. It is of the late 3rd
or early 2nd millennium B.C.
and measures 43 metres in
diameter and 6 metres in height.

Nether Largie Mid Cairn
measures 30 metres in diameter
with traces of a kerb around it
and in both the north-west and
south quadrants of the cairn a
cist is inserted. Inside the
capstone of the cist inserted in

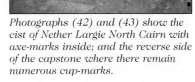

42

*Photographs (42) and (43) show the
cist of Nether Largie North Cairn with
axe-marks inside; and the reverse side
of the capstone where there remain
numerous cup-marks.*

the south quadrant remain a single cup-mark and an axe mark, the
significance of which is a mystery.

Nether Largie North Cairn measures 21 metres in diameter and is
3 metres high. In its centre is inserted a stone cist, 1.5 metres by 0.7
metres and 0.6 metres deep, and inside the cist are two axe marks,
similar to those seen on the capstone of one cist of Ri Cruin Cairn
nearby, and on the reverse side of its capstone are vast numbers of
cup-marks.

Dunchraigaig
Cairn is a conical
cairn which lies
in a small wood
and measures 30
metres in dia-
meter and 2
metres in height.
One cist 3 metres
by 1.5 metres was
found in the
south-east
quadrant, and

43

inhumed bodies, cremated bone and fragments of flint have been excavated. In the small cist near the top of the cairn, food vessels have been found.

44

Photograph (44) shows an overall view of Dunchraigaig Cairn.

Ri Cruin Cairn (The Round Cairn of the King) also lies in a small wood and measures some 20 metres in diameter. The mound, now not very high, has a concave facade. Two cists were inserted there and the capstone of the cist inserted in the north of the cairn is grooved and devised so as to make it fit tightly to the cist. The capstone of the cist inserted in the southern-most end of the cairn is decorated with seven pecked axe-marks. Cremation deposits have been found.

Cat Cairn is an oval cairn which measures 22 metres by 19 metres and 2.5 metres high. It co-exists with three other cairns on the ridge of Tullos Hill: Baron's Cairn, 18 metres in diameter and 1.5 metres in height; Tullos Cairn, 20 metres in diameter and 2.5 metres in height; and Crab's Cairn, 14 metres in diameter and 1.7 metres in height.

Memsie Round Cairn is the sole survivor of the cairns that once clustered on the low ridge of Cairn Muir where Bronze Age people densely thronged as the name "Cairn Muir" indicates. The cairn is 25 metres in diameter and 4.5 metres in height and from it a beaker and a leaf-shaped sword have been excavated. It might have been built for a clan chief or a noble.

45

*Photograph (45) shows the capstone of a cist of Ri
Cruin Cairn displaying seven axe-marks.*

46

*Photograph (46) shows an overall view of Memsie
Round Cairn.*

Huly Hill Round Cairn, 30 metres in diameter and 3 metres in height, is surrounded by three upright stones, the nearest one standing over 2 metres high, 30 metres north-west of the cairn; the second one, some 2 metres high, stands nearly 50 metres to the south-west; and the third one, 53 metres to the east, is 1.3 metres high. Though the original number of the stones is unknown, it seems to have been a cairn inserted in a huge stone circle, a colossal site for ritual and astronomical observation.

Fairy Knowe Cairn is a conical cairn which has a concave facade. It originally measured 24 metres in diameter and 6 metres in height, but now measures 18 metres in diameter and 2.5 metres in height. Pieces of bone and cremated skulls have been discovered in the cist inserted at the centre of the cairn and beakers and vessels of an unspecified kind have been excavated from the cist 0.6 metres under the top of the cairn.

47

Photograph (47) shows the Huly Hill Round Cairn and one of its standing stones.

48

Photograph (48) shows an overall view of Fairy Knowe Cairn which has a concave facade.

Nether Cairn is one of nine conical cairns clustered on the south-east slopes of North Muir in Tweedsdale. It measures 15 metres in diameter and is 4 metres high with a ditch in its circumference. The Upper Cairn, situated some 730 metres north-east of the Nether Cairn, is 20 metres in diameter and 4.2 metres in height with no ditch. This site and its surrounds were also once densely populated by Bronze Age people and thus many cairns are distributed there.

Auchagallon Cairn, a burial ground built in the late Neolithic or early Bronze Age, is surrounded by an intermittent ring of fifteen boulders. The measurement is 14 metres in diameter and a large number of cup-marks remain on the surface of one standing stone on the north-west side. This cairn has not yet been excavated.

49

Photograph (49) shows an overall view of Nether Cairn.

50

Photograph (50) shows Auchagallon Cairn and the standing stone bearing a large number of cup-marks on its surface.

51

Photograph (51) shows an overall view of Judge's Cairn.

Judge's Cairn is a conical cairn situated north-west of Dunblane and measures 12 metres in diameter and 2 metres in height. In front of it was held, in the late Iron Age, "a judgment court", just as with "the Judge's Seat" or "Suidhe A' Bhritheimh" on the Hill of Severie east of Callander, which carries [6] the tradition that people were judged at this stone and, when found guilty, were hanged at Kilbride near Dunblane.

2. HENGE MONUMENTS

The henge is a monument peculiar to the Bronze Age. Ordinarily it has one or two concentric outer banks and ditches and one or two entrance causeways through the ditches and banks. The internal area is an open space and a sacred precinct, the size varying considerably in each arrangement, and it is accompanied by a circle of standing wooden pillars or upright stones. Its function is not known precisely but the most likely explanation is that it was a social and religious centre for each autonomous community, akin to stone circles, standing stones, and alignments, though a form of cairn was inserted in later days.

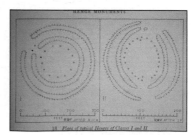

Figure 7

52

*Photograph (52) shows the site of the timber circle of Balfarg Henge and the
remaining two stones, surmised to have been the position of the entrance.*

Henge monuments are customarily divided into two classes
according to the number of entrances leading into the internal area as
shown in Figure (7). Class (I) has a single entrance and class (II) has
two opposed entrances. Henges of Class (I) include Balfarg Henge in
Fife; Conon Bridge Henge in Ross and Cromarty (now gone); and
Stenness Henge in mainland Orkney. Henges of Class (II) include
Normangill Henge in Lanarkshire; Cairnpapple Henge in West
Lothian; Ballymeanoch Henge in Mid Argyle; Broomend of Crichei
Ceremonial Centre in Aberdeenshire; Muir of Ord Henge in Ross and
Cromarty (now gone); and Ring of Brodgar in mainland Orkney. The
small-scale henge served a minor autonomous group while the larger
ones, imagined to have needed immense man hours to complete, seem
to have belonged to huge, centralized hierarchical groups of a tribal
system.

Balfarg Henge is a monument which was re-sited to the south-east
of its original site in the New House Building Plan by Glenrothes
Development Corporation. Several phases of re-construction have
been detected and excavations have revealed that the facilities in the
first phase comprised a timber circle of sixteen upright posts some 25
metres in diameter, and that it was later re-arranged into two
concentric stone rings about 60 metres in diameter, with its entrance
on the west side, surrounded by a ditch 5 metres wide and 2.5 metres
deep in an area of some 4,000 square metres. Though the original
number of stones is not clear and most of the stones are now gone

except for two, there were insertions of cairns, and many items of burial and a large quantity of pottery have been excavated, and in the centre of the sanctuary the burial of a young person has been found along with a beaker and a flint knife.

53

Photographs (53) and (54) show the five stones of Stenness Henge, and "The Watch Stone."

Stenness Henge is a monument with five surviving stones, the tallest over 6 metres high. The original number of stones was thirteen, set in a circle some 30 metres in diameter. Ploughing has levelled the henge earthworks but the circle once stood in an open space some 44 metres in diameter, comprising a bank and a rock-cut ditch some 7 metres wide and 2 metres deep with a single entrance causeway in the north. In the centre of the sanctuary remains the site of a square setting of flat slab called a "table tomb" (a kind of mortuary), and

54

the bones of sheep, dogs, cattle and wolves, for feasting or sacrificing, have been excavated along with an item of grooved pottery ware. It is presumed to have been the site of a fire-festival or a primeval fire-cult.

Some 700 metres north-north-west of the circle is a standing stone known as "The Watch Stone" which until 1814 had been paired with "The Stone of Odin", which Sir Walter Scott (1771–1832) mentions in his novel *The Pirate* (1821), and similarly served those who plighted a bargain or engagement by grasping hands through the hole at the upper part of the stone. From the circle it is located in the direction of sunset at the summer solstice and is thought to have been part of a structure for astronomical observation. Another outlying stone, "Burnhouse Stone," is some 700 metres to the south-south-east of the circle.

The henge of Cairnpapple, the name of which means "the Cairn for the People", is one of several monuments built there in different phases of age between 2800 B.C. and the 2nd millennium B.C., though most of the structures are now gone. This monument is situated on the isolated Cairnpapple Hill in the outskirts of Edinburgh. The facilities made there in the first phase comprised an arc of seven small pits from which deposits of cremated bone have been excavated. This was followed by the construction of a henge monument of an egg-shaped setting of stones which measured 35 metres by 28 metres. The ditch measured 3.5 metres wide and 1 metre deep and the two entrance causeways, one on the north and the other on the south, led to the sanctuary inside. The ring of twenty-four standing stones was set near to the edge of this rock-cut ditch, the debris of which was upcast to form an outer bank, and at the centre of the complex is supposed to have been set a table tomb or a series of them as seen in the Stenness Henge.

This henge monument, however, was taken down round about 1800 to 1700 B.C. and a small free-standing round cairn 15 metres in diameter with a kerb was built on the south-west of the original structure of the henge, as shown in Figure (8), with a standing stone remaining at the west end. Early in the Iron Age this cairn was enlarged to a diameter of 30 metres. Excavations include two pottery vessels of beaker ware, inhumation burials, two burial deposits in cinerary urns, fragmentary pins of horn or bone, and Neolithic stone axe chips which are surmised to have come from the Cumbrian region. This

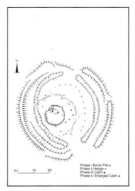

Figure 8

55

Photographs (55) and (56) show the remains of an arc of seven small pits left in the henge site along with the sockets of the standing stones of the henge monument and its ditch (in the background); and the Cairnpapple Round Cairn, built in the Bronze Age, though what we now see is a replica.

56

site was originally and for a long period a place for meeting and ritual and later for burial. It seems also to have been a centre for barter.

Broomend of Crichei Ceremonial Centre, built on a terrace of the River Don in the late Neolithic Age, is also a henge monument, its diameter being 34 metres with entrances on the north and south. There are two crescent ditches, 25 metres long, 7 metres wide and 1.5 metres deep, inside the outer banks on the east and west sides; and there remain three standing stones and the remains of six stone holes. Two of the stones stand near the inner edge of the sanctuary while the third one, which is in the centre, is a stone decorated with Pictish symbolic carvings of a sea-elephant and a crown-and-V-shaped rod. At the base of each stone have been found deposits of cremated bone in decorated urns; pins; and, at the centre of the sanctuary, a shaft grave some 2 metres deep. These facilities are said to have had a close resemblance in size and structure to that of Muir of Ord Henge, no longer extant.

57

Photograph (57) shows a panoramic view of Broomend of Crichei Ceremonial Centre.

58

Photograph (58) shows the stone row and the ditch of the Ring of Brodgar.

Ring of Brodgar is a well-preserved, huge henge monument situated on a low promontory between Loch Harry and Loch Stenness. No trace remains of the outer bank. The ditch is 113 metres in diameter, 9 metres wide and 3 metres deep and the opposed entrance causeways are 3.5 metres wide on the north-west and south-east quadrants. The ring is 124 megalithic yards (103 metres) in diameter. Twenty-seven upright slabs, from 2 metres to 4.5 metres in height, stand 3 metres from the inner edge of the ditch. The ring originally consisted of 60 upright slabs and was almost certainly a site where observations of solar or lunar movements were carried out by using a number of horizontal points as markers. Presumed to have served for social and religious meeting as well, its period as an active monument was from 1700 B.C. to 1400 B.C.

3. MONOLITHS, STONE CIRCLES (CROMLECH), STANDING STONES (MENHIR) AND ALIGNMENTS.

Stone circles, monoliths, standing stones and alignments are also presumed to have been facilities for ritual, social meeting and astronomical observation by Bronze Age people. They were all built in the late Neolithic Age or in the early Bronze Age, and some of them were handed down to the later Druidical La Tene people in the Iron Age, though burials were later inserted in the sites. Differences of size and scale of facilities seem to be mainly due to the size of autonomous groups, as is the case with chambered cairns and henge monuments. Differences of structure, mode and number of stones seem to have stemmed from differences in the settlers, their geometrical talents and numeration systems. When the facilities served specifically as an instrument for astronomical observation, the number of stones used to obtain a spatial diagram took on an important significance. However, even stones are perishable by weathering, damage by earthquake, thunderbolt, intentional destruction, stone robbery and so on, and it is quite difficult to know the original size, scale, mode and number of stones of each set of facilities.

The thirteen standing stones appended to the Callanish Chambered Cairn can be construed as indicators to mensurate the passage of the thirteen lunar months of the year and suggest the prototype of the later Druidical Tree Calendar in the Iron Age in which, as Caesar explains, [7] the day begins and ends with the evening, and the months revolve thus: Birch (Dec 24 – Jan 21); Rowan (Jan 22 – Feb 18); Ash (Feb 19 – Mar 18); Alder (Mar 19 – Apr 15); Willow (Apr16 – May 13); Whitethorn (May 14 – Jun 10); Oak (Jun 11 – Jul 8); Holly(Jul 9 – Aug 5); Hazel (Aug 6 – Sept 2); Vine (Sept 3 –

Sept 30); Ivy (Oct 1 – Oct 28); Reed (Oct 29 – Nov 25); Elder (Nov 26
– Dec 22), containing the special days of five tree names beginning
with the capital letters of the five Gaelic vowels: Ailm (Silver Fir, Dec
24, New Year's Day, which was shifted to the Birthday of Jesus Christ
by early Christians); Onn (Furze, the Spring Equinox); Ur (Heather,
the Summer Solstice, or Beltane); Eadha (White Poplar or Aspen, the
Autumn Equinox); and Iodh (Yew, the Winter Solstice, or Hallowe'en).
The year revolved with the next day of the winter solstice (Dec 23) as
a day missing from the calendar. [8] This is the origin of the phrase "a
year and a day" and is the reason why it is exactly one year, meaning
thirteen lunar months plus a missing day.

As the days consisted of two halves of day and night, so the year
consisted of summer and winter. The former began with Beltane and
the latter with Samhuinn (or Hallowe'en). However, of the two
occurrences of solstice, Hallowe'en (New Year's Eve) was perhaps older
and the more important, since the Celts seem to have dated the
beginning of the year from it rather than from Beltane, as pointed out
by J. Frazer, the author of *The Golden Bough*. As to the coincidence
of feasts and solstices, it may be inferred that this was not accidental,
but supposed that the ancients had purposely timed ceremonies of fire
on earth to coincide with the arrival of the sun at both the highest and
lowest points of its course in the sky. [9]

The number 13 is certainly a very important and convenient
number. However, in addition, the numbers 1, 2, 3, 4, 6, 7, 8, 9 and 12
are supposed to have been fundamental and convenient numbers
which Bronze Age people employed in their numeration system. The
multiple of 4 and 7 is the number of days of one lunar month; the
multiple of 3 and 9 almost coincides with the number of days which
the moon takes to fulfill its tour of one cycle if one missing day (or
holy day) is added. Twenty-eight is the number comprising the
constellation of the lunar zodiac as it is told in Hindu and Chinese
mythology where the Moon has twenty-eight star wives, with each of
whom he spends one night every month. The fundamental numbers
which Bronze Age people had adopted and used are supposed to be full
of varied combinations and, in consequence, the number of stones
used in constructing stone circles, standing stones and alignments are
necessarily full of variety.

However, the megalithic yard (0.83 m), which it is supposed
some groups of settlers invented or brought with them, began to be
used in the Bronze Age as the standard "yardstick" to measure the
distance and the intervals between the stones of standing stones
and stone circles. This standard was used in constructing the
Callanish Standing Stones (see p 58), Achavanish Standing Stones
(see p 57), Burgh Hill Stone Setting (see p 57) and Borrowstoun
Rig Stone Setting (see p 57).

59

60

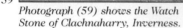

Photograph (59) shows the Watch Stone of Clachnaharry, Inverness.

Photograph (60) shows the Kirkland Hill Standing Stone.

a. Monolithic Monuments

Among noteworthy examples are the Watch Stone (or Clach na h-Aire) near Clachnaharry in Inverness; Kirkland Hill Standing Stone and Pencraig Hill Standing Stone in East Linton, East Lothian; Strontoiller Standing Stone (which has the other name of "Clach Diamid") and Kintraw Standing Stone near Oban; Clackmannan (The Stone of the Mannan) Stone in Clackmannanshire; and Clockmaben (The Stone of the Mabon) Stone, 1 mile south-west of Gretna. Each of these stones carries the probability that it was once part of dual or triple architecture or of a henge or a setting of huge standing stones, even though now seeming to be a single standing stone or a landmark stone.

As to the function, there are many references suggesting that it was a stone for the atonement of sins and to stimulate the procreation of progeny and so on, according to folklore and tradition, but no one really knows the original number and function of these stones.

The Watch Stone in Inverness was presumably the partner of Clachnaharry (Clach na h-aithrighe, or the Stone for Atonement), the name of which became established as the proper name of the place. Clach na h-aithrighe is now gone, leaving its name behind, and only the Watch Stone survives, just as is the case with the Watch Stone in the annex of Stenness Henge (see p43). The Watch Stone in Inverness is a monolith which is in essence a small lump of rock some 4 metres high.

Kirkland Hill Standing Stone is 3 metres high and 0.5 by 0.5 metres in girth and stands looking over Traprain Law, due south, and Kirkland Hill in the south-west, the direction of sunset at the winter solstice. Pencraig Hill Standing Stone is 3.5 metres high and 1 metre in girth at its base, thickening as it goes upwards. It stands overlooking far-distant North Berwick Law in the north-west, the exposure point of midsummer sunset. Each seems to have been an instrument for astronomical observation or a landmark stone.

Strontoiller Standing Stone is 4 metres high and 0.9 metres by 1.2 metres in girth, accompanied by a cairn 4.5 metres in diameter with a kerb of large boulders built in the 2nd millennium B.C. To the cairn clings a tradition that it was the burial ground of the Irish hero Diamid. A monolith stands as if it were a phallus to the "Womb of Earth" nearby. Kintraw Standing Stone, also a monolith, is 4 metres high, accompanied by a cairn 15 metres in diameter and 2 metres high with a kerb and three other small cairns. The stone stands 5.5 metres south-west of the largest cairn and according to tradition is said to have been for a long time a stone for promoting the fertility of progeny, as with Strontoiller Standing Stone.

61

Photograph (61) shows Strontoiller Standing Stone. In Japan, similar facilities consisting of a standing stone and spherical stones often stand at a diverging point of a road. However, it merely represents a phallic god which people implored for the prosperity of offspring.

62

Photograph (62) shows the monolith and cairn of Kintraw Standing Stone.

63   64

Photographs (63) and (64) show the Clackmannan Stone and the Clockmaben Stone.

A natural whinstone boulder, Clackmannan Stone now stands adjoining Clackmannan Tolbooth and Mercat Cross. It was a fertility boulder which came from the foot of Lookabouty Brae about 0.6 miles to the south. Mannan was the tribal name of the Votadinii of the Iron Age whose ancestry can be traced back to Manannan, the sea-god and Lord of Tir nan Og of the Tuatha De Danann.

Clockmaben Stone, which is near the confluence of Kirtle Water and the River Esk at the northern end of the Solway crossing, is a round boulder like the sun, as the name "Maben" was associated with the Gaulish sun-god and fertility-giver, Maponos. Both stones were once placed at a tribal meeting place.

65

66

Photograph (65) shows the alignment of Fingall's Limpet Hammer.

Photograph (66) shows the Brothers' Stone Standing Stones.

b. Dual Stone Monuments

Among typical examples are: "Giant's Grave" in mainland Shetland (see p24); "Fingall's Limpet Hammer" in Colonsay; Ballinaby Standing Stones in Islay; and Brothers' Stone Standing Stones on the slope of Brothers' Stone Farm in Ettrick and Lauderdale. These facilities seem to have possessed functions similar to those of the monolith, such as astronomical observation, ritual, social meeting and so on, though again the original structure and number of stones can not be proved. In Japan, a couple of rocks in the sea near the shore ordinarily served as a site for fixed point observation and they also represented a harmonious couple of god and goddess whom people implored for the well-being of their family and the prosperity of offspring.

67

*Photographs (67) and (68) show Tuilyies Standing
Stones and the stone having many decorations of cup-
marks on its surface.*

"Fingall's Limpet Hammer" is a stone setting where the two stones
stand aligned from north-west to south-east some 15 metres apart.
The height of the stones is 3.5 metres and 2.5 metres respectively.

Ballinaby Standing Stones also have two stones aligned from
north-east to south-west some 200 metres apart. The southern stone,
which stands in a cattle-pen, is nearly 5 metres high and 0.3 metres in
diameter at the base. The
northern stone on the hillside is broken.

Brothers' Stone Standing
Stones comprise two stones
aligned from south-east to
north-west some 13 metres
apart. The southern stone is
2.5 metres and the other 1.5
metres high. This setting
commands a beautiful view of
the Eildon Hills in the south-
west.

c. Monuments Comprising
Three or More Stones

Good examples of structures
comprising three or more

68

megaliths are: Drumtroddan Standing Stones 2 miles east-north-east of Port William in Wigtown; Moss Farm Machrie Standing Stones in the Isle of Arran; Ballymeanoch Standing Stones near Dunchraigaig Cairn in Mid Argyle; Dervaig Standing Stones at the northern end of the Isle of Mull; and Lundin Links Standing Stones in North East Fife. Though the functions of these stone settings seem to have been similar to those of monolithic and dual megalithic monuments, they do stir the imaginiation more strongly as to whether they would once have been much larger complexes. Tuilyies Standing Stones in Torryburn, Dunfermline, and Caiy Stane Standing Stone on the north side of Oxgangs Road, Fairmilehead, Midlothian, are each now reduced to a single stone, but it can be deduced that they were once part of huge constructions for astronomical observation, in view of the fact that they bear many decorations of cup-marks on their surfaces and that the stone sizes are comparatively large.

Drumtroddan Standing Stones is a structural alignment which comprises two megaliths over 3 metres high. The stones stand aligned from north-east to south-west some 20 metres apart with a recumbent megalith lying at the base of the southern stone as if it were some form of altar for ritual.

Moss Farm Machrie Standing Stones originally consisted of seven or eight megaliths but now only three megaliths survive. The tallest is 5.5 metres high and the surface of one megalith displays a great number of cup-marks, presumably the diagram of a constellation. Two cists have been found inside and from one of them there has been excavated a food-vessel containing cremation ash, along with a crouched inhumation burial.

Ballymeanoch Standing Stones is an alignment of three groups. Four stones stand in a line from north to

69

Photograph (69) shows the stone row of Drumtroddan Standing Stones.

south in the easterly position. The tallest is 3.6 metres high and one of these stones bears 23 cup-and-ring marks, of which some 15 have two rings, and there are also over one hundred and thirty cup-marks.

70

Photograph (70) shows Moss Farm Machrie Standing Stones, one of which bears decoration consisting of a quantity of cup-marks.

The second group, comprising two stones, stands 40 metres west of the first group. Some 18 metres to the north-west of the second group there was once a stone which had cup-marks and a hole at the top like Odin's Stone in the annex of Stenness Henge. It is suggestive of multilithic architecture, though its original scale and structure are unknown.

Dervaig Standing Stones is a setting in the form of a parallelogram composed of four megaliths. It is suggestive of the ritual setting for the ancient Japanese Shintoist ceremony of "Jichinsai" which took place to propitiate the soul of the tutelary god of earth. The stones are all substantial blocks over 2 metres high and three are still upright while the fourth, to the north, lies prostrate.

71

Photographs (71) and (72) show the stone rows of Ballymeanoch Standing Stones and the decoration of cup-marks and cup-and-ring marks left on the surface of one megalith.

Lundin Links Standing Stones is also a monument in the form of a parallelogram. However, it was conceivably a huge construction comprising a great many megaliths as in the case of the Callanish Standing Stones in Lewis (see p58). Though now only three stones survive, they are all megaliths. The north stone is 5.5 metres and the south 5 metres high, both tapering towards the top. The southeast one is 4 metres high and 1.5 metres wide. It is said that until the late 18th century there was a fourth stone nearby.

72

d. Stone Settings and Multilithic Monuments

In the classification of multilithic monuments are: Mid Clyth Stone Row Setting on the Hill o' Many Stanes, 9 miles south of Wick; Rearable Hill Stone Rows near Kildonan Lodge in Sutherland, the famous site of the "Kildonan Gold Rush" in 1869; Burgh Hill Stone Setting near Hawick, Roxburgh; Borrowstoun Rig Stone Setting in Ettrick and Lauderdale; Achavanish Standing Stones at the head of Loch Stemster near

73

Photograph (73) shows an overall view of Lundin Links Standing Stones.

Lybster in Wick; and Callanish Standing Stones in Lewis. However, the first two, Mid Clyth Stone Row Setting and the stone rows on Rearable Hill, are presumed to have been settings for the purpose of astronomical observation while the others were for both rituals and astronomical observation.

Mid Clyth Stone Row Setting, built in the 2nd millennium B.C., is composed of nearly two hundred earthfast boulders less than 1 metre high. The stones, in arrangements over twenty, in rows, run from north to south on the southern slope of a low hill called "Hill o' Many Stanes," fanning out towards the south end of the hill as shown in Figure (9). The original number of boulders is said to have been over six hundred.

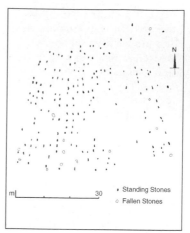

Figure 9

74

Photograph (74) shows an overall view of Mid Clyth Stone Row Setting.

Rearable Hill Stone Rows fan out on the edge of the south-east slope of a hill 190 metres above sea-level near the confluence of the Suisgill Burn and the River Helmsdale which once drew many gold prospectors. Though now very ruinous, the setting co-exists with circular Bronze Age cairns for cist graves with a stone kerb and a standing stone from the Bronze Age some 1.6 metres high on which was engraved a simple cross similar to the Creich Cross Slab (see p224) near Bonar Bridge.

75

Photograph (75) shows Rearable Hill Stone Rows.

Burgh Hill Stone Setting is a structure which originally comprised 25 or 26 slabs (13 times 2 ?) and measured 16.3 megalithic yards (13.5.metres) in diameter, but, having been once remodelled according to a definite geometrical rule, it now forms an egg-shape with 13 slabs. It measures 20 megalithic yards (16.5 metres) by 16.3 megalithic yards (13.5 metres) with the axis running south-west to north-east.

Borrowstoun Rig Stone Setting is a similar arrangement with an original setting once measuring 50 megalithic yards (41.5 metres) in diameter, but finally remodelled into a setting measuring 55.5 megalithic yards (46 metres) by 52 megalithic yards (43 metres) with the axis running west to east. Some thirty stones survive.

Achavanish Standing Stones is an oval stone setting which once comprised 60 stones but now only 36 stones survive to form a long U-shaped setting opening to the south-east. Broad stones about 2 metres high protrude on average 1.5 metres above

76

Photograph (76) shows the stone row of Achavanish Standing Stones.

the ground and are set at intervals of some 3 megalithic yards (2.5 metres) as in the case of the Callanish Standing Stones.   A   cist measuring 1.5 metres by 1 metre, formed by four slabs, was at the north-east corner just outside the setting.

Callanish Standing Stones at the head of East Loch Roag is an alignment in which a stone circle 13 metres in diameter was built with thirteen megaliths (stone numbers 41-53) from 2.5 to 3.7 metres in   height   and   a monumental pillar or the "Callanish Phallus" (stone number 29) 4.7 metres in height. This stone circle presumably formed   facilities   for ritual and astronomical observation.   Although the original number of stones   has   not   been determined, it is a huge construction where the total   of   48   stones (except for 5 stones, stone   numbers   36-40 used   to   form   the chambered   cairn) survive   and   form   a setting of 123 metres from   north   to   south (stone numbers 19-10 and 28-24) and 42.7 metres from east to west (stone   numbers   23-20

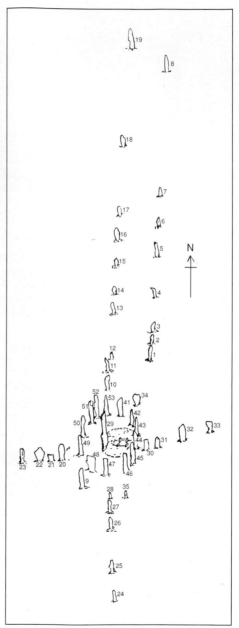

Figure 10

and 30-33), each stone aligned at an interval of 3 megalithic yards (2.5 metres).

[10] Admiral Boyle Somerville, who introduced the numbering system of the stones in 1912 as shown in Figure (10), explains that the prolonged line of five stones (stone numbers 24-28), aligned south to north, was the direction in which Bronze Age people had observed Capella early in the winter twilight of the 1800's B.C. and it points due north. The line from stone number 28 to 24 was the direction of the rocky outcrop of Cnoc na Tursa above which the full moon of midwinter used to pass some 2 degrees lower than usual every 18.61 years.

77

Photograph (77) show an overall view of Callanish Standing Stones.

78

Photograph (78) shows the stones of the north row. On the right-hand side are the stones of stone numbers 34 (the nearest one) and 1 to 8; on the left-hand side are those of 10 (the nearest) and 11 to 19.

79

Photograph (79) shows the stones of stone numbers 27, 26, 25 and 24 of the south row.

80

Photograph (80) shows the stone circle 13 metres in diameter built with fourteen megaliths, conceivably a ritual site; the highest stone is the "Callanish Phallus" (see p58).

The prolonged line of four stones from 23 to 20 is the direction in which people of the 1750's B.C. had observed Grigirean (the Pleiades) or the "Clock" and is the direction of the sunrise at each equinox (6:27 GMT), azimuth 90; the line from 33 to 30 is the direction of the sunset at each equinox (18.27 GMT), azimuth 270; 29 to 34 is the direction of midsummer sunrise (4:15 GMT), azimuth 40; the line from 9 to 20 is the direction of the midsummer sunset (10:15 GMT), azimuth 320; the line from 20 to 9 is the direction of midwinter sunrise (9:15 GMT), azimuth 140; the line from 34 to 29 is the direction of the midwinter sunset (15:45 GMT), azimuth 220; and the line of stone numbers 9 to 34 is the direction of the northern extreme of the midwinter full moon. It was a complex whereby the foreseeing

81

*Photograph (81) shows the stones of the west row: the
stone on the right-hand side is 49; the stone on the left-
hand side is 47 (nearest); and the stone row on the left-
hand side 48, 20, 21, 22 and 23.*

of the northern and southern extremes of moonrise and moonset at
minor and major standstill was possible.

The Outer Hebrides is an area which has a deep association with
the Tuatha De Danann who,
migrating from the north of
Scotland to Ireland, demanded
of the Fir Bolg (or the People of
the Leather Bag) that they
cede half of Ireland to them.
With negotiations broken off,
they then fought with the
natives "the Battle of Moytura",
near Cong in County Mayo. The
original arrangement was to
fight with bronze spears,
shields and swords of the same
number, but it was finally
fought with camans (or wooden
clubs) as used in "camanachd,"
the prototype of "shinty" which
is now the national sport of
Scotland.

The time of the arrival of
the Tuatha De Danann and the
contents of negotiations
between the two hosts are
precisely described by J. Fraser

82

*Photograph (82) shows the stones of
stone numbers 44 (nearest on the
right-hand side), 30, 31, 32 and 33 of
the east row; the stone on the left-hand
side is stone number 43.*

in his book *Erin VIII, 29* and by J. N. MacDonald, equally precisely, in his book *Shinty*. The date of the battle is circa 1896 B.C. according to *The Annals of Ireland*, and 1750 B.C. according to *The Book of Leinster*, and this coincides with the age when Bronze Age people in the area of the Callanish Standing Stones had observed Capella and the Pleiades in the northern and eastern skies of winter twilights. It was an age when the principal weapon was the "caman" or wooden club as bronze weapons were not so easily obtainable.

4. STONE CIRCLES

This type of monument is a small-scale henge structure comprising a small circle of standing stones and was probably a site for primeval religion where people of a minor autonomous community had once prayed to the Earth-mother goddess and the Sun-god in the heavens for the fertility of crops and animals. It is also presumed to have been a site which people used to observe the points where the sun and the moon rose and set. This arrangement acquired the name of "navity" (neimhidh) in the later Iron Age, meaning "an enclosure or sanctuary in oak-trees", though most of these constructions have burial insertions, just as is the case with Neolithic chambered cairns, henges, and other structures of standing stones.

The structure classified as a stone circle is widely distributed throughout the country, some well-preserved but others severely decayed or destroyed, thus making it impossible to eradicate doubt as to the original number of stones. Good examples of these structures are: the Twelve Apostles' Stone Circle near New Bridge in Nithsdale, Dumfries and Galloway; Torhouskie Stone Circle in Wigtown; Moss Farm Machrie Stone Circle in Arran; Templewood Stone Circles near Nether Largie South Chambered Cairn in Mid Argyle; Croft Moraig Stone Circle, 2 miles north-east of Kenmore in Perth and Kinross; Balbirnie Stone Circle in Kirkcaldy in Fife; and Kingside Hill Stone Circle, 6 miles south-south-east of Gifford, East Lothian.

Twelve Apostles' Stone Circle is a neimhidh of the Bronze Age, though its name is associated with a Christian ritual site. The structure was originally made up of 12 stones but now, of the 11 stones surviving, only 5 are still upright. It measures 90 metres by 75 metres and is the biggest stone circle on the mainland of Scotland and the fifth largest in Britain. One of the fallen stones has many cup-marks on its surface. The symbol "twelve," which is found in Eurasia as the "zodiacal twelve", is certainly older and more widespread than the start of Christianity. However, it is uncertain what function it had in those earlier days.

83

*Photograph (83) shows a part of Twelve Apostles'
Stone Circle. The nearest stone bears a quantity of
decoration of cup-marks.*

84

*Photograph (84) shows a part of Torhouskie Stone
Circle.*

Torhousekie Stone Circle consists of 19 stones and measures some
21 metres by 20 metres. In the centre of the circle is an altar-like
setting called "King Galdus's Tomb" where a massive recumbent stone
was flanked by two other massive stones. A standing stone is some 25
metres off to the south and an alignment of three stones stands to the
east.

Moss Farm Machrie Stone Circle consists of two concentric rings
of stones. The outer circle comprises fifteen small boulders and
measures 20 metres in diameter. The inner circle has eight large
boulders and measures 12 metres in diameter. This stone circle carries
the tradition that Fingall, an Irish hero, tethered his dog Bran to the
holed stone in the outer circle while he was in the inner circle, boiling

his cauldron, and so the inner circle has the other name of "The Seat of Fingall's Cauldron." The holed stone, though now gone, is presumed to have been an instrument for astronomical observation, as with Odin's Stone in the annex of Stenness Henge in mainland Orkney. A cist has been found at the centre of the circle.

85

Photograph (85) shows an overall view of Moss Farm Machrie Stone Circle.

86

Photographs (86) and (87) show an overall view of Templewood Stone Circles North and South, and the engraving of a spiral motif on a stone surface in the South circle.

The name Templewood is literally "neimhidh" or "the wood of the Druidical temple", presumably acquired in later days by reason of its existence, and the stone circles there consist of two structures built in the 4th or 3rd millennium B.C. One is Templewood Stone Circle North and the other Templewood Stone Circle South. The North circle is said to be the oldest stone circle in Scotland and measures some 10

metres in diameter, but it was
originally a timber circle similar
to Balfarg Henge in Fife (see
pp41-42). It was remodelled into
a stone circle, most of the
uprights of which have been
removed. Now only the remains
of the original posts of the
timber circle survive, marked by
round concrete pillars.

Templewood Stone Circle
South, adjoining the North,
measures some 12.5 metres in
diameter and consists of 13
stones about 1 metre high,
though the original number of
stones is uncertain. Within it
only ritual activities had been
practised for a long period of
time. The site is presumed to

87

have been the last phase of rebuilding and it was not until the 1700's
B.C. that burial settings were inserted inside and outside the
structure. One of the stones has a stone-pecked engraving of a spiral
motif on its surface. A beaker vessel and flint arrowheads have been
excavated.

Croft Moraig Stone Circle was revealed by excavations in 1965
as having its earliest setting in the late Neolithic Age. A penannular
setting of wooden posts was succeeded by a stone circle. The
original timber setting had its entrance in the south-west and
measured about 8 metres by 9 metres with an altar of flat stone at
the centre, and, from the depth of the post-holes, the height of the
timbers has been estimated at about 2 metres. About 2000 B.C.,
based on the same axis, it was remodelled into a stone circle which
measured 6 metres by 7.5 metres, comprising 8 large slabs from 1.4
metres to 1.6 metres high, with
three new outlying stones
appended on the southern arc.
Finally, it was remodelled into a
stone circle some 12 metres in
diameter, the arrangement
consisting of nine new stones,
three other outlying stones of
the earlier phase and two
entrance stones in the east-by-
south as shown in Figure (11).

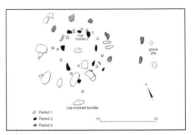

Figure 11

Some of the stones have cup-marks and cup-and-ring marks on their surfaces.

88

Photograph (88) shows Croft Moraig Stone Circle.

89

Photograph (89) shows an overall view of Balbirnie Stone Circle. A cup-and-ring mark is seen on the stone surface on the nearest right-hand side.

Balbirnie Stone Circle was excavated previous to the new road development plan, transferred to Balbirnie Park 125 metres south-east of the original site and re-erected as it had been. The circle is 15 metres by 14 metres, consisting of nine uprights. One of the stones on the south-east has a cup-and-ring mark on its surface. It has a hearth-like setting 3 metres by 4 metres at the centre and, as if encompassing it, there is an insertion of a cist 1.5 metres by 1 metre on both the east and west sides. On the inside wall of the easterly cist there are also decorations of cup-marks and cup-and-ring marks. Much cremated bone has been found inside the circle.

90

Photograph (90) shows an overall view of Kingside Hill Stone Circle.

Kingside Hill Stone Circle is a setting which stands in moorland called "Nine Stane Rig" or "Degsastan" which is presumed to be the site of the "Battle of Degsastan" fought between Aedhan of Dalriada and Aethelfrith of Northumbria in 600 or 603 A.D, (see p190). Though it is uncertain whether or not the setting is the original one, the circle is some 12 metres in diameter. It comprises some thirty small stones, the transport of which seems to have been easily possible, and a cairn is inserted at the centre, forming a low mound 3 metres in diameter surrounded by boulders.

In the later La Tene Age, Druids succeeded to some of these stone settings and remodelled or reconstructed them as sites for their own ritual and astronomical observations. A typical example is the "navity," which is the Anglicised form of "neimhidh" (sanctuary or enclosure in the wood) in Old Irish, surviving as Navity in Cromarty, in the Black Isle; Navitie in Ballingry near Loch Leven, Kinross (though now demolished); Dalnavie in Ross-shire; Navidale near Helmsdale in Sutherland;

91

Photograph (91) shows the road sign indicating the site of "Navity" in Cromarty.

Nemoth, the other name of Invernochty; and Neved near Dumbarton which has retained the root of the name "neimhidh."

Who and what were the Druids?   The principal sources of information about them are in the writings of Greek and Roman classical authors because the Druids were oral tramsmitters of their knowledge. Strabo (? 63 B.C.-21 A.D.?) describes them as a group of special honour consisting of Bards (bardoi) who were singers and poets; Vates (ouateis) who interpreted sacrifices and studied natural phenomena; and Druids who were concerned with both natural phenomena and moral philosophy. Diodorus (Siculus) lists them as Bards or poets chanting both eulogies and satires; Druids who were philosophers and theologians; and Manties who divined from sacrifices and auguries. And Strabo, referring to sacrifices of humans and animals, mentions that they were appallingly cruel, highlighting in particular a holocaust of humans and animals in a huge wickerwork device. [11]

Caesar (Gaius Julius, 100 B.C.– 44 B.C.) writes that the Druids were a high-ranking class of learned, non-combatant, respected and holy men within a barbarian society of a heroic type. He considered that the doctrine of the Druids was invented in Britain, describing the Druids as moral philosophers preaching the immortality of the soul; physical scientists deeply versed in the movements of the heavenly bodies, the size of the universe and the nature of the physical world; and, at the same time, theologians well versed in the power and properties of the immortal gods. Furthermore, he states that they were priests who took charge of religion and public and private sacrifices, and, at times, they were judges who settled disputes between communities and individuals. [12]

As seen in the case of Cairnpapple Henge (see pp43-44), many of the neimhidh built in the Bronze Age and presumably transferred in the Iron Age to the Druids, who also used the lunar calendar, survive in Grampian region as sites called " The Circle of the Moon".

5. THE CIRCLE OF THE MOON

In the early Bronze Age, North-East Scotland's Grampian region was the heartland of the users of the lunar calendar. Stone settings called " The Circle of the Moon" or stone circles, the centres of which had a massive recumbent stone and two flankers, were ordinarily built in the depths of a wood on the crest or saddle of a hill with a wide southerly view. The diameter was from 20 metres to 25 metres on average and the flankers and recumbent stone were normally set in the direction of moonrise or moonset, supposedly to show the points of moonrise and moonset at major and minor standstills. Some of the stones comprising the circle have cup-marks on their surfaces.

Ian A. G. Shepherd, the author of *Grampian, Exploring Scotland's Heritage* writes [13] that "these (settings), it is now known, were arranged to frame the rising or setting of the (major standstill) moon in the southern sky, when viewed from inside the circle. It follows that, for the monument to fulfill this primary function, the centre would have had to be unemcumbered by rising cairns. Furthermore, such lunar observations would have been helpful to define broad, seasonal changes for the small egalitarian farming communities which had co-operated to build the circles, and other relevant rituals can be imagined in the central space. The fertility of crops and animals may have been ensured by acts of sympathetic or imitative magic performed within bonfire-lit circles to the urgent, entrancing drumming that faded into night's blackness all around."

Innumerable structures of "the Circle of the Moon" survive in the woods of Grampian region. In Kincardine and Deeside district are: Tomnaverie Recumbent Stone Circle in Tarland; Nine Stane Recumbent Stone Circle in Mulloch; and Garrol Hill and Eslie the Greater Recumbent Stone Circle in Banchory. In Banff and Buchan district are: Louden Wood Recumbent Stone Circle and Strichen Recumbent Stone Circle near Old Deer. In Gordon district are: Midmar Kirk Recumbent Stone Circle in Echt; Sunhoney Recumbent Stone Circle in Echt; Loanhead of Daviot Recumbent Stone Circle in Daviot; and Easter Aquhorthies Recumbent Stone Circle in Inverurie. However, "the Circles of the Moon" to be dealt with here as monuments unique to this Grampian region are limited to four: Eslie the Greater Recumbent Stone Circle; Strichen Recumbent Stone Circle; Sunhoney Recumbent Stone Circle; and Loanhead of Daviot Recumbent Stone Circle.

Eslie the Greater Recumbent Stone Circle is a facility which was situated on the low shoulder of a hill half a mile to the south-west of Eslie the Lesser. The circle, with wide views to the south and west, is 27 metres by 24 metres in diameter, and five stones of the original eight still stand, along with a recumbent stone and two flankers. There is an insertion of a ring cairn 18 metres in diameter.

Strichen Recumbent Stone Circle is a monument which Dr Johnson (Samuel, 1709-84) and Boswell (James, 1740-95) visited on 25th August 1773. "We set out at about nine. Dr Johnson was curious to see one of those structures which northern antiquarians call a Druids' temple. I had a recollection of one at Strichen, which I had seen fifteen years ago; so we went four miles out of our road, after passing Old Deer, and went thither. Mr Fraser, the proprietor, was at home and showed it to us. But I had augmented it in my mind; for all that remains is two stones set up on end, with a long one laid upon

92

Photograph (92) shows the altar of Eslie the Greater Recumbent Stone Circle.

93

Photograph (93) shows an overall view of Strichen Recumbent Stone Circle.

them, as was usual, and one stone at a little distance from them. That stone was the capital one of the circle which surrounded what now remains." So Boswell writes in the passage of August 25th in his *Journal of a Tour to the Hebrides.*

This monument is now situated on a crest below the summit of the rounded Buchan Hill but it was in woodland when Dr Johnson and Boswell made their visit. This Circle of the Moon is some 12 metres in diameter, built on a slight bank. The circle comprises thirteen stones in all and the flankers and recumbent stone are orientated to the extreme southern moonrise. However, what now remains was reconstructed after the excavations of 1979-83. This structure had once been pulled down by a tenant farmer some twenty years after Dr Johnson and Boswell had visited it but it was re-erected to the south

of the original site by demand of the land-owner. It is said that near
the recumbent stone of the original site there has been found a great
deal of quartzite flakes which are presumed to have been used for
enhancing the cheering effect of moonlight.

94

*Photograph (94) shows the recumbent and flanking
stones of Sunhoney Recumbent Stone Circle.*

Sunhoney Recumbent Stone Circle is also a "neimhidh" which is in
a quiet wood on a low hill shoulder in Echt, 125 metres above sea-
level. It measures 25 metres in diameter, now having nine uprights
and a recumbent stone with two flankers which were orientated to the
points of the extreme southern moonrise. The recumbent stone is
cracked but it has thirty-one cup-marks on its surface and a low ring
cairn has been inserted inside the circle. Deposits of cremated bone
and a circular cist have been found along with the fragments of a stone
vessel.

Loanhead of Daviot Recumbent Stone Circle is also situated on a
gentle hill crest, 155 metres above sea-level. The circle is some 20
metres in diameter, comprising eight uprights. One of the standing
stones has five cup-marks engraved in a vertical line on its surface. Two
flankers and a massive recumbent stone of some 20 tons are
orientated to the direction of the extreme southern moonset. A low
cairn with a kerb occupies the whole inside area of the circle, and
beaker sherds, charcoal and cremated human bone have been
excavated. Just on the south east of this structure lies a cremation
cemetery some 15 metres in diameter with entrances at the west and
east, presumably built in the later Iron Age. Within the two arcs of a
ditch and the lines of a stone bank (with entrances at the west and the
east) was enclosed a grave-pit, and cremated bone and cinerary urns
have been excavated from there.

95

Photograph (95) shows an overall view of Loanhead of Daviot Recumbent Stone Circle and the cremation cemetery of the Iron Age.

6. CUP-MARKS AND CUP-AND-RING MARKS

Cup-marks and cup-and-ring marks are both puzzling. These markings, once widespread in Northern Spain and Ireland in the Bronze Age and eventually making their appearance in Scotland in the first half of the 2nd millennium, were marks chiselled on the surfaces of standing stones and outcropping rock.

A cup-mark is a single depression some one inch in diameter and depth, while a cup-and-ring mark is a complex mark which constitutes a single depression with double or triple concentric rings encircling it. Both appear mostly in plural numbers on stone surfaces, though it is not known whether the marks were contemporaneous or not.

As to the function of cup-marks, they have been conjectured as being copies of a certain constellation or a diagram to show the extreme points of the moonrise or moonset at major and minor standstills. However, as to the function of cup-and-ring marks, no acceptable explanation has come forward but, though the mark has remained as an enigma which perhaps only Bronze Age people understood, it is a fact that stones having these marks are dotted mainly in Northumbria, and, as far as Scotland is concerned, to the south of the line linking Oban in Mid Argyle with Arbroath in Angus.

Good examples are: High Banks Cup-and-Ring Mark Stone, 2 miles south-east of Kirkcudbright; Drumtroddan Cup-and-Ring Mark Stone, 1.5 miles east-north-east of Port William, Wigtownshire; Kilmichael Glassary Cup-and-Ring Mark Stone and the Cup-and-Ring Mark Stone of Achanabreck, north of Lochgilphead in Mid Argyle; and Tormain

96

*Photograph (96) shows the markings of High Banks
Cup-and-Ring Mark Stone.*

97

*Photograph (97) shows the markings of Drumtroddan
Cup-and-Ring Mark Stone.*

Hill Cup-and-Ring Mark Stone 3 miles south-west of Ratho near
Edinburgh. However, these marks are also seen on stones in the Croft
Moraig Stone Circle (see pp65-66), Balbirnie Stone Circle (see p66)
and Ballymeanoch Standing Stones (see pp53-54)

The geographical distribution of these stones, which suggest
moulds or casting moulds for wrought metals as well, is roughly
limited to the Kirkcudbright, Wigtown, Perth and Mid Argyle regions
in Scotland. Most of these stones have both cup-marks and cup-and-
ring marks. Stones having only a cup-mark or cup-marks are mainly
found to the north of the line connecting Oban and Arbroath.

High Banks Cup-and-Ring Mark Stone bears several groups of cup-
and-ring marks on rock surfaces nearly 30 metres long. A remarkable

Photograph (98) shows the markings of Kilmichael Glassary Cup-and-Ring Mark Stone.

feature is the close massing of great numbers of simple cup-marks which were carved around cup-and-ring markings.

The Stone of Drumtroddan has markings on a flat exposed rock. They comprise cup-marks and cup-and-ring marks (with concentric rings), both with and without radial grooves. The markings of Kilmichael Glassary Cup-and-Ring Mark Stone is an assembly of a variety of marks. Deep and large cup-marks are surrounded by a single ring groove and double, triple and quadrupple ring grooves. These marks seems to have been carved by different settlers, according to differences in the chiselling.

CHAPTER III

SETTLEMENTS OF THE PREHISTORIC AGE

I t is quite rare for dwelling houses from the prehistoric age to survive intact. Unfortunately, with a few exceptions, it is difficult to find instances on the mainland of Scotland where urbanization and development of farmland have been comparatively active. However, good examples can be seen in the outlying islands such as the Orkney and Shetland Islands. Such dwelling houses are: Skara Brae Settlement near the Ring of Brodgar in mainland Orkney; Rinyo Settlement in Rousay, Orkney; and Sumburgh or Jarlshof Settlements, Stanydale Settlements, including the Settlements of "Temple," Ness of Gruting and Scord of Brouster in Shetland.

Skara Brae Settlement (Old Norse "Skari" (Shore) plus Scottish "brae" (bank)) consists of some ten houses clustered together, connected by complicated passages (see Figure 12). The settlement

Figure 12

99

Photograph (99) shows a part of the overall view of
Skara Brae Prehistoric Village.

had been underneath the blown sands of the seashore until it was
exposed by high sea water after a violent storm in December, 1850.
Radiocarbon dating shows its construction to have been carried out
between 3000 B.C. and 2500 B.C., and the inhabitation term to have
been 600 years, during which period took place the reconstructions
and modifications of the houses and passages which now remain.
Based on excavations, the inhabitants numbered some thirty and they
are presumed to have been fishermen who could also cope with
farming, keeping cattle, sheep, goats and pigs, and at times took part
in hunting wild animals for the economic benefit of the whole
community.

Each house is rectangular in shape. The bigger ones are 6.5 metres
by 6 metres and the smaller ones 4.5 metres by 4 metres. The walling,
some 2.5 metres high, is of thick drystones and the roofs seem to have

100

Photograph (100) shows the interior and fixtures of House No.1. of Skara Brae Settlement.

been corbelled at the top of the wall and spanned by a frame such as a timber or a beam.

The entrance of each house is 1.1 metres high and 0.6 metres wide. Inside the house is a set of furniture and utensils for daily life, such as a hearth some 1.5 metres by 1 metre; a pair of box beds (from 1.8 metres by 1 metre to 1.2 metres by 0.8 metres) which seems to indicate the height of the inhabitants of those days; a wall cupboard of two shelves, probably designed to store food and vessels; a stone box; and a stone kneading trough and mortar.

Rinyo Settlement, a similar type to that of Skara Brae, was partially excavated in 1938 and awaits a full-scale excavation. Implements for the daily life of prehistoric settlers, amounting to some 250 items (including beaker ware, flint knives, stone hammers, axes and balls), have been uncovered and show that the cultural tradition was similar to that of Skara Brae.

Sumburgh Settlements (Swymbrocht: the former half represents a Scandinavian personal name and the latter half Old Norse "borg" or "fort")

101

Photograph (101) shows the passage connecting each house of Skara Brae Settlement.

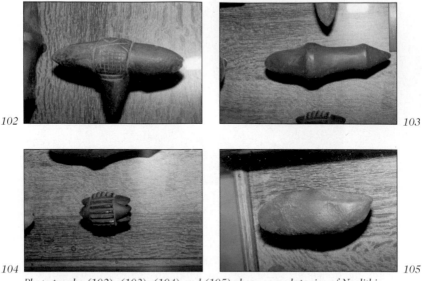

Photographs (102), (103), (104) and (105) show some legacies of Neolithic civilization: a stone hammer; a stone axe; a stone ball; and a spatula.

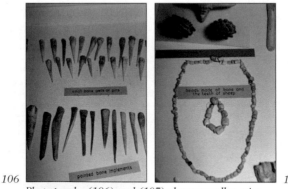

Photographs (106) and (107) shows needles, pins and beads made of bone and the teeth of sheep.

is a complex of settlements which comprised heterogeneous settlers. It commenced with the settlement of Bronze Age people in the early or middle period of the 2nd millennium B.C. Their houses were oval stone-built huts surrounded by a thick drystone walling.

Next, late Bronze Age settlers built houses with the inside complicated like a labyrinth, some 8 metres by 5 metres and 1.5

108

*Photograph (108) shows the type of hut which Bronze
Age people built.*

metres high with a hearth at the centre.
Then early Iron Age settlers migrated
there and built circular houses and, after
a span of time, in came the Picts, the
builders of the "broch." The next arrivals
were the builders of an aisled round
house or "wheel-house" (see Figure 13)
which, measuring from 5 metres to 8
metres in diameter and from 1.5 metres
to 2.5 metres in height, had rooms some
2 metres long and 1.5 metres wide
radially divided towards the
circumference with the hearth at the
centre as an axis. People were able to
come and go from house to house
through a passage as in the case of Skara
Brae village. Throughout the days of the

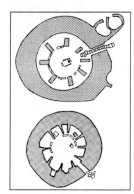

*Fig. 13 shows the plan of
a "wheel-house."*

Vikings, who were fond of a rectangular form of house, the settlement
survived until about 1600 A.D. when the laird's house was built there
(named "Jarlshof" or "Earl's temple" in *The Pirate* by Sir Walter Scott
who visited there in 1816).

Judging from the contents of the excavations, the earliest
inhabitants seem to have burned peat and cooked fish and shellfish.
The fact that some of the earliest houses had an extension
compartment for cattle suggests that the life of the Bronze Age people
seems to have been much more pastoral. From sites of wheel-houses
there have been excavated some 200 items of clay moulds for casting
axes, swords and spears, a legacy of the smiths who moved there
around 650 B.C.

109   110

Photographs (109) and (110) show the interior and fixtures of the wheel-house and the passage by which each house was connected to the others.

111

Photograph (111) shows a Viking Age settlement.

  Stanydale House, called "Temple", 1.5 miles east-south-east of Bridge of Walls, is a late Bronze Age house, the appearance of which reminds us of a heel-shaped chambered cairn from the Neolithic Age: hence it is called "Temple." The external measurement is 13 metres by 19 metres and the thickness of the wall is 3.5 metres with large boulders arranged at places like the kerb of a chambered cairn. Its

112

*Photograph (112) shows a grinding quern from the
Bronze Age.*

113

*Photograph (113) shows a bronze spear-head and axe
and their clay moulds.*

circumference encloses an oval area measuring some 12 metres by 6
metres. The entrance on the south-east, some 2 metres long, opens
from the centre of the facade and the interior near the entrance is
slightly narrower than the north-west end. The fixture of this house is
plain and at the north-westerly depth of the house are six recesses
similar to the chambers seen in the wheel-house. At the centre are two
post sockets for timber uprights, some 0.3 metres in diameter, which
presumably once supported the central ridge of the roof. Since the
inside is very spacious, it was probably a building for public assembly.

The settlement of Ness of Gruting is 2 miles south-east of Bridge
of Walls and is an oval house with half an oval room appended to the
main chamber opposite the entrance. The main chamber measures
some 6 metres in length by 4.5 metres in breadth, while the apse is

114

Photographs (114) and (115) show an overall view of "Temple" and its interior.

some 2.2 metres by 1.8 metres. The wall is about 2.7 metres thick and the entrance, with a porch, is at the south-east side. The house seems to have been used by a potter. Along with stone articles and artefacts from the late Neolithic Age, great quantities of domestic pottery and the commonest sherds, decorated with sheveron and herring bone patterns, have been excavated and surely reflect a ceramic tradition in the builders of Hebridean chambered cairns (see Figure 1). The patterns of sheveron and herring bone were to become the prototype and basis of the Hebridean textile patterns in later days.

115

116

Photograph (116) shows an overall view of the settlement of Ness of Gruting.

CHAPTER IV

THE IMMIGRATION OF IRON AGE SETTLERS

With the dawn of the 7th century B.C., devotees of the Halstatt civilization, who were a mixture of Teutons and Brythons, began to flow from the continent into Scotland (where the aboriginal inhabitants at that time were Bronze Age people), though the names and homelands of these tribes are not known. They were the ancient British, descendants of Celts who had made their appearance in the 2nd millennium B.C. in central Europe, east of the Rhine, and enlarged their domains by successive raids. They were people well versed in the art of metal-working, having a thorough knowledge of bronze and iron, and their livelihood is presumed to have been based upon both farming and stock raising.

Following the influx of these new people, another new group, devotees of the La Tene civilization which originated in the eastern area of Lake Neuchatel in Switzerland, began to arrive from about the middle of the 5th century B.C. They were cremationists and fire-worshippers highly skilled in the art of iron working. Caesar writes in his *De Bello Gallico* that [14] although Gaul was not a rich country, funerals there were splendid and costly; everything the dead man was thought to have been fond of was put on the pyre, even including animals; until latter times, slaves and dependents known to have been their master's favourites were burned with him at the end of the funeral.

They were roughly contemporary with the people who penetrated the Iberian Peninsula; sacked Rome in 386 B.C.; within a century raided Delphi; and established the colony of Galatia in Asia Minor. Those who moved to Britain were mainly Britons and Druidists.

[15] Strabo writes that when the three Celtic tribes, the Tectosages, the Troemi and the Tolistobogii, settled in the district called after them, Galatia, "the land of the Gauls," in Asia Minor in 280 B.C., the first thing they did was to establish a central council of three hundred to judge

cases of bloodshed; other offences were left to the chiefs of districts, or tetrarchs, and local judges. Strabo adds that this great council functioned at a place called Drunemeton," the chief Nemeton" or "chief sacred place." Nemeton is "neimhidh" in Gaelic, a place of judgment and worship. Caesar also writes in corroboration that the Druids met at a fixed time of the year in a sacred place (in loco consecrato) in the tribal territory of the Carnutes and judged all disputes. [16]

Their society was tribal in organization though linked by a common culture, custom, language and religion. They seem to have been a factional people who, over-concerned with trifles, could not renounce their quarrelsome tribal traits and form a stable coalition with other tribes. Tacitus writes: "Fortune can give no greater boon than discord among our foes, and we pray that the tribes might retain their traditional hatred one for another indefinitely." The Romans built up the powerful Roman Empire as a result of political union but the Celts could not put political unity into practice because they tended to fractionalise their society.

Caesar says that the Celts with whom he came into contact were not a nation: they were a complex of tribal groups in different stages of social development (BFG, VI,12). Their tribal organization was a monarchy headed by a noble and his family. After them, two privileged Druids and knights were ranked; and then craftsmen, who took charge of iron working, were followed by freemen engaged in food production. At the lowest rank were groups of unfreemen or slaves who chiefly took

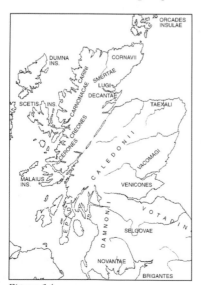

charge of farming and stock raising. The noble owned large tracts of farmland and large herds of cattle and at times hired them out to farmer-clients in return for food and service [17]: it was the prototype of the tenant farming system in later days. In their households, husbands had power of life and death over their wives and children. However, property management between husband and wife was based on co-ownership. [18]

The vicissitudes of the tribe or clan depended upon the choice and competence of the knights, craftsmen and freemen allied to a particular chieftain to whom they pledged their loyalty and received patronage in return.

Figure 14

*Illustration (1) is an artist's impression of an unenclosed
platform settlement in the Bronze Age.*

117

*Photograph (117) shows the site of Green Knowe Unenclosed Platform
Settlement in the Bronze Age. It is 3 miles north-west of White Meldon Hill on
the opposite side of the Meldon Burn, 3 miles north-west of Peebles. There were
nine unenclosed hut platforms, on average 15 metres in diameter, each
platform bearing evidence of ten or eleven circular timber posts in a circle
some 8 metres in diameter.*

According to Claudius Ptolemaeus, geographer of Alexandria in the 2nd century, the tribes which moved into Scotland up until the 2nd century A.D. numbered sixteen or eighteen, large and small ones mixed together, as shown in Figure (14).

The Brigantes occupied the north of Northumbria; the Selgovae, the Borders, including Ettrick and Lauderdale; the Votadinii (the Gododdin), the Lothians and Berwick; the Novantae, Dumfries and Galloway, including a part of Strathclyde; the Damnonii, Strathclyde and Central districts; the Venicones, Fife and Tayside; the Vacomagi, Grampian; the Taezali, the northern part of Grampian; the Caledonii, the central Highland districts from Perth to Inverness between Grampian and Argyle districts; the Epidii, Argyle; the Creones or Cerones, the north of Argyle; the Carnonacae, Wester Ross and a part of the north of Wester Ross; the Carinii, the north of Wester Ross; the Cornavii, Caithness; the Lugi, Sutherland; the Smeartae (the Painted Folk, i.e. the Pictish?), central Sutherland; and the Decantae, Easter Ross.

Caesar writes that [19] the most important deity whom the Celts worshipped was the deity of arts and crafts, corresponding to the Roman Mercury and Minerva. Next were ranked Apollo, Mars and Jupiter. Among the names of newly immigrated tribes were those which associated themselves with Celtic deities as is shown by the names of the Brigantes, the Epidii, and the Lugi. The Brigantes were associated with Brigantia, the Halstattan Minerva; the Epidii with Epos, "the horse", or the Celtic Apollo; and the Lugi with Lougos or "the raven", the Celtic Jupiter.

118

Photograph (118) shows the site of Normangill Rig Unenclosed Platform Settlement along the Campus Water road. Well-preserved platforms which had originally supported circular timber-houses in the Bronze Age have been excavated.

1. HILL-FORTS: SETTLEMENTS OF THE IRON AGE

Illustration (2) is an artist's impression of an Iron Age settlement.

Structures built by the new-comers to Scotland in the Iron Age were hill-forts, brochs, galleried duns and crannogs.   Hill-forts were constructed on the crests and saddles of hills to protect tribal men and their stock from outer and inter-tribal warfare and cattle larceny. They were defended structures, dissimilar to the unenclosed and defenceless ones which Bronze Age people had built. In plan the hill-fort resembles the Bronze Age henge monument where part of the sanctuary was reformed into residential quarters and its outer ditch and bank into a defensive arrangement, at times appending a palisade, or timber-laced stone wall. The defence mechanism all resulted from the technological advance of producing iron weapons, and a huge complex of these facilities was called an "oppidum."

Defence structures built in island and coastal districts were brochs and galleried duns. A broch is a structure supposedly constructed by the Picts who are presumed to have begun their influx about the 8th century B.C. It is a cylindrical structure, the whole walling of which was made of stone slabs with the base slightly broader than the upper section. Usually, it has one entrance and the height is some 10 metres, the external diameter being some 20 metres. The courtyard inside is 10 metres in diameter with a hearth and a well. The interior walling structure is 5 metres thick and has passages and chambers inside it. The galleried dun is also a low cylindrical structure, the internal diameter of which is some 10 metres to 15 metres with a stone walling from 3 metres to 6 metres high and 5 metres thick, in which are enclosed rooms and passages with footholds at places. Its external diameter is from 20 metres to 25 metres. The structure can be categorized as a lowered broch with one entrance. A crannog was a defended homestead built on an artificial island with a palisade, but no traces have been left of this type of structure.

Crabs make their hole dwellings to suit their carapace, and the ancients, whose environments were suited to their inherent natural states, built masterpieces of defensive structure, making the best and wisest use of natural features along with the advantage of location. But merciless are the ferocity of nature and the passage of time. These structures were free from the protection of the human taboos attached to cairns and ceremonial sites, and thus most hill-forts, brochs and galleried duns were destined to be weathered or readily destroyed, or both together, leaving only their sites behind.

a. Hill-forts in the Borders and Lothian Region

In the Borders there is quite a large number of hill-forts. These include: Eildon Hill North Fort and Tollis Hill Fort in Ettrick and Lauderdale; Woden Law Fort with Roman siege works in Roxburghshire; Dreva Craig Fort with settlements and field-systems in Peebles-shire; Traprain Law Fort and Chesters Drem Fort in East Lothian; Braidwood Settlement; and Castle Law Fort with souterrain in Midlothian.

Eildon Hill North Fort, 1 mile south-east of Melrose, was an oppidum of the Selgovae who occupied the Upper Tweed area. The life span of the fort is interpreted as having ended when the Roman army arrived in Tweedsdale in 79 A.D. The earliest structural feature is now almost invisible but the defence was a single wall or rampart enclosing the hill-top for a length of some 180 metres and to a width of some 50 metres. The earlier works of the north and north-east flanks were in later times remodelled into a small oppidum of some 10 acres and it was finally surrounded by two heavy ramparts to form a hill-fort some 40 acres in extent.

With some 300 platforms remaining in the west of the hill-top, there still exists a shallow ditch, part of it overlapped by the foundation of a Roman signal station which was presumably erected in relation to the Newstead Roman supply station at the foot of this hill in the second century (see pp137, 143).

Woden Law is about 9 miles south-east of Jedburgh and Woden Law Fort, with Roman siege work, is on the crest of this hill 423 metres

119

Photograph (119) shows a view of Woden Law; the road is the old "Dere Street."

120

Photograph (120) shows the earthworks and ditch of Woden Law Fort.

above sea-level, just above the Roman road known as "Dere Street" which was in Roman times one of the main military routes from Corbridge in Northumbria to Newstead. Originally, it was, for a long period, the fort of a native British tribe, though the tribal name is not certain. From the complex sequences of its defences, which are surrounded by multifarious earthworks, ramparts and ditches, the fort on top of the hill seems to have been reconstructed at least twice. The earthworks to the east and south were appended by the Roman army for training soldiers in siege operations.

Dreva Craig Fort with settlements and field-systems is 1 mile south-east of Broughton. The area of some 650 square metres, with a Bronze Age cairn, is defended by two substantial stone walls some 4 metres thick at the base. A great number of stones were set to

121

Photograph (121) shows the stone rampart of Dreva Craig Fort and, in the far distance, a Bronze Age cairn.

discomfort enemies attempting to rush this fort and the build-up of stones acted as a natural barrier to chariots or horsemen approaching the entrance, 3.5 metres wide, on the south-east. On the north-west slope of the fort is an extensive settlement of stone-walled houses with traces of field-systems.

Tollis Hill Fort is located some half a mile west of a farm house at the end of a minor road, north-north-east up Kelphope Burn, Ettrick and Lauderdale. It is a circular henge-like hill-fort which is 90 metres across internally and is enclosed by a double rampart with an intervening ditch. The defences in the west and north sides are well preserved and the inner ramparts are some 4 metres high from the bottom of the ditch. The western entrance, also well-preserved, is some 2.5 metres wide. The location is suitable for farming and stock raising and there is a large number of hut circles within the ramparts.

122

Photograph (122) shows the ditch and rampart of Tollis Hill Fort.

123

*Photograph (123) shows a distant view of Traprain
Law Fort.*

Traprain Law, 2 miles south-west of East Linton, is an oval hill
resembling a recumbent boar, though the north-east part has been
eroded by quarrying. It retains many traces of fortifications, and
excavations and finds show that it had been a settlement site from the
Neolithic Age through to the Bronze Age, though now the visible
structures are all of the Iron Age.

The hill falls steeply on the north while the eastern and southern
flanks and the site in the west (where a rampart 1,100 metres long
and 3.5 metres thick was constructed and enclosed an area of some 30
acres) reveals structures from the Iron Age.

An area of some 40 acres, enclosed by a rampart which takes in a
number of hut-platforms on the lower slopes of the north plateau, was
the tribal capital of the Votadinii, though overlapping to some degree
with the structures of the west side. It was a site where great numbers
of people once massed and were employed in industries such as metal-
working, farming and stock raising, as well as trading with the Romans
and southern countries by way of the east coast sea route.

Chesters Drem Fort is 1 mile south of Drem, East Lothian, and
stands on a low ridge just under the lee of a precipitous hill, some 15
metres high, from which even a primitive missile could be directed to
the interior. The external measurement of the whole structure is 275
metres by 150 metres and three lower ramparts and two shallow
ditches run within it. The entrances are set on the north-west and
east sides, the innermost rampart enclosing an area some 110 metres
by 45 metres, and there are traces of several circular stony
foundations of varied size.

Braidwood Settlement, 0.5 miles south-west of Silverburn, 10
miles south-south-west of Edinburgh, has been remodelled twice to its
present arrangement. The structure surrounds an open space some 55

124

Photograph (124) shows a panoramic view of Chesters Drem Fort.

125

Photograph (125) shows a panoramic view of Braidwood Settlement.

metres by 35 metres, comprising two ditches and an intervening bank with a concentric palisade trench appended in later times. There were three entrances and there remain traces of some ten houses within the earthwork. The first phase was an all-timber structure enclosed by a single palisade inside, but in the second phase an outer palisade 15 metres in length was appended between two entrances and formed a cattle-pen-like structure.

126

Photograph (126) shows a panoramic view of Castle Law Fort and Photograph (127) shows the souterrain.

Castle Law Fort, with souterrain, is 3 miles south-west of Fairmilehead and is an oval hill-fort. It is defended by three ramparts and ditches with enclosing palisades some 80 metres by 40 metres and has an internal souterrain system (some 20 metres long and up to 2 metres in width and height) . Midway along the passage on the west side is the entrance of a souterrain which has a bee-hive chamber 3.5 metres in diameter. Brooches, Roman pottery and glass-ware have been excavated from the souterrain.

127

b. Hill-forts in Dumfries and Galloway, Clydesdale and Strathclyde Region

In Dumfries and Galloway, which was the territory of the Novantae, are Burnswark Hill Fort in Annandale; Tynron Doon Hill Fort in Nithsdale; and Rispain Camp in Wigtown. In Clydesdale region are Abory Hill Fort; Fallburn Fort; Black Hill Lesmahagow Fort (with settlement and cairn); and Cow Castle Fort. In Strathclyde region, once the territory of the Damnonii, are Walls Hill Fort in Renfrewshire and Dumbarton Rock on the North shore of the River Clyde (see photo 232).

Burnswark Hill Fort, on the spectacular plateau of Burnswark Hill, named after the fort, is a fortification which dominates most of Annandale. Its earliest structure was an enclosure defended by a palisade trench some 275 metres by 200 metres at the east end of the hill, and it is presumed to have been built about 600 B.C.

The structure in the second phase was a gourd-shaped fort some 17 acres in extent, lying lengthwise from north-east to south-west some 500 metres in length with its south-western half 250 metres and its north-eastern half 100 metres wide. This structure was most likely an oppidum of the Novantae and is thought to have been demolished by the 1st century when the Romans arrived. In the 2nd century there were appended two Roman siege camps, one 300 metres by 80 metres and the other 100 metres by 200 metres in extent on the north-west and south-east flanks of the hill. The latter, on the south-east flank, is thought to have been the facilities in the time of the second Roman incursion into the north under the reign of Emperor Antoninus (see p137). These siege camps were once bases for Roman soldiers on field exercises, practising the use of ballistae to attack British forts. However, they were used in punitive expeditions after the uprisings in 155 A.D. when the nearby Roman fort at Birrens was demolished (see p138).

128

Photograph (128) shows Burnswark Hill.

Tynron Doon Hill Fort is a small fort and stands on a hill-top rising abruptly to a height of 289 metres above sea-level some 2 miles west-by-south of Penpont in Dumfriesshire. The defence on the summit, where there is a hut circle some 5 metres in diameter, measures 45 metres by 40 metres and is surrounded by a boulder rampart. The north-eastern side, just below the summit, forms a scarp of natural terraces of three steps and has crescent-shaped enclosures surrounded by stone parapets. Only to the west and south-western sides, on slopes just below the summit, are there man-made oval defences. In its construction it resembles Dun Nosebridge Fort in Islay (see p112).

Rispain Camp, situated north-west of Rispain Farm, is a settlement of the late Iron Age surrounded by rectangular earthworks. It measures some 70 metres by 50 metres, surrounded by a deep V-

129

Photograph (129) shows a distant view of Tynron Doon Hill Fort; the fort is on the hill-top.

130

Photograph (130) shows the V-shaped ditch of Rispain Camp.

shaped ditch originally 5.8 metres in depth. The upcast diggings of the ditch have provided material for the bank on either side of the settlement, and the south and east sides have a further outer ditch. The entrance is at the centre of the north-east side and on the north-western side is the site of a circular house some 15 metres in diameter.

Abory Hill Fort, which is on an elevated plateau at a height of 429 metres above sea-level, has a series of defences representing two periods of fortification. The earlier defence, consisting of two sets of ramparts with outer ditches and counterscarp banks, measures some 80 metres by 70 metres. The outer rampart has one entrance and the inner rampart five, which suggests that the area between the ramparts was once a cattle-pen. In the second period there was an insertion of a stone-walled enclosure some 45 metres in diameter with no rampart nor ditch within the inner rampart. There are two entrances, and traces of some houses with a ring-ditch are detectable within the enclosure.

Fallburn Fort is a well-preserved fort situated on a slight knoll on the access to Tinto Hill Cairn. The defences consist of two ramparts and ditches with a low counterscarp bank around the verge of the outer ditch, and a stone-walled enclosure is inserted within it. It probably represents a second period of fortification and, in plan, its sequence resembles that of Abory Hill Fort. This fort has two entrances but there are no traces of houses within the inner enclosure.

131

Photographs (131) and (132) show a distant view of Fallburn Fort and its ditches and ramparts.

132

133

*Photograph (133) shows the single stone wall of Black
Hill Lesmahagow Fort, now in a ruinous state.*

Black Hill Lesmahagow Fort, with settlement and cairn, is on the
top of Black Hill, 290 metres above sea-level, dominating the Clyde
Valley. The fort is oval and measures 255 metres by 110 metres within
a single stone wall which is now greatly ruined. The cairn, from the
Bronze Age, is some 18 metres in diameter and 1 metre high, and it
is in the uppermost position of the fort. On the south-east side of the
fort there is a settlement enclosed by earthworks built at a later stage.
Cow Castle Fort is a hill-fort of two main periods of fortification,
though, more precisely, probably of multi-periods, and is situated on
the south-west end of an isolated ridge near Nisbet Farm 1.5 miles
south-east of Culter. The earlier and larger one is D-shaped with its
chord in the western side, fitting it to the geographical features of the
eastern and western sides on steep scarps. It measures some 70
metres by 50 metres, with entrances on both north and west sides, and

is set within a single heavy rampart and ditch. The later and smaller one, also D-shaped but almost an oval, measures 42 metres by 30 metres and is inserted within an earlier D-shaped enclosure with subsidiary minor stretches of rampart and ditch. A site of timber-framed houses is traceable inside and there are two entrances in the north-west and two in the south-east sides.

134

Photograph (134) shows a distant view of Walls Hill Fort.

Walls Hill Fort is on the summit of a steep-sided lava plateau 230 metres above sea-level and is roughly oval. It measures 460 metres in length and 200 metres at its greatest width. The southern third of the interior is now farmland, much of the defences having been removed. The northern side retains a considerable stretch of rampart measuring 3.5 metres in thickness by approximately 1 metre in height. This fort is some 18 acres in extent, comparable to Burnswark Hill Fort, and excavations have revealed two early Iron Age occupations with circular timber-framed houses. It is presumed to have been a form of oppidum, if not the oppidum itself, of the Damnonii.

c. Hill-forts and souterrains in Perth, Fife and Angus regions

The Antonine Wall, totalling in length 36.5 miles, from Bridgeness on the Firth of Forth to Old Kilpatrick on the River Clyde, was built in the early 140's A.D. by the Roman Governor in Britain, Lorius Urbicus.

This area was the territory of the Damnonii, while the region north of this Wall was that of the Vacomagi, the Vinecones, the Caledonii (or the Caledonians) and the Maetae in the Iron Age (see Figure 14).

Surviving hill-forts in these regions include Dumyat Fort in Stirling; Moncrieffe Hill Fort; Evelick Fort; Dundurn Fort; Machany Fort in Perthshire; East Lomond Hill Fort; Norman's Law Fort in Fife; White Caterthun Fort; Brown Caterthun Fort; Finavon Fort; and souterrain monuments in Angus.

Dumyat Fort near Stirling Castle is a fort of multi-period fortification and is on the summit of a hill over 300 metres above sea-level. The east side of the fort is protected by natural, steep, rugged rocks and the main emphasis of the fortification is thought to have been put on the west where access is comparatively easy. Two stone ramparts enclose an area some 150 metres by 50 metres with an entrance on the west, and outside the entrance there is also a series of outworks arranged in ramparts. The work, extending to the higher point of the hill, is connected to earlier ramparts and forms a dun-like structure some 30 metres by 15 metres. The name "Dumyat" is thought to have derived from "Dun Myat" (the Dun of the Maetae) as with the Myot Hill Fort nearby. The Maetae was a local tribe which flourished from the late Iron Age to circa 600 A.D. in the Dark Age (see p103).

135

Photograph (135) shows an overall view of Dumyat Hill.

Moncrieffe Hill Fort is on a ridge of the diverging point of the Rivers Tay and Earn and is an oval fortress akin to Dumyat Fort in Stirling. It measures 170 metres by 100 metres, enclosed by two ruined ramparts some 4 metres thick. It has a dun-like structure inside, measuring some 50 metres by 35 metres, which may have been built after the outer fort had been abandoned. Part of the site of the inner structure overlies a sector of the inner wall of the larger enclosure, with traces of the circular stone foundations of houses.

Evelick Fort is also an oval fortification which is situated on the south-west extremity of the Sidlaw Hills. It measures some 75 metres by 60 metres and the main defences are placed on the north and north-west sides to which access is comparatively easy. There are five-fold ramparts and defence is entirely absent on the south side where the site is bordered by a steep slope. Dundurn Fort is on an isolated and craggy hill in the flood plain of the River Earn, 4 miles west of Comrie. It commands the east and west of Strathearn, once the main route which connected Scottish Dalriada and southern Pictland in the later Dark Age. The whole hill is enclosed by a series of ruined walls forming defended compounds and courtyards covering the flanks of the hill, with an enclosure some 20 metres in diameter uppermost. The fort is presumably the place referred to in *The Annals of Ulster*: "Scottish Dalriada was under siege by the southern Picts in 683 A.D." Some of the compounds are supposed to have been built in those days by the Picts, based on the observation that the defences have a resemblance to those of Dunadd Fort which was under siege many times by the Picts. A series of earthern banks and scarps supposedly represent stock enclosures and cultivation terraces. However, it is thought to be basically an Iron Age fort, the earliest fortification of which dates back to the 2nd century B.C.

136

Photograph (136) shows an overall view of Dundurn Fort.

Machany Fort is on a low ridge 0.3 miles north of Machany, close to the right bank of the Machany Water. It is an oval fort, the wall of which measures some 50 metres by 35 metres. Within the wall, vitrified matter can be detected.

The Caledonians and the Maetae

Xiphilinus, the translator of A History of Rome by Dio Cassius, writes, in a passage referring to Septimus Severus's activities in later times, that [20] "the most important tribes of the Britons in the North (Northern Scotland) were the Caledonians and the Maetae. Practically all the names of the other tribes were absorbed in these. The Maetae dwelt close to the wall (the Antonine Wall), which divided the island into two parts, and the Caledonians lived next to them. Each tribe inhabited rugged hills with swamps intervening, possessing neither walled places nor towns nor cultivated lands, but living by pastoral pursuits and hunting and on certain kinds of hard-shelled fruits (or nuts). They ate no fish, though their waters teemed with all kinds of them. They lived in tents, naked and shoeless (Roman soldiers used sandals); they had their women in common and reared all of their offspring (i.e. they did not, as the Romans did, practise the exposure of undesired infants); their government was democratic and they took the utmost delight in forays for plunder; they fought from chariots and had small swift horses; their infants were extremely swift of foot and enduring; their weapons were a shield and short spear with a knob of brass on the end of the butt (which means they knew the art of alloy), and they had daggers; they could endure hunger and thirst and every kind of hardship; they plunged into marshes and lasted many days with only their heads above water; and in the woods they lived on bark and roots; above all, they prepared and consumed a certain foodstuff of such a nature that, if they only ate the bulk of a bean of it, they felt neither hunger nor thirst."

The fort to which Dio Cassius refers in A History of Rome is presumed to have been one of these: Dumyat Fort, Moncrieffe Hill Fort, Dundurn Fort or Machany Fort. Though now not always accomapanied by swamps, these forts are all on "rugged hills."

East Lomond Hill Fort in Fife, which was the territory of the Venicones, is a fort of two structural periods, situated on a steep hill summit 425 metres above sea-level, 1 mile south-west of Falkland. The fort measures some 60 metres by 30 metres and is, together with a large Bronze Age cairn some 13 metres in diameter, encircled by a ruined outer wall on a lower terrace on the north of the summit. Several other ramparts, both long and short, stretch out on the slopes below, while to the south, on the only easy line of access, a heavy bank and ditch provide an obstacle. It is thought to be an example of the standard early Iron Age fort. However, there is evidence that it was occupied until a very much later date. A mould for casting ingots, glass beads and a Pictish symbol stone bearing a bull image have been found among the debris of the walls.

137

Photograph (137) shows the hill-top of East Lomond Hill.

138

Photograph (138) shows the hill-top of Norman's Law.

Norman's Law Fort, which crowns Norman's Law, is in the east end of the Orchil Massif and is a multi-period fortification. The earliest one encloses the hill-top with a heavy stone wall 210 metres by 80 metres in extent. The second one is a rampart which accommodates all the south-west foot of the hill, enclosing an area measuring some 300 metres from north-east to south-west by 170 metres across. The latest one is oval and, built on the north-western side of the hill-top, measures 50 metres by 30 metres within a wall some 4 metres thick.

139

*Photograph (139) shows the site of the hill-top
settlement of White Caterthun Fort and the ruined
rampart.*

The Angus area was the territory of the Vacomagi. White
Caterthun Fort is situated in this Angus area and is a huge henge-like
settlement associated with an oppidum of this tribe. It is on the
summit of a low hill 5 miles north-west of Brechin. An open space
some 150 metres by 70 metres is enclosed by a wall which now
consists of only a heavy pile of boulders, with entrances on the north-
east and south-west sides of the hill-top within an outer ruined wall
some 500 metres by 270 metres and 6 metres in thickness. This wall,
furthermore, is enclosed by a low rampart and ditch accompanied by
two other outer ramparts. Within the fort are traces of a wall, the
foundations of houses, and a well. There was once a large boulder
some 2 metres by 1 metre bearing a number of cup-marks.

Brown Caterthun Fort is situated 1 mile north-east of White
Caterthun Fort and is a similar hill-fort settlement. The circumference
of the outermost defence is 330 metres by 300 metres. An open area
some 90 metres by 60 metres is enclosed in an area some 180 metres
by 150 metres with several lines of outer defences consisting of stone
ramparts and quarry ditches set in the slopes just a little below the
hill-top. Defences are quadruplicated and each rampart has many
entrances. The open spaces between ramparts could once have been
cattle-pens, as in the case of Abory Hill Fort.

Finavon Fort is also a fort in what was once the territory of the
Vacomagi and is 1 mile west of Aberlemno. The fort occupies the
summit of a rocky knoll and was built between the 8th and 6th
centuries B.C. The plan is oblong and measures 150 metres by 35
metres within a massive timber-laced wall measuring from 4.5 metres
to 6 metres in thickness. Inside the fort can still be seen large
amounts of vitrified material which shows that fire had broken out

once or twice. Excavation within the interior has revealed two wells, one at the east end, the other at the west.

The souterrain is a monument of curiosity found in the Angus and Kincardine & Deeside areas in Grampian which was once the territory of the Vacomagi. Three souterrains have been discovered so far in this area. They are Carlungie, Tealing and Ardestie Souterrains, facilities associated with a kind of workshop for iron refining or a warehouse for food (see pp127-128).

140

Photograph (140) shows the main gallery of Carlungie Souterrain.

Carlungie Souterrain is situated to the north of the A 92 Dundee-Arbroath road in Angus and was discovered in the course of ploughing in October 1949. It was an L-shaped underground paved gallery set into a trench with an entrance at the east end. The main gallery is about 39 metres long with the side walls built of boulders and flagstones some 2 metres both in height and width, while another narrow entrance passage joins with the main one halfway to the entrance in the north. The roof is gone but the corbelling of the side walls remains. At the southern corner of the souterrain is a small chamber which it is conjectured was a workshop for metal-working, and in the gallery there has been found a cup-and-ring-mark stone associated with a mould or casting mould to make wrought metals.

Tealing Souterrain is also on the north side of the A 92 Dundee-Arbroath road. It was discovered in 1871, also in the course of farmwork. The souterrain is roughly oval, measuring 24 metres in length and 2.5 metres, on average, in breadth. The corbelled walls still stand to a height of 2 metres with large boulders forming the walls. On the surface of the wall on the north side, near the entrance, are large boulders decorated with cup-and-ring marks and cup-marks. Broken pottery and quern stones have been found along with fragments of Roman pottery and glass of the 1st or 2nd century.

Ardestie Souterrain is north-west of the Mains of Ardestie and is similar to the Tealing and Carlungie Souterrains. It has a banana-shaped paved gallery with chambers at the centre. The gallery is composed of massive boulders at the foundation of the corbelled side-walls. A kind of "fire-bowl" with a draft ventilator, a Roman amphora, a pitted stone, and a stone-made water tank have been excavated.

141

Photograph (141) shows the gallery of Tealing Souterrain and the cup-and-ring-mark stones.

142

Photograph (142) shows an overall view of Ardestie Souterrain.

d. Hill-forts in the Isle of Arran, Knapdale, Kintyre and the Western Isles

The south-western area, the Isle of Arran, Knapdale, Kintyre and the Southern Hebrides, was mainly the territory of the Epidii in the Iron Age. Hill-forts there include: Dun Torr a' Chaisteil in the Isle of Arran; Dunadd Fort and Duntroon Fort in Mid Argyle; Dun Skeig Fort in Kintyre, 10 miles south-west of Tarbert in Argyle; Dun Nosebridge in Islay; and Dun Cholla Fort in Colonsay. Most of the defensive structures in the coastal areas are "duns" or structures accompanied by them. A "dun" is a circular, oval or oblong fortified enclosure.

143

Photograph (143) shows an overall view of Dun Torr a' Chaisteil in the Isle of Arran.

Dun Torr a' Chaisteil is a fortress which is peculiar to south-western Scotland in the Iron Age, making good use of the natural terraces of a knoll just as with Dundurn Fort and Dunadd Fort (see below). Its interior structure, an area only 14 metres in diameter on top, is surrounded by a wall 3.7 metres thick and 2 metres high, with an entrance on the east, and is protected by an outer bank which crosses the knoll from north to south. The top stone of a rotary quern and bones of both domesticated and wild animals have been excavated.

Dunadd Fort is a fortification, resembling a recumbent boar, on a small rocky eminence in the east of Moin Mhor. Its use is presumed to have begun in the 1st millennium B.C. and it is defended by four lines of walling of natural terraces rimmed by several different levels with a sub-fort just below the peak at the northern end. The uppermost summit area in the west end is surmounted by the fort which measures about 30 metres by 14 metres at maximum width with an entrance on the east. Just below this there is a terrace where in 498 or 500 A.D. men of Scottish Dalriada (see p201) placed their coronation rock (Lin Fail) or "Stone of Destiny," a legendary slab of sandstone now gone. There is also a rock with a sculpture of a rock-cut basin, a foot-print and a boar image with several lines of ogham letters as yet undeciphered. Just under this terrace is a settlement area which measures some 60 metres by 30 metres with a well in the northern end and an entrance in the south-east end.

144

Photograph (144) shows an overall view of Dunadd Fort.

145

*Photograph (145) shows the natural rampart of
Dunadd Fort.*

After this fort had come into the hands of Scottish Dalriada, it was
occupied by the Picts in the 560's and 680's A.D. until it went up in
flames in 698 A.D., after which it was reconstructed and re-occupied
by the Picts from the 730's to the 740's A.D. However, the upper
terrace, where there remains a sculptured stone, is presumed to have
been the site of the inauguration ceremonies of new kings of any of
the Epidii, the Picts or the Scots, since there is a similar stone on
which there are two foot prints just under a canopy of stones on the

causeway near Clickhimin Broch in Shetland where a great number of
Picts and Iron Age people settled. Legend has it that new kings stood
barefooted on it and made a sacred oath of enthronement during their
inauguration ceremony.

"Lin Fail" [21] was removed by the Scots to Dunstaffnage,
Forteviot and finally to Scone and this indicates that it belonged to
them and they had possessed their own ceremonial stone. Though
purely conjectural, it might have been the ceremonial stone of the
Picts or a tribe in the Iron Age.   Another enigma is the inscription of
a boar image. When this fort was first occupied in 560 A.D. by the
Picts, the Pictish high king Brude was recorded by historians thus:
"His word is the law of Orkney," [22]   (the isles of "Orcoi" or the
"Boar"), while the Celts, it is said, used to admire the boar image as
"a war-hound" (archu) for its strength and ferocity and used its figure
as a fitting emblem to adorn their shields and helmets. [23]

There remain enigmatic questions such as to whether the Epidii
might have bequeathed it and, in addition, whether it was a totem or
merely an emblem, but what enabled the stone of the boar image to
survive through the war-torn civil war age is that, most likely, it was an
image acceptable to all, or alternatively a tabooed image which no
party could bring itself to destroy.

146

Photograph (146) shows the stone of the boar image.

Highlanders' prejudice against swine's flesh is referred to in Dr
Samuel Johnson's account of his Hebridean tour (JWI p.51), and,
earlier, in *The Masque of the Gypsies Metamorphosed* by English
dramatist Ben Jonson (1573?-1637) [24] which entertained James I
at the Duke of Buckingham's seat of Burley-on-the Hill on August 3rd
1621. Sir Walter Scott writes in a footnote in *The Fortunes of Nigel*
(WAV, XXVII, p.281) that "the Scots, till within the last generation,

disliked swine's flesh as an article of food as much as the Highlanders do at present." Such an unusual abhorrence or avoidance of the flesh of the swine or swine itself, which is mythologically as well as zoologically perceived as the same as the boar, might have been a sign of reverence to the ancestors of the Scots whose totem might have been a "boar." "Till within the last generation", in Sir Walter Scott's words, coincides with the time when the Stewarts came to an end with the defeat of the Jacobites at Culloden in 1746. Again this abhorrence or avoidance might have been a sign of reverence for the Royal House of Stewart (Sty-ward), which was the benign protector of the totem of this member of even-toed ungulates, Artiodactyla.

Duntroon Fort, which is near Dunadd Fort, is a small fort measuring 42 metres by 27 metres within an outer timber-laced enclosure, some 90 metres by 55 metres, with two other defences where a number of saddle querns of the early Iron Age has been excavated.

147

Photograph (147) shows a distant view of Dun Skeig Fort.

Dun Skeig Fort is a fortification on a hill summit which rises steeply to a height of some 143 metres from a point near the south-east shore of the mouth of West Loch Tarbert. It consists of a fort and a dun which were built at different times. The fort is oval in plan measuring 27 metres by 20 metres within a vitrified wall, and the dun, appended 45 metres to the north-east, measures some 14 metres in diameter within a wall some 4 metres thick with an entrance on the east.

Benderloch Fort, built in two periods, is situated on a rocky ridge on a promontory of Ardmucknish Bay. The earlier structure was a timber-laced wall fort enclosing the entire summit of the ridge, measuring some 210 metres by 30 metres at maximum width. This was superseded by a small rectangular and now vitrified fort, about 50 metres by 20 metres, and a circular and vitrified dun measuring about 18 metres in diameter. In a low-lying seaside district, a dun was thought to have been indispensable for defence.

148

Photograph (148) shows an overall view of Dun Nosebridge.

149

Photograph (149) shows a distant view of Dun Cholla.

Dun Nosebridge is a hill-fort situated on an isolated ridge 0.5 miles south-east of Bridgend. The main defence consists of a wall parapet which encloses the summit of the ridge, measuring some 25 metres by 15 metres, and parapet wall works, extending some 50 metres in length and 5 metres in width, partly enclose the defence at a lower level with an entrance on the south-west. Just under this work there is a rectangular defence-structure measuring 75 metres by 25 metres.

Dun Cholla Fort is a small insular hill-fort, or a dun, which encloses the summit of a ridge 2 miles south-south-west of Scalasaig with a wall some 3 metres thick and 1 metre high. There remains an area some 7.5 metres in diameter with a ring of several post-holes. The entrance is some 1.5 metres wide on the north-east of the wall.

e. Hill-forts and Settlements in Grampian Region

Kincardine and Deeside, and Gordon districts are located east and south-east of the Grampian Massif, (mainly the former territory of the Vacomagi), while the Banff and Buchan area is to the north of the Massif and was the territory of the Taezali. There is a considerable number of hill-forts in these regions. Barra Hill Fort in Oldmeldrum, Barmekin Fort of Echt, the Fort of Mither Tap of Bennachie, Dunindeer Fort, and the Fort of Tap of Noth are all in Gordon district. Mortlich Fort is in Kincardine and Deeside district, together with Old Kinrod Settlement and New Kinrod Settlement. In Banff and Buchan district are Cullykhan Promontory Fort and Burghead Promontory Fort, both presumably once in the possession of the Taezali.

150

Photograph (150) shows an overall view of Barra Hill Fort.

Barra Hill Fort was a fortification built in two periods. The earlier structure was the innermost defence line which enclosed an area some 120 metres in length and 100 metres in width with a single entrance on the east. The two outer ramparts and ditches, 2 metres in height and depth, constituted the second phase of fortification. They enclosed the earlier defence line and had three entrances. The structure resembles Barmekin Fort of Echt and Brown Caterthun Fort from the view-point of its multi-entrance design.

Barmekin Fort of Echt has an unusual number of ramparts and entrances similar to Brown Caterthun Fort already mentioned. The outermost defence comprises three ramparts which enclose an area measuring 150 metres in diameter with five entrances. The inner rampart is some 135 metres in diameter with three entrances and the innermost defence line encloses an area some 110 metres in diameter with two entrances. It is a defence structure of a two or three-period fortification.

151

Photograph (151) shows a distant view of Barmekin Fort of Echt.

The Fort of Mither Tap of Bennachie is situated on a pointed rough granite hill 518 metres above sea-level near a large Roman camp, Durno, which has been claimed as being the site where the supposed "Battle of Mons Grapius" (see p132) took place in 84 A.D. The outermost wall, some 4.5 metres thick, encircles the contour some 30 metres lower than the summit and, halfway up to the summit, a secondary wall, composed only of enormous masses of tumbled blocks and boulders, encircles the main area of the summit. Presumed to have been built before the Iron Age, its true scale and size have not been clearly defined.

Dunindeer Fort is situated on a hill consisting of three steep terraces 267 metres above sea-level and is encircled by three outer defences approximately 400 metres by 200 metres, now somewhat disconnected. The innermost defence at the top is a vitrified and oblong enclosure some 65 metres by 25 metres, encircled by a stone wall. In the west side is the ruin of a cistern, and the outer low stony

*Photograph (152) shows a distant view of The Fort of
Mither Tap of Bennachie.*

*Photograph (153) shows a distant view of Dunindeer
Fort.*

bank, some 125 metres in length, encircles the main defence. A
ruined medieval tower survives.

The Fort of Tap of Noth is on a conical eminence, some 565 metres
above sea-level, on the west end of the steep Hill of Noth. The second
highest hill-fort in Scotland, it consists of a single vitrified wall over 5
metres thick and 3 metres high. The fortification is presumed to be
from the early first millennium B.C., as with the Fort of Mither Tap of
Bennachie. The interior measures 105 metres by 40 metres. At the
south end, ruins of a cistern exist and in the north-west and north-
east, 145 platforms of houses have been found.

New Kinrod Settlement is in a birch wood of Muir of Dinnet. Built
in the late 1st millennium B.C., as with the similar settlement built in
Old Kinrod nearby, it consists of five or six houses encircled by a stone

wall, some 2 metres thick, with gates. The diameter of the houses is
some 20 metres on average and very akin to the house of Ness of
Gruting in Shetland. Some have an enclosure, approximately 2 metres
in width, presumably for the keeping of livestock.

154

*Photograph (154) shows a house site of the New Kinrod
Settlement.*

Cullykhan Promontory Fort is a sea fortress on a promontory 10
miles west of Fraserburgh. It was built in the early 1st millennium
B.C., refortified around the 4th century B.C. and used as a Pictish fort
in later days. The initial defence seems to have been built on the
landward point of the promontory, probably consisting of one palisade,
but after refortification a vertical stone wall was appended along a
narrow knife-edged isthmus, less than 4 metres wide.

Burghead Promontory Fort is also a sea fortress, built on the tip
end of Burghead, but it is difficult to define the details of its original
structure or its earlier fortifications because nearly half of the
structure was destroyed in 1805 – 9 and used to build the present
village of Burghead. The final structures, before dismantling,
consisted of an enclosure some 225 metres by 75 metres with a
rampart 7 metres wide and 6 metres high along the north-eastern
seaside; a rectangular plateau enclosed by a rampart 150 metres by
100 metres on the south-western side with an entrance in the east of
the plateau; and two pairs of triple ramparts, some 100 metres and 75
metres long and 5 metres wide, in the south-eastern depth of the
promontory. Where the two pairs of triple ramparts were once placed
became the residential quarters and the ramparts were arranged at
intervals of 10 metres and ran from north-east to south-west.

In the Dark Ages this fort became a Pictish oppidum, probably of
Moray or Mar, and their naval base. Today its harbour is Burghead Bay.

155

*Photograph (155) shows a part of Burghead
Promontory Fort.*

157

*Photograph (157) shows
a slab, decorated with
the image of a bull,
excavated from
Burghead Well, now in
the possession of the
British Museum.*

156

*Photograph (156) shows the entrance
to Burghead Well.*

Burghead Well is a rock-cut basin 3 metres square and 1.2 metres deep
enshrined in a subterranean chamber 5 metres square and 3.5 metres
high with an entrance, near the south-eastern end of an enclosure 225
metres by 75 metres. It is presumed once to have been a wishing well
or a holy water shrine for the Earth-mother goddess and several stone
slabs decorated with the image of a "bull," ceremonial tablets of the

Pictish people in the Iron Age, have been excavated from the well. The folk belief that it may have functioned as a place for execution by drowning, the historically documented Pictish method, should be dismissed.

f. Hill-forts, Settlements and Brochs in Highland Region

In Highland region there are numerous hill-forts, some weathered, some destroyed and those vitrified by fire intermingled. Among those are Laggan Fort or Dun-da-Lamh in Badenoch and Strathspey; Craig Phadrig Fort in Inverness; Knock Farril Fort, Dun Canna Fort and Dun Lagaidh Fort with a dun in Ross and Cromarty; the Ord Hut Circles and Duchary Rock Fort in Sutherland; and Ben Freiceadain Fort and Farse Wag Broch with settlement in Caithness. Forts by the seaside in Caithness and Sutherland were often accompanied by a dun.

Laggan Fort, or Dun-da-Lamh, which means " the Fort of the Two Hands" in Gaelic, is on one summit of two knolls at the east end of a long steep-sided ridge known as "Black Craig," 6 miles north-north-west of Dalwhinnie. The flanks of the promontory fall steeply from the summit to the flood-plain 180 metres below. The rampart, 4 metres to 6 metres in width, climbs up and falls down following the contours of the crag and encircles an area 140 metres by 80 metres with an entrance in the middle of the north wall. The position of the fort, the craggy knoll and the use of rock outcrops encourage the imagination to suppose that the fort was contemporary with other strongholds on rocky hills such as Dunadd and Dumbarton Rock.

Craig Phadrig Fort is also a hill-fort built in the first millennium B.C. on a wooded eminence, 1.5 miles west of Inverness. An inner heavily vitrified wall, extending to a thickness of some 8 metres, encloses an elevated ground area 75 metres by 25 metres and 5 metres high, and the outer wall, also heavily vitrified, encircles it at a distance of some 15 to 25 metres from the inner one. Excavation has revealed evidence of reconstruction in the 6th or 7th century and it reminds us of the presumed presence of the high king of the Northern Picts, Brude I Mac Maelcon, who ruled over the whole of Pictland from 555 A.D. to 584 A.D., and also St Columba's visit to him in 565 A.D. as Adamnan describes in his *Vita Sancti Columbae* (or *Life of St Columba*).

Knock Farril Fort is on the summit of an eminence standing high above Strathpeffer west of Dingwall. The fort is sub-rectangular and a heavily vitrified rampart encloses an area some 130 metres by 40 metres.

*Photograph (158) shows a distant view of Craig
Phadrig Fort.*

*Photograph (159) shows an overall view of Knock
Farril Fort*

Dun Canna is a fort which stands on a promontory protruding into
the sea 1 mile north of the mouth of the River Kanaird. The main
defence is a massive wall, which is now heavily vitrified and collapsed,
and it follows the edge of the high rocky cliffs and encircles an inside
area measuring 42 metres by 12 metres. The outer landward defence
of the western extremity is long and narrow and is also heavily
vitrified.

Dun Lagaidh Fort, accompanied by a dun, is on a ridge on the
south-west shore of Loch Broom opposite Ullapool. On the highest
part of the ridge are the remains of a dun with piles of loose stones
around it. The fort, built in the early first millennium B.C., occupies
the western end of the ridge and measures some 100 metres by 36
metres with a massive vitrified rampart some 3.5 metres thick. There

is no trace of ramparts on the precipitous north and south sides of the hill but a stretch of rampart is in the east end of the fort where the dun is located. Inside the fort there are the ruins of a well or a basin.

Ord Hut Circles are on a low hill near Lairg at the south end of Loch Shin and the specification of these Iron Age hut circles is nearly the same as that of the New Kinrod Settlement (see pp115-116). There are the remains of some twenty circles, together with Neolithic chambered cairns and Bronze Age burial cairns (see pp17-18), and the site was presumably in an environment quite well-suited to the settlers of each era since there survives a variety of historical monuments from the Neolithic Age onwards.

160

Photograph (160) shows an overall view of the site of the Ord Hut Circles.

Duchary Rock Fort, 3.5 miles west of Brora, is on a rocky ledge some 300 metres long on the east flank of a massif between Strathbrora and Dunrobin Glen. The north-west and south-east ends, to which access is comparatively easy, are defended by a single stone wall, now tumbled but originally some 4 metres thick. The shorter south-east rampart utilizes natural rock outcrops at places and the longer northern rampart cuts off access from the hills behind. The eastern and western sides border on precipices and the interior measures 240 metres by 55 metres. The stronghold is an impressive set-up which commands Loch Brora from the south of the fort.

Ben Freiceadain Fort (Hill Fort for Lookout) is the northern-most hill-fort of any size on the mainland of Britain and is on the flank of Ben Freiceadain 8 miles south-east of Reáy. Measuring some 270 metres in length and 145 metres in width, it is encircled by a single wall to a thickness of some 4 metres, though now quite weathered. The entrance

161

*Photograph (161) shows an overall view of Ben
Freiceadain Fort.*

is on the north-west side and on the summit there are Neolithic
chambered cairns some 2,000 years older.

Farse Wag Settlement (the name "wag" meaning " a little cave" in
Gaelic) is situated 1 mile north-north-east of Latheron. This
settlement is an assembly of hut sites which were built in oval yards
some 38 metres by 30 metres. The hut circles are, on average, some
14 metres in diameter within a wall 1.2 metres thick. Its identity is
comparable to that of the earliest Iron Age house in the Sumburgh
Settlement (see pp78-79).

2. BROCHS, GALLERIED DUNS AND EARTH HOUSES.

A broch is a structure of antiquity which is presumed to have been
built by Pictish people who began to settle about the beginning of the
8th century B.C. and continued to increase in numbers. Many of the
sites remain chiefly by the seaside in Caithness, Sutherland, the
Western Isles, Orkney and Shetland, but the well-preserved are not
many, as with galleried duns, because they are all antiquities over
2,000 years old and were chiefly shelters from a foreign enemy or
piracy: thus they are sometimes accompanied by a fort or a dun.

Good examples are: Dun Mor, Vaul in Tiree; Dun Telve and Dun
Troddan in Glenelg near Lochalsh; Dun Beag and Dun Hallin in Skye;
Dun Carloway in Lewis, Outer Hebrides; Gurness Broch and Midhowe
Broch in Orkney; Mousa Broch and Clickhimn Broch in Shetland;
Ousedale Broch and Keiss Broch in Caithness; Carn Liath, Dun na
Maigh, and Kilphedir Broch with hut circles and souterrain in
Sutherland; and Edinshall Broch in Berwickshire.

162

Photograph (162) shows one of the entrances and the inside of Dun Mor Broch.

Among the earth houses are: Culsh Earth House in Kincardine and Deeside; and Grain Earth House and Rennibister Earth House in mainland Orkney. Stone-made structures such as brochs and galleried duns tend to be thought of as being too cold to live in, especially in the frozen winter time, but they were rather warm and habitable residences or shelters, once the inside was heated up by fire.

Dun Mor was originally a broch built in the 6th century B.C. and is situated by the seaside in Vaul Bay, 3 miles north of Scarinish in Tiree. The central court measures some 9 metres in diameter within a wall 4.5 metres thick. The original height was about 8 metres but is now only some .2 metres. Within the wall are a basal gallery and a mural cell.

The main entrance is nearby the north-west side of the structure where there is a doorway leading to a staircase to the upper area. Two more similar doorways, lintelled by massive slabs, give approach from the central court to the gallery. In the south-east side of the structure there is another entrance, its pivot-stone showing traces that there was once a strong wooden door, and there is a guard cell, some 2 metres in diameter with a low lintelled doorway, on the north side of the entrance. The interior suggests that there were once timbered buildings.

Dun Telve, built in the late 1st century B.C., is also a broch and stands on a valley floor near a riverside in Glenelg. The wall is some 18 metres in external diameter, tapering slightly inward as it goes up, and the courtyard inside is some 10 metres in diameter within a wall some 4 metres thick, the wall being double with approximately one third of the original standing to a height of some 10 metres. The base is solid with four galleries still above it, the entrance is on the south and there is a crescent-like cell on the left side. To it adjoins a doorway with a

stairway leading to an upper gallery with a corbelled roof and
scarcement ledge which provided support for the upper storey and
timber roof, the first gallery being on the same level as the first
scarcement ledge. In the courtyard are traces of postholes and a
hearth, and outside there are traces of a stone rampart which seems
once to have surrounded the whole structure.

Dun Troddan is a broch of similar structure and scale, with similar
fixtures, and is situated nearby Dun Telve.

Dun Beag is a galleried dun built on a knoll to the west of
Bracadale in Skye in the late 1st millennium B.C. The external
diameter is some 20 metres and the courtyard inside measures 11
metres within a wall 4.5 metres thick and 3 metres high. The entrance
is on the east and nearby on the right is a cell some 2 metres in
diameter while another cell has a stairway of some twenty steps
leading to an upper gallery on the left. On the north-west side of the
inside wall there is a crescent-formed chamber some 1.6 metres wide
and 13 metres long with an entrance leading to a courtyard in the
centre.

163

164

*Photograph (163) shows an overall
view of Dun Telve.*

*Photograph (164) shows the
intramural passage of Dun Troddan.*

165

Photograph (165) shows an overall view of Dun Troddan.

166

Photograph (166) shows the gallery inside the wall of Dun Beag.

167

Photograph (167) shows an overall view of Dun Carloway.

168

Photograph (168) shows the intramural passage of Dun Carloway.

Dun Carloway is a broch which stands on a knoll south of Carloway. The wall of the broch is 15 metres in external diameter with its base just a little wider. The courtyard inside is some 7 metres in diameter within a wall some 4.5 metres thick. The base is on solid rock outcrops and nearly half of the original wall remains standing to a height of some 9 metres, along with some parts of its three galleries. The entrance is on the north side with a guard cell on the right and, opposite, a passage provides an approach to an intramural staircase which leads to the upper galleries. Between this and the entrance there is a cell some 7 metres in length and 3 metres at maximum width with an entrance on the inside courtyard. On the north-east side is another cell 4.5 metres in length and 3 metres in width.

169

Photograph (169) shows a front view of Gurness Broch.

Gurness Broch stands on a solid rock some 4.5 metres above the high water mark of Aikerness, facing Eynhallow Sound. Around the broch are multi-period residential quarters such as large oblong Viking houses and Pictish houses consisting of five cells around a central axis. They are surrounded by triple ramparts and quarry ditches, except for the area facing the seaside. The wall of the remaining broch is some 4 metres thick and 4 metres high on average and the courtyard inside is 10 metres in diameter with a hearth in the centre. The entrance is on the east facing the seaside and there are guard cells with short galleries on either side. Under the ground are a well and a storage cell for food.

Midhowe Broch stands on a rock ledge protruding over the shore of Eynhallow Sound opposite Gurness Broch. The entrance faces the south, and the inside of the broch, some 9 metres in diameter, is

170

171

Photograph (170) shows the passage-
way leading to the basement of
Gurness Broch.

Photograph (171) shows the dwelling
quarters of Midhowe Broch.

divided into two rooms by large upright stones. The wall is some 4.5 metres thick, standing to a height of some 4 metres with an internal ledge as the upper floor. Near the entrance is a guard cell and under the ground is a cellar for storing food. Each dwelling has its own fixtures such as a hearth, a cupboard, a cubicle and a water tank.

Mousa Broch, on an island of flagstone near the west coast of Mousa, retains its actual-size original form, having an external diameter of 15 metres at the base and 12 metres at the top and a height of 13 metres. The entrance passage, facing the south, is very long and the interior is only 6 metres across. There is no guard cell adjoining the entrance passage while three large cells some 5 metres by 2 metres lie inside the wall which is 4.5 metres thick at the base and divided like that of a wheel-house. On the internal wall-face, two ledges protrude and they represent the original position of the floor and the roof height. Inside the wall there are stairways leading to the top of this well-preserved broch.

Dun na Maigh is a broch which stands on a rocky knoll at the head of Kyle of Tongue. The courtyard inside is 8.5 metres in diameter and it has defences on the north and south sides with an entrance passage some 5 metres long on the east.

Edinshall Broch is a galleried dun on the north-east flank of Cockburn Law in Berwickshire, standing in the north-west corner of an earlier hill-fort which measures 135 metres by 75 metres. The courtyard of the broch is 17 metres in diameter within a wall some 5 metres thick and 4 metres high. The entrance is on the east, and on either side of the passage, 5 metres long, is a guard cell. An aisle in the wall south of the entrance gives approach to a stairway which leads to a small chamber on the left and by another stairway to the top of the wall on the right. There are two more intramural cells in the wall, conforming to the bend of the wall, and each of them leads to a small compartment. Similar brochs at Torwoodlee and Bow in this central Tweedsdale region were all destroyed by the Romans in the early years of the 2nd century. The

172

Photograph (172) shows an overall view of Dun na Maigh.

territory was that of the Votadinii and the name of the broch derives from "Woden's" or "Odin's Hall," the naming seeming to have stemmed from the later age of the Vikings. It is uncertain, therefore, who were the builders of this broch.

Though one type of earth house or souterrain is presumed to have been a workshop for metallic processing work, as in Tealing, Carlungie and Ardestie Souterrains (see pp106-107), the earth house made by

173

Photographs (173) and (174) show the entrance of Edinshall Broch and its interior.

174

excavating the rock under the earth with little room in height and width of its chamber seems to have been a kind of warehouse. Being located in the heartland of a grain-producing district increases the probability of its being a warehouse, a monument suggesting the centralization and control of food by a pre-historic autonomy.

Culsh Earth House in Tarland, 4.5 miles north of Aboyne, was a structure which, between the 1st millennium B.C. and the 1st millennium A.D., was made into a rocky underground house by excavating a trench some 14 metres in length and 1.7 metres in width and height, lined with drystone walling. Grain Earth House, in an industrial estate on the outskirts of Kirkwall in mainland Orkney, is a similar structure presumably dug for the purpose of storing food, as the name indicates, in the first millennium B.C. It is under the earth some 2 metres deep and the entrance leads to a trench, some 5 metres long, which bends in a gentle arc. It is lined by drystone walling and roofed by flat slabs some 1 metre high. It gives access to a small oval chamber some 1.5 metres high supported by four pillars. A similar one is Rennibister Earth House in a granary district of mainland Orkney some 4 miles north-west of Kirkwall.

175

Photograph (175) shows the trench of Grain Earth House.

CHAPTER V

THE INVASION OF THE ROMAN ARMY INTO SCOTLAND

Caesar, in his *De Bello Gallico*, writes with regard to his expedition to Great Britain from 55 to 54 B.C.: [25] "Not much of the summer is left and winter sets in early in these regions because the whole of this part of Gaul faces north. Nevertheless, I proceed with plans for an expedition to Britain because I know that in almost all of our campaigns in Gaul our enemies have received reinforcements from the Britons. Even if we should not have enough time for conducting a campaign this season, I think it would be very useful merely to visit the island, to see what sort of people live there and to get some idea of the terrain and the harbours and landing places."

He continues: "In the ordinary way, no one goes to Britain except traders and even they are acquainted only with the sea coast and areas opposite Gaul. And so, although I summoned traders from all parts, I cannot find out about the size of the island, the names and populations of the tribes who live there, their methods of fighting, the customs they have, or which harbours there could accommodate a large numbers of big ships."

Caesar's mobilization of his army to Britain might have been, for his own prestige, a punitive expedition against the Britons who had helped his antagonists in Gaul, but behind it all lay a great hidden significance for the strategic reconnaissance of the land and people of Britain.

A series of Roman campaigns which began less than one century after the death of Caesar was for the purpose of territorial expansion. Augustus Octavianus (27 B.C. – 14 A.D.), Caesar's adopted son, broke off a series of internal wars which had continued for a long time under his control and, subjugating Africa, Italy, Sardinia and Sicily, gained ascendancy over these areas. Tiberius (14 – 37 A.D.), before his accession to the throne, carried out an expedition to subjugate Armenia in 20 B.C. and throughout the ten years from 4 to 14 A.D. he carried out campaigns against Germany, Dalmatia and Pannonia and gained these fertile lands.

When, under the reign of Claudius I (Tiberius Drusus Nero Germanicus, 41 – 54 A.D.), the Romans set up a great frontier-line along the Danube and the Rhine, they had taken little notice of the potential worry of Britain in their north-western flank. But at long last they began to embark on a definite plan for the conquest of Britain.

1. THE FIRST EXPEDITION OF THE ROMAN ARMY INTO SCOTLAND

The invasion of the Romans to Great Britain began in 43 A.D. They landed on the south-east coast of Britain and steadily pushed up to the west and north, setting up their garrison forts at each strategic point. In 80 A.D., under the reign of Titus (Flavius Sabinus Vespasianus. 79 – 81 A.D.), they made their first appearance in Scotland. This was thirty-seven years after the first four legions of the Roman regular army of Claudius I invaded south-east Britain. The first expedition of the Roman army into Scotland was carried out by Julius Agricola (b.37 – d.94 A.D.) who entered Britain in 77–A.D. as a strategic consul and took office as Roman governor of Britain in 78–A.D. He had accomplished the subjugation of Wales and Northumbria, having constructed commissariats and military roads (known as "Stanegate") within two years of his entering Britain. It was his firm intention to secure a grip on the Brigantes in the north of England so that he might enter Scotland in safety.

He appeared in the south of Scotland in 80 A.D., with a troop 20,000 strong, and took two routes. One was by Dere Street running from York over the Cheviots, across the Tweed near Newstead, up Lauderdale and into the Lothians. The other was by the route running from Carlisle, up Annandale to Crawford, and along the River Clyde to Castledykes and the Clyde estuary. On arriving in the Forth-Clyde area, Agricola halted further progress and then began to construct a chain of strongholds, on the north of the isthmus between the two Firths, to cut off invasions of Northern forces from the Highland region, linking each stronghold with a military road. Clearly, he seems to have intended establishing a Roman province in the southern region, making the isthmus his northern-most front line. Roman occupation in Scotland thus began and was to last for nearly three hundred years, though intermittently.

Figure (15) shows the distribution of forts which Agricola constructed, each fort being situated at points of traffic importance leading to the main Highland glens and to the south of the two Firths. Forts in Ardoch, Dunblane in Strathallan, and Fendoch at the gateway to Strath Almond, were 30 acres on scale, while Dunning in

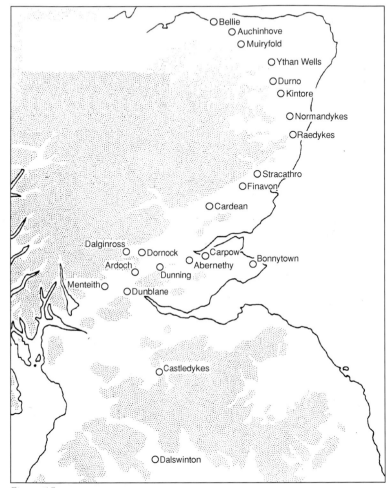

Figure 15

Strathallan was 115 acres. Cardean, Dornock and Bonnytown in
Strathmore were 30 acres, Carpow and Abernethy in North Fife were
115 acres, while those in Menteith, which led to the western end of the
Firth of Clyde via Drymen and Dalginross at the gateway to Strath
Earn, were 7 acres. They were forts of the same scale as those of
Castledykes and Dalswinton which Agricola built in 82 A.D. when he
organized a fleet and sent his army to Galloway.

The normal official term of Roman governorship was three years.
In the year 81 A.D., as his governorship was about to terminate, the

Emperor Titus died and his brother Domitianus (Titus Flavius, 81 – 96 A.D.), with eyes fixed on the far north of Britain, ascended the throne and his governorship extended for another three years, during which time he was to dispatch his forces to the Highlands.

In the spring of 84 A.D. he set out by sea and land on an expedition to the North with a troop 20,000 strong with his fleet, skirting the eastern coast, serving as a commissariat. He chose the route of the flatlands along the eastern coast and pushed up to the north via Finavon, Stracathro, Raedykes, Normandykes, Kintore, Durno, Ythan Wells, Muiryfold, Auchinhove and Bellie, setting up a camp of some 110 acres at each army post. En route, at Durno (see p114) or somewhere in the Grampian region, he supposedly fought the Battle of "Mons Grapius," the site of which has not yet been identified and the name of which has been misread and now survives as the "Grampian Massif." The enemy was the allied Celtic forces, some 30,000 strong, whom "Calgacus" or "Swordsman" commanded.

Tacitus (Publius Cornelius, 55 – 117 A.D.), conveniently the son-in-law of Agricola, mentions that Agricola gained a triumphant victory over them, with 360 casualties to 10,000 of the Highland tribes! Tacitus writes: "Agricola had "Dutch" forces (Batavorum cohorts) placed in the centre, with cavalry on the wings, and his Roman legions were in the second line, in front of the "vallum." The Highlanders arrayed their first line on the level ground while their supports occupied the heights. Chariots and horsemen scoured the plain. To avoid being outflanked, Agricola then extended his front while he himself dismounted and stood by his colours.

The battle began with a discharge of arrows and other missiles, in which the Highlanders seemed to have had some superiority. Agricola therefore ordered his Batavian and other foreign forces to charge. In the melee the claymore and targe (ingentes gladii, breves cetrae), and the swashing blows of the Highlanders were less successful than the point delivered by the Batavians. Against spears, as against bayonets, the broadsword might have held its own but the short Roman sword came within the guard of the two-handed claymore. The Roman lines then charged up the slopes. The Highland chariots swooped down and apparently were broken by the Roman cavalry who, in turn, were impeded by difficult ground. Meanwhile the Highland supports, descending from the hill, attacked the legions in the rear, or were about to do so, when they were assailed by fresh Roman cavalry from the wings. They fled and were pursued; some ran, some rushed unarmed on certain death."

After this great "triumph," Agricola marched further north and, organizing a fleet, carried out an expedition to Orkney, being also confident of the conquest of Ireland as Tacitus relates. But in the same year 84 A.D., he was summoned back to Rome. Tacitus writes:

"Perdomita Britannia et statim omissa" and suggests that the recall was due to imperial jealousy. However, it is also a fact that Agricola mobilized, on his expedition, a large portion of Rome's regular army, some 20,000 strong (three legions out of thirty), and gained no fertile land nor any great plunder. How then should his merits and demerits be appraised?

Figure (16) shows the disposition of the Roman army in Scotland between 85 and 90 A.D. after Agricola had been recalled. The emphasis of the disposition was put on the consolidation of the southern region, making the Firths the northern-most frontier-line as Agricola had envisioned. Some of the forts which Agricola had built had fallen into disuse, but some were rebuilt. North of the Firths, forts like Inchtuthil, Fendoch, Dalginross, Bochastle, Menteith and Drymen were disposed in an oblique line down to the south-west, together with the newly-built Barochan to the west of Glasgow with Inchtuthil as the northern-most frontier fort. Emperor Domitianus strengthened the forts to the south of the Firths as seen in Figure (16), but having deployed his many troops

Figure 16

in Britain, he undertook a campaign against the Chatti in 83 A.D., in
the course of which he began the construction of a boundary wall
between the Danube and the Rhine. Between 86 A.D. and 90 A.D. he
fell into an embarrassing situation carrying on unsuccessful wars
against the Dacians under Decebalus and finally he was compelled to
purchase peace under promise of a yearly tribute.

Figure (17) shows the disposition of the Roman army in Scotland
between 90 and 105 A.D., under the reigns of Domitianus, his
successor Marcus Cocceius Nerva (96 – 98 A.D.), and Marcus Ulpius
Trajanus (98 – 117 A.D.). Most of the Roman units disappeared from
Scotland during that time with Newstead as the northern-most
frontier-line, leaving a chain of forts comprising Cappuck, Chew
Green, High Rochester and Learchild and another line consisting of
Oakwood, Milton, Dalswinton and Glenlochar, diagonally from
Newstead down to the south-west, with Broomholm as a relay station
leading to Carlisle.

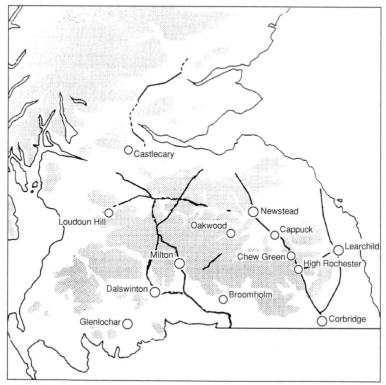

Figure 17

The last years of Domitianus were tragic. His reputation was sullied by his disgraceful peace with Dacia and by his cruelty and tyrany. He was impelled by fear of revolt and assassination and was finally murdered in 96 A.D. by a freedman, the result of a conspiracy between Empress Domitia and officers in the court. Marcus Cocceius Nerva succeeded him. Trajanus, the adopted son and successor of Nerva, was an able Emperor who, after serving as a military tribune in various provinces before his enthronement, completed fortifications on the Rhine in 98–99 A.D. In 101–102 A.D. he conducted his first Dacian campaign in which Decebalus of Dacia was defeated and in his second campaign (102–103 A.D.) he completely defeated the Dacians and made Dacia a Roman province. Between 114 A.D. and 116 A.D. he again conducted successful wars against the Armenians and the Parthians but throughout his reign his eyes never turned towards Britain.

2. THE CONSTRUCTION OF HADRIAN'S WALL AND THE ANTONINE WALL

In 117 A.D. the 9th Legion suffered a crucial disaster in the territory of the Brigantes and in the year 119 A.D. Emperor Hadrianus (Publius, Aelius, 117–38 A.D.), who was a nephew of Trajanus and had accompanied him on many of his campaigns, arrived in Britain. He carried out a personal survey of the isthmus between the Solway Firth and the mouth of the River Tyne and ordered the construction of a great stone wall on the isthmus. The total length was 73.5 miles, with a mile castle or watch tower provided with shrines and workshops at each Roman mile (1,482 m). It was a gigantic offensive and defensive wall designed to control Scotland and was the base for commissariats from either extremity of which the maritime transportation of troops and military commodities was possible. Work began in 120 A.D. and was completed in 128 A.D.

176

Photograph (176) shows a part of Hadrian's Wall near Haltwhistle, 16 miles east of Brampton.

The wall starts with a base near Bo'ness. 1 Carriden; 2 Kinneil; 3 Inveravon; 4 Mumrills; 5 Falkirk; 6 Camelon; 7 Watling Lodge; 8 Rough Castle; 9 Seabegs; 10 Castlecary; 11 Westerwood; 12 Croy Hill; 13 Bar Hill; 14 Auchindavy; 15 Kirkintilloch; 16 Glasgow Bridge; 17 Cadder; 18 Wilderness Plantation; 19 Balmuildy; 20 Summerston; 21 Bearsden; 22 Castlehill; 23 Cleddans; 24 Duntocher; 25 Old Kilpatrick; 26 Bishopton.

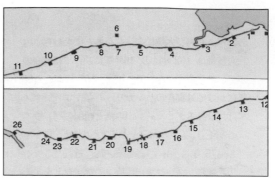

Fig. 18 shows the Plan of the Antonine Wall

The completion of this Wall was indirectly to encourage the next emperor Antoninus Pius (138–61 A.D.) to carry out the Second Expedition of the Roman army to Scotland in 142 A.D. However, the movements of the Northern tribes were constantly serious and Lorius Urbicus, the new governor of Britain, after having once put down their disturbance, proposed to Pius that they should build another defence line or "the Antonine Wall" on the isthmus between Bo'ness on the Forth and Bishopton on the River Clyde. Its total length was 36. 5 miles and its rampart was 6 metres wide and 3 metres high, consisting of a solid foundation made of rough boulders and a ditch 12 metres wide and 3.6 metres deep. It was provided with some 26 forts or signal stations of various sizes from 0.65 to 7.3 acres, at intervals of two Roman miles, connected by a road system (see Figure 18) and accompanied by workshops, shrines and civil settlements. The work was done by the co-operative efforts of the 6th Legion at York, the 21st

177

Photograph (177) shows the ditch and rampart of Watling Lodge near Falkirk. The width of the wall is 12 metres and the ditch is 4.5 metres deep.

Legion at Chester and the 2nd Legion at Caerleon, but with the completion of this wall, Stracathro, Cardean, Inchtuthil in Tayside, Fendoch, Dalginross, Bochastle, Menteith and Drymen to the north of the Wall were abandoned.

178

Photograph (178) shows the fort site of Croy Hill, 12 miles south of Kilsyth, where altars dedicated to nymphs, Mars and the Eastern god Jupiter Dolichenus (see p157) have been excavated. Measuring 0.75 acres with the headquarters building in the centre, it was equipped with a workshop to make ballistae.

3. THE SECOND EXPEDITION OF THE ROMAN ARMY INTO SCOTLAND

The Second Expedition of the Roman army to Scotland started in 142 A.D. while awaiting the completion of the Antonine Wall. The headquarters site was Newstead at the foot of Eildon Hill North as shown in Figure (19). Along Dere Street, Oxton was rebuilt between the remodelled forts of Inveresk and Newstead, and Risingham near the border was also rebuilt. Learchild and Oakwood were abandoned and in their place Cappuck was remodelled, while Lyne Roman Fort was reconstructed as a relay station between Newstead and Castledykes in Strathclyde. In Annandale, at the western gate of Hadrian's Wall, Netherby and Birrens were newly built while Broomholm, built in the Flavian Dynasty, was abandoned. In Nithsdale, Dalswinton was abandoned and Durisdeer rebuilt, and in Dumfries and Galloway region Glenlochar was remodelled into a fort of Newstead-class. In Clydesdale, the forts of Crawford, Milton and Castledykes were remodelled and Redshaw Burn was newly built. In Strathclyde, Bothwellhaugh and Loudoun Hill were constructed while Barochan was abandoned.

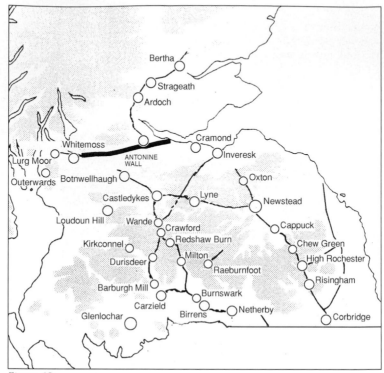

Figure 19

The Romans stood face to face with the Northern tribes with the
Antonine Wall as the front line and Bertha, Strageath and Ardoch as
their outposts. The wall, a commissariat for the maritime
transportation of troops and military goods from both Firths, was
garrisoned by a Roman regular army of some seven thousand in the
early years of the 140's A.D. However, it was once abandoned due to a
revolt of Roman soldiers in the 150's A.D. and after that it was
defended by garrisons of auxiliaries who came from Gaul, Tungria,
Germany, Spain and Thrace.

In this expedition the Romans remained in Scotland for sixteen
years but with the second half of the 150's A.D. as a turning point, a
series of revolts began to occur successively among Roman soldiers in
many forts, though the causes are unexplained. In Netherby, where the
First Alien Cohort of Hispani was garrisoned, there occurred revolts in
the middle of the 150's A.D., and the fort of Birrens, where Reatian
Spearmen and the 2nd Cohort of Tungrians were garrisoned, was
destroyed by an uprising in 155 A.D.

The second expedition, begun by the injunction of Antoninus Pius, came to an end with his death in 161 A.D. Roman soldiers commenced evacuation and the Antonine Wall was formally abandoned. It was a necessary consequence of the planned dispatch of troops to the Continent by two great successors of Pius, the joint emperors Antoninus Marcus Aurelius (161–80) and Lucius Aurelius Verus (161–69 A.D.). They initiated a series of campaigns to Parthia from 162 A.D. to 167 A.D., to Pannonia and Quadi from 167 A.D. to 168 A.D., and to Marcomanni from 170 A.D. to 175 A.D.

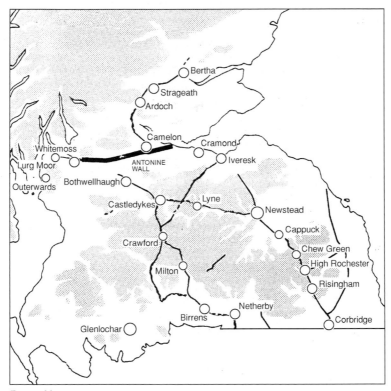

Figure 20

Figure (20) shows the disposition of the Roman army from 158 A.D. to 163 A.D. Newstead was still the headquarters but along Dere Street there were left only Risingham, High Rochester, Chew Green, Cappuck, Inveresk and Cramond while to the north of the Antonine Wall there remained Bertha, Strageath and Ardoch, and in Clydesdale, Milton, Crawford and Castledykes connected to Newstead through

Lyne. In Annandale there still existed garrisons at Netherby and Birrens, and in Dumfries and Galloway only one large-scale garrison at Glenlochar.

Antoninus Marcus Aurelius died in 180 A.D. and a son unworthy of him, Emperor Commodus (Lucius Aelius Aurelius, 180–92 A.D.) was enthroned. In 184 A.D. northern Scotland was subjugated to an expedition by Ulpius Marcellus, the British governor of the time. It was a punitive expedition against Northern tribes who had invaded a Roman province somewhere to the south of the Wall, killing a Roman general and annihilating his army. Northern tribes were steadily gaining power.

The reign of Commodus was marked by scandals of his violence, prodigality and unrestrained indulgence to such an extent that Rome was unable to manifest its real power. Commodus made a disgraceful peace with the Marcomanni and Quadi on his father's death. He was proud of his physical strength which he showed in gladiatorial combats until, as a result of a conspiracy, he was strangled by an athlete.

In 193 A.D. the Roman regime changed to that of Emperor Severus. In the Central Highlands there was a further increase in the powers of the Caledonians and the Maetae. In 197 A.D., according to Xiphilinus in his abridgement of Dio Cassius, [26] "Virus Lupus, the new governor, arrived and was at once obliged to make peace, for a large sum, with the Maetae, because the Caledonians did not abide by their promises and were preparing to assist the Maetae." However, even this agreement with the Maetae was cancelled in 205 A.D. and in 208 A.D. Emperor Severus himself was obliged to come to Scotland.

4. THE THIRD EXPEDITION OF THE ROMAN ARMY INTO SCOTLAND

Emperor Severus (193–211 A.D.) was born in Africa. After serving as questor and praetor under Marcus Aurelius, he commanded as chief of the army in a campaign to Pannonia and Illyria and was proclaimed emperor by the soldiers. After overcoming his rival Didus Julianus in Rome in 193 A.D., he waged successful wars against Pescennius Niger in northern Syria in 194 A.D., Albinus in Gaul in 197 A.D. and Parthia from 197 A.D. to 202 A.D. The Third Expedition of the Roman army to Scotland, carried out by this skilful strategist, was a large-scale punitive campaign against the Caledonians and the Maetae.

Severus began his expedition with the consolidation of a commissariat system, as shown in Figure (21). The forts at Pathhead, Channelkirk and St Leonards, between Inveresk and Newstead along

Figure 21

Dere Street, were all 165 acres in extent. To the north of the Wall, in
the territories of the Caledonians and the Maetae, he constructed
forts of 130 acres at Kair House, Balmakewan, Oathlaw, Cardean,
Grassy Walls and Ardoch, slanting from north-east to south-west with
Kair House as the northern-most base. And between these large-scale
forts he disposed smaller scale forts (some 60 acres) such as those at
Keithock, Marcus, Lunanhead, Kinneil, Essie, Kirkbuddo, Lintrose,
Scone, Broomhill and Craigarhall, and he connected all of them by
military roads, one of them extending to the Moray Firth in the far
north. He also constructed forts some 60 acres in extent at Carpow
and Auchtermuchty in Fife, once the territory of the Vinecones or
"Swamp Hounds."

Severus seems to have strengthened the Wall between the Forth
and the Clyde. Xiphilinus again writes in the abridgement of Dio
Cassius: [27] "Severus lost heavily in a *swampy* country without
bringing his enemy to action," though the locality cannot be

identified. Roman units seem again to have suffered stubborn
resistance from the Northern tribes.

Andrew Lang, author of *A History of Scotland*, writes, "Dio reckons
the Roman casualties in this expedition at 50,000 men. Some died in
skirmishes with the Northern tribes which they happened to
encounter and others by ill climate and disease resulting from
overwork in the construction of forts and roads." However, accounts of
historical fact are often distorted by the partiality of the historian.
(The supposed number of Roman casualties in the Battle of Mons
Grapius in the First Expedition, 360 men according to Tacitus, the
son-in-law of Agricola, seems incredible.)

Dio writes, "Severus, after reaching the extreme North (Burghead
probably), felt quite worn out and was carried in a litter to Eboracum
(York). Having given carte blanche, with regard to the expedition, to
Caracalla (Marcus Aurelius Antonius, 211–17 A.D.), his son and
successor, he died there in 211 A.D." [28] His reward was the security

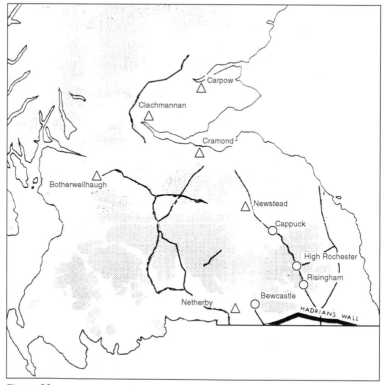

Figure 22

of the province as far as the Tay but only for four years and the death
of Severus brought a speedy conclusion to the Third Expedition. It
seems that Caracalla had to consolidate his position in Rome or he
might have made a secret transaction to conclude a peace treaty with
the Northern tribes. Evidence for this is that there was no Roman
interference in Scotland for the next hundred years. In any event,
Caracalla required a means to ensure that British affairs were brought
to a satisfactory end.

Figure (22) shows the disposition of Roman units for about one
hundred years after Severus's expedition. A few units of mercenaries
were disposed in Bewcastle, Risingham, High Rochester and Cappuck
near Hadrian's Wall. Newstead, the Roman headquarters of each
campaign from the days of the Flavian Dynasty, was now guarded by a
small unit of the Segloes, presumably descendants of the Selgovae.
Near Netherby there was garrisoned a unit of a Welsh tribe, the Mabon,
descendants of the Celtic sun-god Maponos; in Strathclyde a unit of
the descendants of the Damnonii; and near Stirling a unit of the
descendants of Mannan or Manannan, the Celtic sea-god, leaving the
origin of the word in the "Isle of Man".   This disposition was
maintained until the early fourth century when the Picts gained power
in place of the Caledonians.

5. THE EVACUATION OF THE ROMAN ARMY FROM SCOTLAND

The end of the 3rd century was a period when provincial officers
arbitrarily set themselves up as emperors taking advantage of discord
in the imperial authority of Rome and its consequent loss of power.
Thus in Britain, Carausius (Marcus Aurelius, originally a Menapian
pilot) set himself up as emperor in 287 A.D. Because the imperial
authority had no power, open insubordinations and internal disorders
were overlapped by raids of Scots from Ireland and incursions of
Teutonic tribes by sea. In 297 A.D. the situation was so serious that
Constantius I (Flavius Valerius, or Chlorus, 305–6 A.D.), a junior
partner of the imperial "firm" and father of Constantine the Great
(Flavius Valerius Aurelius Constantinus, 306–37 A.D.), had to come to
Britain in person to restore order.

Eumenius, the panegyrist of Constantius, writes concerning the
Picts in a passage of 297 A.D. that [29] "they were new barbarian
tribes." Hegemony over northern Scotland had already transferred
from the hands of the Caledonians to those of the Picts whose
repetitions of racial mixture by matriarchal exogamy had made
themselves predominant. Eumenius writes that Constantius made an
expedition to Orkney (the homeland of the Picts) and, referring to the

Britons (the mercenaries of Roman units), he also mentions that "they had already been accustomed to Picti and Hiberni (Irish) as enemies." [30]

In a passage of 310 A.D. Eumenius writes: "The Emperor did not deign to acquire the woods and marshes of the Caledonians, the Picts and others", though the locality of the reference is not certain.

In 342 A.D. the forts of Bewcastle, Risingham and High Rochester were destroyed and abandoned. In the winter of the same year, Emperor Constans (Flavius Julius, 337 – 50 A.D.), the youngest son of Constantine the Great, came in person to Britain, though the exact reason for the trouble is uncertain.

Ammianus writes in a passage of 360 A.D. that "the savage tribes of Scots and Picts, having broken the truce, ravaged the parts of Roman Britain in the neighbourhood of the Walls" (probably Hadrian's Wall). By the year 365 A.D., Roman units were steadily losing their foothold and in 367 A.D. the Roman provinces to the south of Hadrian's Wall suffered a dreadful incursion of Picts, Saxons, Scots, Attacotti and Franks (see p149). Fullofaudes, the Duke of Britain, and Nectaridus, the Count of Saxony shore, two great Roman officers, were killed, though the precise location has not been identified. A field army was dispatched from Gaul, the invaders were driven out and order was restored. However, in the next year, 368 A.D., all the frontier scouts disbanded and all the Roman garrisons of the outpost forts in Scotland withdrew.

The weakening of the Roman army seems to have been due to the fact that a lot of manpower had to be allocated to coastal defences against the incursions of Teutonic tribes by sea. Each fort had necessarily to reduce armaments. In addition, for a long time legions had been recruited from among the Britons, and the importance of heavy cavalry, which could respond to sudden attacks, had been neglected. Rome seems to have had become exceedingly worn out.

Even though the invasion of the Roman army to Scotland came to an end in 368 A.D., relations between Scotland and the Roman army still continued for another forty years, for Britain south of Hadrian's Wall remained as a Roman province. After the withdrawal, campaigns of the Roman army were carried out three times: the campaign of 382 A.D. was conducted by Theodosius (Flavius) the Great, Roman general and later emperor (East, 379 – 95 A.D.); the one in 383 A.D. was conducted by Maximus (Magnus Clemens, West, 383 – 88 A.D.) who, taking many good troops back over to the Continent after the campaign to Scotland, was recognized by Theodosius as "Augustus" in Gaul, Spain and Britain; and the final campaign was carried out by Stilicho (Flavius) who was the last Roman governor in Britain and commander in chief of the army under Emperor Theodosius in the

390's A.D. All the campaigns were a means of self-defence to protect
the Roman province in southern Britain from the Picts and the Scots.

6. ROMAN SOLDIERS: THEIR DAILY LIVES AND THEIR DEITIES

The Roman legacy in Britain is manifold: Roman blood; the
institutions that Britain adopted as a model for the organisation
and administration of the army in later days; a "rotary" traffic
system, turning clockwise to the right in a roundabout fashion; and
the sites the Romans bequeathed as historical monuments. It is
delightful that many of these sites have already been excavated and
many items from excavations have been collected. However, at the
same time, it is a pity that so many sites have not been restored to
their actual original state for display to the public, as has been
done with the Roman forts and museums situated along Hadrian's
Wall. There now follows comment on the daily life of Roman soldiers
and the deities they held in high esteem, selecting photographs
mainly from the Roman forts along Hadrian's Wall where most
soldiers were billeted before entering Scotland.

a. Roman Forts

It seems to have been an invariable principle for Roman forts to have
been built near riversides to maintain hygiene and soldiers' health,
but those in the first century were mostly tented camps with earthern
ramparts and ditches in their circumferences. At the centre of the
camp were the headquarters tents for the storage of important
documents, valuables and the standard of the unit. Surrounding this
were tents for a granary, a commandant or legate, and for soldiers.

However, in the second century masonry was introduced and old
forts were replaced by timber buildings constructed on stone bases
with an aqueduct system of earthernware pipes. The headquarters
building was in the centre of the fort and had an open courtyard at the
front with rooms for administrative staff and a shrine for altars and the
standard of the unit at the back. In the basement was a room in which
to store important documents and valuables. Adjacent to the
headquarters office were placed buildings for the commandant and his
family, for granaries, a hospital, workshops, storehouses, blocks for
barracks and stables.

Outermost was a wall with four or six gates, and inside the wall were
fitted soldiers' catering ovens or hearths with the stone statue or frame

Illustration (3) is an artist's impression of the inside of the shrine in the headquarters office of a Roman Fort.

of Vesta, goddess of fire and the fireplace. The bath-house, an important military installation, was built just outside the fort, and within it there were dedicated stone images or frames of gods and goddesses whom the soldiers loved and respected. Near these forts, civil settlements, shops and shrines were built.

Photograph (179) shows the site of Easter Happrew (or Lyne) Roman Fort at Hallyne where Lyne Water flows into the River Tweed. It was a relay station located midway between Newstead and Strathclyde and was constructed during the First Expedition by Julius Agricola and remodelled previous to the Second Expedition. Figure (23) shows the plan of the fort after remodelling. The fort stretches out 180 metres from east to west, 150 metres from north to south and encompasses

7.75 acres with four gates. The circumference was enclosed by a ditch
and rampart on the north and west sides. On the east and south sides
respectively there were three and two ramparts with ditches. The site
of the commandant's building was near the southern gate and the
headquarters office was as usual situated in the centre of the fort. The
granary was near the north gate with barracks on the east and west
sides.

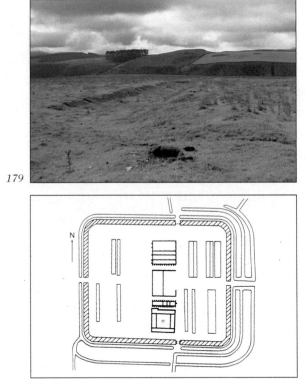

179

Figure 23

Photograph (180) and Figure (24) show the site and plan of
Fendoch Roman Fort by the River Almond, to the north of which was
the gateway to the Highland glens leading to the north. This fort was
constructed in the Flavian Dynasty and was remodelled previous to the
Third Expedition by Severus. It is similar in its composition to Easter
Happrew Roman Fort and measures 4.5 acres in extent.

180

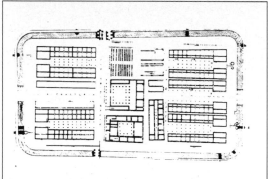

Figure 24

The following photographs show the fixtures of Chesters Roman Fort which was constructed by the side of the River North Tyne, 4.5 miles north of Hexham, as part of Hadrian's Wall under the reign of Emperor Hadrianus. Photograph (181) shows the foundation of the Commandant's house of Chesters Roman Fort; (182) the site of the headquarters office with shrine; (183) the entrance to the basement which kept important documents and valuables; (184) the foundations of the barracks and stables; and (185) the bath house and dressing room where there survive seven niches enshrining images of Roman deities whose names were presumably those of the days of the week.

Chesters Roman Fort stretches from north to south some 180 metres and from east to west some 140 metres, totalling 7.5 acres in extent, once with six gates and a wall 2.3 metres high and 1.5 metres thick. This fort, remodelled previous to the Second Expedition with a fully-equipped aqueduct system, became the garrison for the cavalry. Soon after remodelling, the five hundred men of the Second Asturian Horse, recruited in Spain, were garrisoned there and after that it was used by cavalry squadrons until about the end of the 4th century when it was annihilated by a concerted attack of Picts, Saxons, Scots and Attacotti in 367 A.D. The fixtures are those common to all Roman forts and the fort has been restored to its actual and original state in the best of condition.

181

Corbridge Roman Fort, the biggest commissariat in the forts of Hadrian's Wall, constructed in the reign of Hadrianus and remodelled previous to the 2nd and 3rd Expeditions, is also a fort which was destroyed in 367 A.D. by another concerted attack of the same Picts, Saxons, Scots and Attacotti. There remain many granary sites, the foundations of which measure 26 metres by 7 metres on average. Photograph (186) shows one granary site. Photograph (187) shows the water tank before the Shrine of the Fountain, taking its water from a stream nearby. The water tank was part of a decorative fountain-house, designed in the fashion of a shrine, where soldiers whetted their swords and spears.

182

183

184

185

186

187

Photograph (188) shows the restored castle gate and an overall view of the inside of South Shields Roman Fort for maritime transportation built at Tynemouth in 129 A.D., measuring some 190 metres by 110 metres in extent. It was turned into a supply base previous to the 3rd Expedition and abandoned late in the 3rd century. There were fourteen granaries and the aqueduct system was appended in 222 A.D. by the 5th Cohort of Gaul. In the lower part can be seen the site of the headquarters office with a basement and a well.

188

b. The Organization of the Roman Army

[31] The Roman army consisted of three main units: cohorts, legions and auxiliaries. The cohorts acted as praetorian guards, a fire-brigade and a city police, and at times accompanied very important persons on their campaigns. The legions were the pivot of the provincial army and consisted of well-disciplined and well-armoured infantrymen who participated in actual combats. Each legion consisted of some five thousand men organised into ten cohorts (one cohort originally comprising 500 men). Each cohort was subdivided into five "centuries" (one "century" consisting of 80 to 100 men) except for the first cohort which was organised into double five (2 x 5) centuries (800 - 1000 men). Each legion had its own small cavalry detachment, artillery unit, building maintenance unit, and medical service unit.

The legion was put under the supervision of the governor or a legate, a senator in his early thirties, and his deputy was a tribune, a young senatorial aristocrat. Their normal term of service was three years. The third-in-command to the legate was a prefect of the camp, a soldier in his fifties or sixties who had served as a centurion. He supervised the legion to ensure that everything went well, based on his long experience. Also among the senior officers were junior tribunes who had served in the legion for three years and had commanded auxiliary units. In the legion there were some sixty centurions who supervised the centuries. They were mostly battle-trained soldiers who had served in the army for over fifteen years.

The legion in the first century was composed of Roman citizens and they were employed in ordinary battles and military engineering works, building Roman garrisons and forts at strategic points. Hadrian's Wall and the Antonine Wall (see pp136-137) were constructed by them. Odd items of works, such as frontier controls and small units of combat, were left to the auxiliaries.

Auxiliaries were originally recruited from among men of countries friendly with Rome, but in the Battle of Mons Grapius mercenary soldiers of Britons seem to have been already employed as auxiliaries to fight in support of Agricola. A series of revolts in many Roman forts in the 150's A.D. acted as a turning point and from then on soldiers of the Roman regular army gradually began to disappear and in Scotland auxiliaries and mercenaries from southern Scotland and northern England began to play leading roles. A tombstone discovered at Mumrills, a fort of the Antonine Wall, is that of a Brigantian from northern England.

Formations of auxiliary units were of six types, comprising infantry, cavalry and both. One auxiliary consisted of mercenaries of some five hundred to one thousand men. The infantry cohorts were subdivided into centuries and each was more or less eighty men, just as in the formation of the legion, and cavalry was formed into a troop some thirty strong. The smaller independent infantry formation consisted of six centuries, though in the larger formation it was ten. The smaller mixed formation consisted of six centuries of infantry and four troops of cavalry while in the larger formation it was ten centuries and eight troops. The smaller independent cavalry formation consisted of sixteen troops and the larger formation twenty-four, both under the supervision of a young tribune. Auxiliaries wore helmets and coats of mail and were armed with oval shields, swords and spears.

Each unit of the Roman army was responsible for its own supervision and its headquarters was obligated to draw up a list of duties to keep each soldier's individual file and to make an annual report as to the activities in which the unit had been engaged. Ordinarily the Roman army was run by volunteer recruits, the motivation being money or salary. Once a soldier enlisted, he was well paid for twenty-five years and on retirement was paid a considerable amount of cash. If he was not a Roman, cash or Roman citizenship was granted, though Roman citizenship came to be granted even to auxiliaries after 212 A.D. in the reign of Caracalla. In the Roman army, the marriage of soldiers was banned, with the exception of officers. Therefore, many were unofficially "married" to local women and many unofficial "families" existed in the civil settlements near each fort.

c. Arms and Daily Utensils used by Roman soldiers

189

Photographs displayed are of the arms and utensils used by Roman soldiers. Photograph (189) shows a replica of a catapult exhibited in Chesterholm Roman Fort. Real ones were greater in size and the Roman army used them in field operations, mainly in destroying British forts; (190) and (191) show replicas of a Roman and a Celtic chariot owned by Chesterholm Roman Fort Museum; (192) shows Roman millstones owned by Chesters Roman Fort Museum; (193) shows a measure for collecting corn-tribute, excavated at Carvoran Roman Fort. (Romans seem to have established the custom of collecting tribute from farmers in the province); (194) shows the sandals and shoes used by Roman soldiers, owned by Chesterholm Roman Fort Museum; and (195) shows pottery with protruding surface designs owned by Corbridge Roman Fort Museum.

190

191

192

193

194

195

d. Deities loved and respected by Roman Soldiers

In Britain until about the middle of the second century Roman soldiers were mostly pagans believing in the deities of Roman mythology but thereafter Christianity steadily secured a foothold. From then on, confrontation between the two sects seems to have been vehement and sometimes it developed into religious revolts in the camps. Pagan Romans were idol worshippers and the gods and goddesses loved and respected by them were Jupiter, the supreme deity, god of the heavens and embodiment of the national dignity of the Romans; Juno, the earth-mother goddess, queen of the heavens after marriage to Jupiter and the goddess presiding over marriage and childbirth; Apollo, god of light, music and prophecy; Mars, the god of war, fertility and agriculture; Fortuna, goddess of fortune and good luck; Mercury, messenger of the gods and goddesses and the deity of commerce, dexterity and eloquence; Genius Loci, the tutelary deity of land and fertility; Neptune, god of the sea; Minerva, goddess of wisdom, art and war; Aesculapius, god of medicine and healing; Venus, goddess of love and beauty; Coventina, the goddess presiding over water; Silvanus, tutelary deity of untilled land; and Hercleus, a mighty hero of extraordinary strength and courage.

In the Roman world of pagan days there was a custom whereby people dedicated, to a certain deity they loved and respected, a kind of stone altar, a statue or tablet on which was carved the image of the deity with an epitaph and the name of the dedicator. These were annually replaced by a new one on the festival day of each deity and in the forts these dedications were chiefly conducted by commissioned officers. They installed their favourite altar, statue and so on in the shrine of the headquarters office, the Shrine of Nymphs and the Genius Loci, and the bath-house, though similar dedications were made in similar shrines in civil settlements by tradesmen, the rich and so on.

What deities did the soldiers who were not Romans hold in high esteem? They loved and respected the deities of their native homelands or deities amalgamated with a Roman deity such as Jupiter Dolichenus, created by the fusion of Jupiter and the Semitic god of weather and iron-working (of Doliche in Commagene); Juno Lucina, a deity who presided over childbirth and nursing; Mars Cocidus, an ancient British war-god amalgamated with the Roman war-god Mars; Mars Thincsus, a war-god attended by two warrior goddesses, (though it is unknown whether "Thincsus" was the name of a place like "Dolichenus" or of a deity such as "Cocidus"); and Sulis Minerva, a Celtic healing goddess of hot springs and health amalgamated with the Roman Minerva.

To these deities, of course, were dedicated stone altars, statues and tablets, and an altar dedicated to Jupiter Dolichenus has been excavated in the fort of Croy. Besides these deities, soldiers who came from Parthia, Syria, Phrysia and Gaul adored Mithras, Cybele, Maponos and Brigantia. Mithras was a Parthian deity of sunlight and fertility. He was a god sent to earth to hunt and kill the primeval bull [32] "Geush Urvan". The release of its blood was believed to give all creation a life-giving force as also seen in the ritual of the Druidic bull-sacrifice (see p241).

Just before the Second Expedition, a vast number of Islamic soldiers were called up to the forts along Hadrian's Wall and sent to Scotland. A series of Mithoreum began to be built along Hadrian's Wall and the Antonine Wall and became hotbeds of religious disputation with pious Christian soldiers. The cult of Cybele, the cyclical myth of which was personified by the death and rebirth of Cybele's lover Atys, was a cult similar to that of Osiris in ancient Egypt (see pp10-12). It originated in a town bearing her surname, Pessinus in Galatia in Gaul. Standing on a pig, she was the great Earth-Mother Goddess in Phrysia and Asia Minor. This cult was carried into Rome in 205 A.D. but banned until the reign of Claudius II (268 – 70 A.D.), although it was already adored in Britain in the reign of Alexander Severus (222 – 235 A.D.).

Maponos was a Gaulish sun-god, called "Mabon" in Wales, and his descendants were the Maben, Roman mercenaries who settled near Loch Maben (see pp51, 143) and became followers of King Arthur in later days. Brigantia was the tutelary goddess of the Brigantes in North Britain, coming from Bregenze in the west of Austria, the cradle of the Hallstatt Iron Civilization.

An altar was a pedestal on which people offered a votive light to a deity and the following are photographs of stone altars, statues, tablets and so on, dedicated by Roman soldiers and mercenaries, showing the co-existent religious faiths in those days.

Photograph (196) shows the altar dedicated to Jupiter and the Genius Loci with the epitaph, " To Jove, Best and Greatest, to the other immortal Gods and to the Genius on the Praetorium by Quintus Petronius Urbicus, son of Quintus of the Fabian tribe, Prefect of the 4th Cohort of Gaul, from Brixia in Italy." It is owned by Chesters Roman Fort Museum.

Photograph (197) shows an altar dedicated to Mars Thincsus, his two warrior goddess attendants, Beda and Fimmilina, and to an Emperor, deifying him as god. It is owned by Chesters Roman Fort Museum.

Photograph (198) shows an altar dedicted to Cocidus by Quintus Frontius Maternus, Prefect of the 1st Cohort of Tungrians. It is owned by Chesters Roman Fort Museum.

Photograph (199) shows
an altar with an image of
Fortuna, dedicated by
Venenus, a German.

Photograph (200)
shows an altar
dedicated to Neptune,
the sea-god, with the
epitaph in Latin,
"Neptune Le(gion) VI
V(ictrix) P(ia)
F(idelis)" or " To
Neptune the 6th
Legion, Victorious,
Pious and Faithful". It
is owned by the
Museum of Antiquities
of the University and
the Society of
Antiquities of
Newcastle-upon-Tyne.

Photograph (201)
shows an altar with,
at its base, a relief of
Mithras slaying a bull
and at the front centre
an epitaph, "Deo
L(vcivus) Sentius
Castus Leg. VI
D(ecvrio) P(osvit)" or
"To the God Lucius
Sentius Castus, a
Decurion of the 6th
Legion, erected". It is
also owned by the
Museum of Antiquities
of the University and
the Society of
Antiquities of
Newcastle-upon-Tyne.

Photograph (202) shows the remains of the Mithras temple or
Mithoreum near Carrawburgh Roman Fort, built early in the 3rd
century and destroyed in 297 A.D. Reconstruction and destruction
took place alternately at the hands of Mithras adorers and Christian
soldiers. Altars now seen in this temple are replicas, the originals
being in the Museum of Antiquities of the University and the Society
of Antiquities of Newcastle-upon-Tyne. The left-hand side altar was
dedicated to the praetor Marcus Simplicius Simplex and has a
sculpture with Mithras as a charioteer of the sun while the central and
right-hand side altars were ones dedicated by the prefects of
Carrawburgh Roman Fort. The names of Lucius Antonius Proculus and
Aulus Cluentius Habitus can be read. Behind these altars there used

to be a stone relief showing Mithras slaying the bull, as seen in
Illustration (4), and near the entrance two statues of Cautes and
Cautopas with a torch turned upwards and downwards in their hands,
symbolizing the sunrise and sunset.

202

Illustration (4)

203

204

Photograph (203) shows a stone statue representing the birth of Mithras from an egg, symbolizing the signs of the zodiac. Mithras holds a torch in one hand and a knife in the other to cut the shell of the zodiac "egg" to enter the world. This statue was excavated in Housteads Roman Fort and is now owned by the Museum of Antiquities of the University and the Society of Antiquities of Newcastle-upon-Tyne.

Photograph (204) shows a statue dedicated to Julia Mammie, the mother of Emperor Alexander Severus (222 – 35 A.D.), identifying her as Juno Cybele or Juno Regina, the consort of the Syrian God whom the Romans worshipped as Jupiter Dolichenus. She stands on a pig, as does Juno, the Earth-mother goddess. It is in the possession of Chesters Roman Fort Museum.

205

Photograph (205) shows a stone tablet of "Celestial Brigantia" identified with the consort of an eastern Baal, Jupiter Dolichenus or Roman Minerva. She wears a spiral crown on her head and holds a spear. In her left hand is the orb of sovereignty and on her shoulders the wings of victory. It was found in Birrens Roman Fort and is owned by Corbridge Roman Fort Museum.

206

Photograph (206) shows a stone tablet dedicated to Genius Loci, the tutelary god of land and fertility, holding a cornucopia for sacrifice on the altar. It is owned by Chesters Roman Fort Museum.

207

Photograph (207) shows a stone statue of the God or River Genius of North Tyne. It is owned by Chesters Roman Fort Museum.

208

Photograph (208) shows a stone tablet with a fine sculpture of Coventina, the water goddess and leader of the Shrine of Nymphs and the Genius Loci, attended by two nymphs holding water vases which pour out streams of water. It is owned by Chesters Roman Fort Museum.

Photograph (209) shows a tablet dedicated to Minerva and Aesculapius, though the latter is gone. It is owned by Chesters Roman Fort Museum.

Photograph (210) shows a stone tablet with a relief representing a stag running through a forest and two young stags feeding in a wood. The tablet is presumably dedicated to Silvanus, the tutelary god of wood, just as the Celtic Cernunnos usually appears in the form of a horned stag. It is owned by Chesters Roman Fort Museum.

Photograph (211) shows an altar with a relief of a ram-horned snake. In the Roman world of pagan days as well as in the Celtic world, a horned animal was a god, as with other animals with tusks and fangs such as a boar or a wolf. However, the snake also seems to have been identified with a god, as with the Celtic Nantosuelta ("Winding River") symbolizing "vitality".

Photograph (212) is of the Eagle Rock by the seaside near Cramond, the eagle being the embodiment of Mercury, the Roman god. The rock has three carved eagles, although it is also said that the images are of three goddesses.

CHAPTER VI

THE ARRIVAL OF THE
DARK AGES

The Dark Ages in Scotland, an unenlightened period in the perspective of European history, followed the evacuation of the Roman army at the end of the 4th century, accompanying the introduction of Christianity. It was a new age of conflict during which the four large tribes, the Picts, the Scots, the Britons and the Angles, sought supremacy over a period of six hundred and fifty years. The Damnonii or Strathclyde Britons, who were somewhat Romanized, held their land from the mouth of the Clyde to Ayrshire and Lanarkshire with Dumbarton as their base. The Votadinii or Welsh Britons, who had once driven out the Scots from North Wales and established the Kingdom of Gwynedd there, were in Dumfries and Galloway, the Borders and the Lothians with Traprain Law and Arthur's Seat as their bases. In Northumbria, south of these areas, the Angles had seized most of the territories by the end of the 6th century.

The whole land to the north of Fife, the Central region, Argyle, Tayside, Grampian and the Highlands was Pictish

Figure 25 shows the distribution of the four tribes just after the evacuation of the Roman army.

165

territory and in 498 A.D. or 500 A.D. the Dalriadic Scots, the descendants of the Scots who had fought with the Romans in the middle of the 4th century, emigrated from Dunseverick in Northern Ireland to settle in the Argyle district. From the end of the 8th century there began invasions and settlements of Vikings to the seaside areas of the mainland and the circumferential islands. Their language was Old Norse; the Scots spoke Q-Celtic, or Irish Gaelic; the Britons P-Celtic or Brythonic, the modern form of which remains as Welsh and Cornish; the Picts pre-Celtic; and the Angles Old English.

1. THE ARRIVAL AND GROWTH OF THE PICTS

It cannot be denied that even Bede (673-735 A.D.), an English historian and scholar, and Nennius, a Welsh compiler of British history in Latin round about 796 A.D, were too far removed in time to deal with the place of origin of the Pictish people, the time of their arrival and the places of their settlement. Bede writes that [33] the Picts came from Scythia in a few ships (without women) and landed on the north coast of Ireland where the Scots would not receive them but advised them to seek settlement in neighbouring isles. So they made for Britain (supplied with wives), and settled in the northern parts. He adds that the Picts arrived in Britain after the Britons but before the Scots.

Nennius writes that [34] the Picts came from Scythia, otherwise called Agathyrsi. They sprang from Gelon, the son of Hercleus, and after various adventures they landed in Leinster and by their skill in magic helped the king of Leinster to win a battle. But they had to leave Leinster for some reason and sailed northward and settled, according to one account, in Tiree beyond Islay, whence they took possession of Alba from the bounds of the Cats (Caithness) to Foirchiu (The Firth of Forth?). Nennius says that the Picts came and occupied the islands called Orcades (the Orkney Islands) and from these islands wasted many districts, occupied the north of Britain and held the third part of Britain up to the time of his writing.

The date of their arrival in the Orcades, Nennius presumes, was the 300's B.C., according to modern chronology, not long after the time when Eli was Judge in Israel. [35] Robert Graves, the author of *The White Goddess*, presumes the date to be about the 800's B.C., the end of the Bronze Age, [36] and W. J. Watson, the author of *A History of the Celtic Place-names of Scotland*, presumes, in view of the fact that the Picts had become the leading tribe to the north of the Wall (the Antonine Wall) by the end of the third century A.D., that they must have been the predominant tribe in the fourth century B.C. [37]

The Picts were advocates of matriarchal exogamy, the custom of marrying a person belonging to another tribe or clan, and were thus a race likely to become predominant by repetition of racial mixtures. If they had arrived in the 300's B.C. they would have had racial mixture with the Celts in the Iron Age, and if they had arrived in the 800's B.C. they ought to have had racial mixture with the aboriginal Bronze Age people who spoke pre-Celtic.

Scythia, according to Bede and Nennius, was the ancient name of sections of Europe and Asia, now included in Russia, and Scythians were a nomadic and savage race, dwelling chiefly in the steppes north and north-east of the Black Sea and in the regions east of the Aral Sea. They are mentioned as early as the 7th century B.C. when they were driven out of Media, but in the 2nd century B.C. they were conquered by the Sarmatians and shortly thereafter they practically disappeared.

Generally, opinion agrees that the Picts first arrived in the North of Britain where there remains a large number of brochs, supposedly the dwellings of Pictish people and mostly built in the Iron Age. The farther one goes north, the greater the number of these brochs. Though most of them are now only sites, [38] there remain 145 in Orkney and Shetland, 150 in Caithness, 67 in Sutherland, 28 in Lewis, 10 in Harris, 5 at least in North Uist, 30 in Skye, 10 in Ross, 3 in Wigtownshire and 6 in Inverness-shire. These facts of distribution prove that the original area of the broch-builders was in the far north and show that the Picts first dwelled in Orkney and Shetland and, attaining a firm position there, gradually extended their power to the

213

Photograph (213) shows St Ninian's Cave looking onto Port Castle Bay in Whithorn in Galloway, the place where Christianity in Scotland started. The saint used it as his cell to evangelize the Brito-Pictish and Britons before he founded "Candida Casa" (the White House or Chapel) in 397 A.D.

mainland. Having once gained a foot-hold in the south, they quickened their advancement as the Vikings did in later times.

W. J. Watson writes that the island Picts were seamen and pirates while the Picts of the mainland were to a considerable extent agriculturists. Once they had become lords of the mainland as far south as Inverness, which they probably accomplished at an early stage, they came into contact with the ruling tribe of the Caledonians, and in the fourth century, when the power of the Caledonians had declined, the Picts assumed the leading role among all the tribes north of the Wall of Antoninus. [39] Ammianus writes in his accounts of 364 A.D. that the Picts divided into two tribes, the Decalydones and the Verturiones, that is, the Northern Picts and the Southern Picts. [40] The former comprised the Cats possessing Caithness and Sutherland as their territory; those of Moray who had Ross and Cromarty, Nairn and Moray; and those of Mar who had Banff and Aberdeenshire. The latter consisted of those of Athole who had Athole and Gowrie; those of Strathearn who had Perth and Clackmannan; those of Angus who had Kincardine and Angus; and those of Fife who had Fife and Kinross. The Picts originally comprised seven tribes but they had been traditionally ruled by one high king, whether Northern or Southern, according to their constitution. It was after the death of

214

Photograph (214) shows Candida Casa in Whithorn in later days, though its original structure is unknown. Dumfries and Galloway gradually became the territory of the Angles through their aggression which began approximately with Aethelfrith's enthronement (593 – 617 A.D.) and Whithorn became a bishopric of the Northumbrian Kingdom. Candida Casa was rebuilt in 720 A.D. and it became a Northumbrian bishopric monastery. It survived the period of the invasion and settlement of the Vikings and became a priory Cathedral through a series of ecclesiastical reforms in the twelfth century.

Brude I Mac Maelcon, the last high king of the Northern Picts, that the division Ammianus describes can be specified.

In the days of Roman occupation, Dumfries and Galloway was a Romanized region which was ruled by a British king, Coel Hen (or Kyle or Howel, the Old). There were many Roman camps and on the occasion when M. C. Maximus carried out his expedition in 383 A.D. (see p144), his blood-line survived in the lineage of Coel Hen. Since this region had been Romanized and was flourishing, St Ninian (360 – 432 A.D.?), (who, born in Cumberland (the land of Cymrie), had made a pilgrimage to Rome when young and was consecrated as a bishop after fourteen years of study), founded his church "Candida Casa" to evangelise the Britons there.

However, the region, which led to the west exit of Hadrian's Wall, had been a rendezvous point for Picts towards the end of the Roman occupation. Their leader was Talorg Mac Keother (or Keocher) who acceded to the position of high king as Keother "the Broad Forehead" (396 – 413 A.D.) after he had fought with Flavius Stilicho, the British governor who made the last expedition to Scotland in 396 A.D. Though most of these Picts could have been involved in attacks on the forts of Hadrian's Wall, some of them could have been descendants of the Brito-Pictish of Dumfries and Galloway, some of whom were connected with St Ninian who was later to tour all over northern Pictland, the Highlands, Orkney and Shetland, mainly to evangelize the Picts.

The presence of a Pictish symbol stone left in Trusty Hill Fort near Gatehouse of Fleet in Stewartry is evidence that the Pictish were in this region. It has a series of Pictish symbols, such as a water-beast and crescent crown-marks traversed with a reversed Z-shaped sign, and was placed to the side of the entrance passage to the fort.

The history of the Picts in their earliest days has not been accurately ascertained and though the pedigree of the Pictish High Kings is inserted at the end

215

Photograph (215) shows a tombstone with a Latin epitaph carved in the middle of the 5th century. It is owned by Whithorn Museum and testifies to the Roman influence over this region. The epitaph runs:
"TE DOMINU(U) LAUDMUS LATINUS ANNORU(M) XXXV FILIA SUA ANN(ORUM) IV (H)ICSI(G)MUM FECERUT NEPUS BARROVA DI."
(We praise thee Lord, Latinus aged thirty-five and his daughter aged four. Grand-son Barrovadus has erected these monuments here.)

216

Photograph (216) shows the legendary church, St Bridgid's Kirk, Dalgety, which Nechtan Mac Erp dedicated to St Bridgid and her successor Darlugdach (Daor Lugdach) of Kildare. The successor's name remains as the place-name, Dalgety, which is situated 2 miles south-west of Aberdour on the shore of the River Forth.

of this book (see pp267-8), the founder has not been identified. Talorg Mac Keother or Keochar, St Ninian's contemporary, is the first identifiable high king. He reigned until 413 A.D. and all Roman units evacuated Britain in the year 410 A.D., just before the end of Talorg's reign. After Talorg Mac Keother came Drust Mac Erp (413 – 53 A.D.), called "the Hundred Battles," a very brave high king who could never resist battle to re-organize the new frontiers of southern Pictland just after the Romans' evacuation. In 432 A.D. during his reign, St Patrick entered Ireland and shortly thereafter the Angles came in force to settle in the Humber region in Northumbria.

In 453 A.D. Talorg Mac Aniel (453 – 56 A.D.) followed Drust Mac Erp and then Nechtan Mac Erp (456 – 80 A.D.), the brother of Drust Mac Erp, who had his domain in Forfar, Perth and Fife, succeeded Talorg. In his reign an Irish Pict and St Ninian's successor, St Buidhe Mac Bronach (St Yellow Belly-band's Son) came with sixty followers to Tayside. Nechtan built for him a fort and church, Caer-Budde (or Kirk-Budde), near his own fort at Dunnichen. Buidhe was a saint who had spent thirty years in Italy and returned through Germany to Ireland. He is known to have died on December 7th, 521 A.D., the day of St Columba's birth.

Drust Mac Gernot (480 – 510 A.D.) followed Nechtan and in 500 A.D. (or 498 A.D) during his reign the Scots of Irish Dalriada arrived in Kintyre which was still Pictish territory. This event, the beginning of important political change, seemed to have received only local attention and only the sovereign protector of the Pictish territories took any action.

Galan Arilith (510 – 22 A.D.) succeeded Drust in 510 A.D. and in 516 A.D. Arthur, a British high king, led his Gwyr y Gogledd (or Men of the North) to a triumphant victory over the Saxons at Bowden Hill (Torphichen), aided by Humber Angles who attempted to settle on the shores of the Forth in later times. Ecclesiastical activity during his reign included St Briog erecting Munross Annat [41] in Montrose, east of Brechin.

From 522 A.D. to 527 A.D. a joint sovereignty of Drust Mac Gyrom (522 – 32 A.D.) and Drust Mac Udrost (522 – 27 A.D.) was established, though the reason for this is not certain. Each had his seat in the capital of his own clan but disposed of affairs that concerned all Pictland. The latter resigned after a reign of five years and from 527 A.D. to 532 A.D. Drust Mac Gyrom reigned by himself. After Drust came Gartnaidh Mac Gyrom (532 – 39 A.D.) and in 537 A.D., during his reign, King Arthur suffered a crushing defeat at Camelon near Stirling on Pictish territory when fighting with Medraut, a son prince of Loth in Edinburgh. Gartnaidh was succeeded by Gelan Mac Gyrom (539 – 40 A.D.).

In Pictland the sceptre did not pass from father to son. This was because of the marriage system based on the archaic practice of exogamous matriarchy. They were all totemists divided into tribes of different animal, fish or bird totems, and the first daughter was the first heiress of each family line. A woman or a man was not allowed to marry a man or woman in the same totem, even in the case of the royal family.

It was the first-born son of the first daughter of each family and her non-royal consort of a different totem who became the chief of each family; when the first son died, the second son inherited the right to be chief; and if the second son died, failing any other son, a nephew, the son of the second sister, had the right of inheritance. The inheritance ranking of heiress was similar to the order applied to the succession of chief of the family. The tribal king was elected from among the chiefs of the families and the high king was elected from among these tribal kings.

The alternating succession of the sons of the Gyrom family to the throne was a typical manifestation of the first son dying and the second son succeeding him. Similar examples are seen in the successions of sons of the Wid family and the Donnel family in later times. Why Nechtan Mac Erp did not succeed his elder brother Drust Mac Erp on his death was presumably due to the fact that Nechtan had been exiled. [42]

The Pictish throne was thus passed from Gelan of the Gyrom family to Talorg Mac Muircholaidh (540 – 51 A.D.), to Talorg Mac Munaidh (551 – 52 A.D.), and then to Gelan or Cenalph (552 – 53 A.D.). In 547 A.D, during the reign of Talorg Mac Muircholaidh, the "Yellow Plague", which had broken out in 544 A.D in St Mobhi Monastery in Ireland and killed off many kings, abbots, chiefs and ordinary people by a rapidly-spreading fever and jaundice, began all of a sudden to rage throughout Britain. Talorg Mac Munaidh, who reigned for only one year, and his successor were probably among the victims.

In 553 A.D. Brude Mac Maelcon (553 – 84 A.D.), the king of Orkney, took over the sovereignty of Pictland with his capital in Inverness. His father Maelcon was a pagan, once the king of Gwynedd, who had his homeland in the Forth region and whose ancestors had once driven out the Scots who had attempted to colonize North Wales near the end of the Roman era.

In 560 A.D. Gabhran, the king of the Scots, began to move his men north and intrude into Argyle which was still a Pictish domain. Brude mobilized the men of the Western Picts and wiped out the invaders with great slaughter, capturing and beheading Gabhran. The survivors were hunted southward from Lorn to the borders of Lennox, and those who did not escape from Pictland were enclosed in Kintyre. Brude buried the dead at Cladh nan Righrean (or Burial Place of the Kings) in Lismore, the holy place of the Western Picts presided over by the Pictish missionary St Moluag. This saint, nicknamed "Hundred Monasteries", had established his base at Lismore (or Enclosure with a big rampart), from which he extended his activities across Drumalban far into eastern Pictland, founding other monasteries at Rosemarkie, Mortlach (near Dufftown) and Clova (near Rhynie), each with its group of dependent churches.

Brude gave the title of "toiseach," or a mere commander, to Comgal's son and Gabhran's nephew, Conail, and also to some of the vassal remnants, and made Dalriada his tributary. [43] In the same year St Drostan, whose father was a prince of Dyfed, by then part of South Wales, and whose sister was the wife of Gabhran, erected a monastery in Deer in north-east Buchan. It is written that Drostan Mac Cosgreg came from Hi (or Iona) with Colum Cille (St Columba) to Aberdour in Buchan, according to the Book of Deer.

It is certain that this ingenious diplomat St Columba, a fellowman of the Scots who settled on Iona in 563 A.D. after having been exiled from Ireland, came to Inverness in 565 A.D. under the care of the Irish Picts [44] St Comgall of Bangor Mor and St Canneeh of Kilkenny in later times, to receive Brude's sanction for the mission he had contemplated in Pictland.

It is not certain whether or not Brude had been Christianized by St Columba but it seems to be true that Columba, with his diplomatic genius, had intended to restore freedom to conquered Dalriada, and with his visit, relations between the Picts and Dalriada calmed down. In Dalriada in 574 A.D. Conail died and his cousin Aedhan, son of Gabhran, ascended the throne as king of Dalriada, through the good offices of St Columba, and in 580 A.D. the dispatch of [45] St Cormac's mission and Aedhan's expedition to Orkney was decided by the sanction of Brude.

The account of Adamnan runs thus: "The full extent of Brude's kingdom is unknown, though it probably included Orkney, since the sub-kings or "regulus" of Orkney were at Brude's court in the time of Colum Cille. Orkney is mentioned again in documents round the year 574 A.D. when Aedhan Mac Gabhran became king of Dalriada. It seems likely that around this time Orkney was in rebellion against its Pictish overlord, for we hear of Aedhan's campaigning in Orkney and his encroaching on a part of southern Pictland." [46]

217

Photograph (217) shows St Drostan's Cave, looking on to Aberdour Bay in Buchan, which the saint used as his cell to evangelize the northern Picts. On the right side of the photograph is St Drostan's Well.

218

Photograph (218) shows the site (now occupied by two churches) where St Columba and his mission built their fort when they visited Brude Mac Maelcon. It is now by the River Ness in the town centre of Inverness.

Brude died in 584 A.D. in the Battle of Circinn (Angus and the Mearns) on Tayside in southern Pictland. It was an internal strife fought by Brude to suppress disturbing elements among the Southern Picts of Angus and Strathmore and those of Strathearn and Menteith, and Aedhan's invasion of the southern part of Pictland might have been a preliminary action by order of Brude; however, Brude was defeated.

After Brude came the Christian high king Gartnaidh Mac Domneth (584 – 99 A.D.) whose capital was in Tayside. The administrative pivot in Pictland transferred from Inverness to Tayside and this trend reflected the growing power of the southern Picts. Among the conspicuous ecclesiastical activities in those days was the erection of the monasteries of Mortlach and Clova by St Moluag, and the antecedents of [47] St Critan (or Boniface) in Fortrose in the Black Isle were also erected by him. The church of Mortlach, at the south end of the town, the seat of a Pictish bishopric, was enlarged by Malcolm II in later times as a thanks-offering for a victory over the Danes in 1006 A.D.

In 590 A.D., during Gartnaidh Mac Domneth's reign, Aedhan threw his force into southern Pictland where Gartnaidh caught up with them at Kirkintilloch and drove them off (see p189). Gartnaidh was also an ecclesiastically learned high king. He copied the Cambridge manuscript of the Chronicle used in the *Scalacronica* and translated it.

In 599 A.D. Nechtan Mac Cannon (599 – 621 A.D.), another pious Christian high king of the Erp family whose capital was on the east coast of the River Tay, succeeded Gartnaidh. He built the Church of Abernethy and contributed to the posterity of Abernethy as a Pictish foundation at Dunkeld. Also in those days, St Blaan and St Donnan took active parts in evangelizing activities. St Blaan, operating from a base at Dunblane near Stirling, erected churches at Kilblane in Kilmahoe; at Kilblane near Caerlaverock; at Southend in Kintyre; at Kilblane in Glenshira near Inveraray, at a site known as "Camas Blathain" facing Loch Shiel; at Dunblane at Caibeal Bhlathain; at Kilblain near Oldmeldrum; and at Petblane in Daviot.

St Donnan the Great, one of the few martyr saints in the history of Celtic Christianity before the days of the Norsemen's invasion, set up Kirkmaiden next door to Whithorn and extended his work to Kildonan in Sutherland, following exactly the footsteps of St Ninian. Many of his church sites, such as Kildonan in Ayrshire and Kildonan in Sutherland, closely adjoined foundations of St Ninian. Along with his fifty-two brethren, he was martyred at the hands of pirates on the Isle of Eigg on Easter Day, 16th April 617 A.D.

The Pictish throne moved successively from Nechtan to Ciniath Mac Luthren (621 – 31 A.D.), Gartnaidh Mac Wid or Foith (631 – 35 A.D.), Brude Mac Wid (635 – 41 A.D.), Talorg Mac Wid (641 – 53 A.D.), Talorgan Mac Enfred (653 – 57 A.D.), Gartnaidh Mac Donnel (657 – 63 A.D.), and Drust Mac Donnel (663 – 72 A.D.).

The father of Talorgan Mac Enfred was Enfred, the eldest son of Aethelfrith, the king of Northumbria and Bernicia who died in 617 A.D. in a battle with his English neighbours of East Anglia, and he was the brother of Oswald and Oswiu who were expelled together with him by Eadwine, the successor of Aethelfrith and king of Northumbria (617 – 633 A.D.) and Deira (585 – 633 A.D.) in 617 A.D. Enfred, seeking refuge, settled in southern Pictland and married a Pictish princess. Both his brothers, Oswald and Oswiu, sought refuge in Iona where they received "Columban Christianity" and after Eadwine's death they returned to Bernicia.

Oswald acceded to the throne of Bernicia in 633 A.D. and to the throne of Northumbria (634 – 42 A.D.) on the death of Osric (633 – 34 A.D.), Eadwine's son and the king of Northumbria and Deira. Oswiu succeeded to the throne of Bernicia (642 – 70 A.D.) on his brother's death and succeeded to the throne of Northumbria (651 – 70 A.D.) on the death of Oswine, the king of Northumbria and the last king of Deira (642 – 51 A.D.). Both were enthusiastic Christians and Oswald established the Christianity of the Celtic Church in Northumbria.

The organization of the church, the shape of tonsure and the method of computing the date of Easter became a kindling charcoal to fire a dispute with those of the Roman Church which Eadwine had introduced in 633 A.D. The dispute concluded in favour of the Roman Easter and tonsure, and as a result of the eloquence of St Wilfrid at the Synod of Whitby in 663 A.D. or 664 A.D., the Celtic Church which Oswald had established deferred to the Roman Church which preferred the authoritative St Peter. However, the Celtic Church, which favoured the sensitive St John, maintained a strong presence in Lindisfarne for forty years.

Brude Mac Bile, who followed Drust Mac Donnel in Pictland in 672 A.D., was the grandson of Talorgan Mac Enfred. His mother was the daughter of Talorgan and his father was a prince of the Strathclyde Britons. He reigned from 672 A.D. to 693 A.D., and was destined to confront Oswiu's son Egfrid who had subjugated the whole land of the Votadinii north of the River Tyne and established the seat of an English bishopric in Abercorn on the Firth of Forth which was Pictish territory.

In 682 A.D. he sent an expedition to Orkney to reduce the power of the rebellious Picts there, and the following year he sent his "Men of Earn" to the home base of Scottish Dalriada, wasted their territories and took away a host of women hostages, a far-sighted action to prevent the co-operation of the Scots and the Angles in a war conjectured to be near at hand.

In 685 A.D. he fought "the Battle of Nechtansmere" against a large army of Angles. However, a short reference should be made here to the "hostages" mentioned above.

Photograph (219) shows the "Stone of the Hill of Hostage" (or Knocnagael (Cnoc na Gial) Stone) situated in the southern suburbs of Inverness, once the capital of Brude Mac Maelcon, and Figure (26) shows the symbols of this stone also known as the

Figure 26

219

"Boar Stone". The stone has sculptures of "mirror and comb" in the upper part and the image of a "boar" in the lower part. Mirror and comb is presumed to represent women or women hostages, and the boar the totem of either Brude Mac Maelcon or the Dalriadic Scots. The stone might mark the site of women hostages which Brude himself took when he conquered Gabhran, or those he took from minor kings of Orkney, which was associated with the "boar", when he sent Aedhan there in 580 (see p172) or those which Brude Mac Bile took from Dalriada in his campaign of 683 A.D.

With reference to the Battle of Nechtansmere, Archibald B. Scott, the author of *The Pictish Nation, its People and its Church*, narrates in his book as follows: [48] "The instrument of Heaven on this occasion was the Army of the Picts, to whom the Scots themselves had given trouble and caused suffering on almost every occasion that the Picts were occupied in repelling the Angles. Egfrid so often found the Celts an easy prey that Brude Mac Bile was soon gladdened to find him expectant, like Edward "the Hammer" in later days, of decisive action. Egfrid marched into Pictland with his entire army and crossed the Forth near Stirling, bent on smashing Brude in his own province of "Fortrenn", or Strath Earn. But Brude had no intention of giving Egfrid battle where he desired it. He "feigned retreat," as the old accounts put it, and, as he retired, lured the enemy ever onward. Egfrid, with his lust for conquest, perhaps saw visions of the subjugation of all Pictland which had been the dream of his predecessors and of their Roman Catholic prelates. With admirable strategy, Brude drew his enemy across the Tay and finally beyond the Sidlaw Hills, far away from his base. He halted the Pictish army near Dunnichen in Forfarshire, the capital of the Picts of Angus and the place where Nechtan the Great had bestowed on St Buidhe a fort in which he built his Church in the days when the Angles had hardly cleared the German mudflats.

Fortune had favoured Brude in his choice of rallying place. It ensured the support of the petty king of the Pictish province of Angus with his ever-powerful clan. The slow retreat had given time for the Picts of the Mearns, Mar, Buchan, and perhaps Moray, to come to the aid of their sovereign, as they were bound to do by the Constitution. Brude's flanks were safe from any treachery on the part of the Scots from across Drum Alban (which would not have been the case in Strath Earn), if the Scots had been treacherously inclined, hardly conceivable considering the foe. But Brude took no risks."

Bede explains that "Egfrid was drawn into a narrow pass among remote mountains." As the "mountains" were the Sidlaws, it looked to Egfrid as if the main army of Brude had retired by Strathmore, while an enticing force had affected to fall back on the strong capital of Angus, rounding the Sidlaws by the Carse of Gowrie road with Egfrid and his army following hard. As soon as Egfrid and his men were thoroughly involved between the surrounding hills and marshes, which at that time fed the tributaries of the Lunan and the Dean, Brude attacked. The day was "Sabbath," our Saturday, 20th May 685 A.D. (or 686 A.D.).

The battle resulted in a crushing catastrophe for the English army. Bede states that "King Egfrid and the greater part of the forces that he had led thither were slain." The historian Archibald B. Scott continues, "The only chance left for the survivors of the Anglic army was to escape into the Braes of Angus, dashing through Athole and crossing Drum Alban into Dalriada, and to throw themselves on the mercy of the Scots whom they had previously ill-treated. In Iona at that time, Aldfrith, an illegitimate son of Oswiu and Fina, a Scottish

220

Photograph (220) shows the site of "the Battle of Nechtansmere" where Egfrid and the greater part of his forces were crushed on 20th May 685 A.D.(or 686 A.D.) by Brude Mac Bile.

woman, had been exiled by Egfrid and he was the only man whom the survivors could rely on. By grace of the Picts the body of Egfrid was allowed to be recovered from the battlefield and carried to Iona where it was permitted to be buried by grace of the Scots."

Brude Mac Bile died in 693 A.D. and the chiefs of Pictland appointed Taran Mac Entifidich (693 – 97 A.D.) as high king, but he was a weak and irresolute sovereign. He was deposed after ruling for four years, two of which were merely nominal. Real power during the latter two years was in the hands of Brude, chief of the house of Derelei.

Brude Mac Derelei (697 – 706 A.D.) became high king after Taran and then Nechtan Mac Derelei (706 – 29 A.D.) succeeded following the death of his elder brother Brude. However, Nechtan was a troublemaking high king, his character irresponsible and careless perhaps as a result of having been born of the second member of the house. It was fifteen years since the end of "the Battle of Nechtansmere" and a time of harmony with Northumbria. Nechtan had been drawn into a friendly but dangerous connection with the Angles over the government and usage of the Church of Pictland. In 710 A.D. he decided to accept the rule of the Roman Church and he himself was baptized in Rosemarkie in the Black Isle by St Boniface (or St Critan) through the offices of Ceolfrid, the Abbot of the monasteries of Wearmouth and Jarrow in Northumbria.

Nechtan's conversion to the Roman Church disrupted both domestic and foreign affairs, causing the conversion of ministers and members of the Church of the Picts and the expulsion of Columban monks. The situation became worse by 724 A.D. as a result of his careless and irresponsible policies to resolve issues, his evident desire to keep the supreme power in his own family, and the dissatisfaction of his colleagues. At that time he was said to be a cleric but Pictland, henceforth, was unavoidably drawn into civil wars for some time.

221

Photograph (221) shows Restenneth Priory near Forfar. Though it was a priory church of Augustinian canons in later times, it was originally the first stone-made church in Pictland, built by Northumbrian masons at the behest of Nechtan and dedicated by him to St Peter whom he had enthroned as the Protector of Pictland. [49]

In that same year 724 A.D. a Drust, whose full name was uncertain and who was said to be of British descent on his father's side, became the man in position of power, while Nechtan still interfered as an administrator until in 726 A.D. Nechtan was put under restraint by Drust. However, in the same year Drust himself was ejected by Elpin Mac Eachach who was a Scot on his father's side. Elpin had had a claim to Pictish sovereignty through his Pictish mother and thus he ascended the throne. His sudden appearance was an attempt to avenge the expulsion of Dalriadic clerics. If Elpin had been allowed to retain power longer, he might have restored matters to their original state, but the Picts rejected this sympathetic attitude to Dalriada. In 728 A.D., after Elpin had ruled for less than two years, Angus Mac Fergus, who was the rightful successor to Nechtan, fought with this Elpin.

In the first battle Angus routed the army which Elpin sent against him but in the same year Elpin reorganized his army and again rose against Angus. At the head of this army mobilized by Elpin was the figure of Nechtan, now allied with the enemies of Angus. Although Elpin was driven from the field and Angus gained victory, the throne remained in Nechtan's hands.

In 729 A.D. Angus and his army were again in the field and caught up with Nechtan at Monith-Carno or Mountain of the Cairn, an undetermined locality, and though Nechtan was defeated, he survived with a few vassals. Nechtan was to die in 732 A.D., but Angus became sovereign on August 12th 729 A.D., having gained victory in the last of a series of civil wars which had gone on for six years. He enthroned St Andrew, first of the Apostles, as the Protector of Pictland, deposing St Peter whom Nechtan had enthroned.

Photograph (222) shows the sites of St Regles, the mother church of St Andrews, and Cill Righ Monaidh (Church of the Royal Hill) or the antecedents of St Andrews which was built by request of Angus some thirty years after his death and dedicated to the patron saint of Scotland, St Andrew. It is said his relics were brought there in the 8th century. In the 4th century a Greek monk Regulus, who had brought the relics of St Andrew with him, ran aground near there and the site became a place of pilgrimage of early Celtic Christians. They built St Regles as a reliquary church for their saint. This church was rebuilt from 1127 to 1144 and the still extant square tower was part of its structure. The building of the great cathedral of the Augustinian foundation (now in ruins) began in 1161, its east-west dimension some 110 metres, enclosed by a wall 1.5 km long and a series of attached round and rectangular towers in the 12 hectares precinct. It was consecrated in 1318 in the presence of King Robert the Bruce after a series of rebuildings and repairings, necessary due to storm and fire damage, but it was destroyed during the Reformation.

222

With regard to Dalriada, at that time it was divided into the two factions of the Gabhran House and the Baedan House (which derived from Loarn, the brother of Fergus Mac Erc, the founder of the Dalriadic Scots). Elpin of the Gabhran House, ousted from Pictland in 728 A.D., was now in Dalriada, seeking power among his father's kinsfolk. On the death of his elder brother Eochaidh Mac Eachach in 733 A.D. he became a claimant to the throne of Dalriada and disputed the throne with Muredach, chief of the Lorn. This strife among the Scots was a constant menace to the Pictish people, who lived on the borders of the Argyle districts of the Scots, because of recurring plunder and skirmishes.

A former king of Dalriada, Dungal Mac Selbach (723 – 26 A.D.) of the Lorn House, had turned freebooter or raider in 733 A.D. after his dethronement and organized two expeditions for plunder. He attacked Innis Cumennraighe (or Comrie) and Toraidh (or Turret). But where Dungal laid violent hands in Toraidh was the "Sanctuary" of Brude, son of Angus. The violation of ecclesiastical or royal sanctuary was the capital crime among all Celts at that time. What Dungal did was a crime demanding death and thus necessitated an essential punitive expedition by Angus against him or the whole clan of Lorn.

In 734 A.D. Angus, locating Dungal at his fort Leithfinn (or Dun Leven) near Loch Leven, sent out his troops and engaged him. At the same time, while he himself stayed in Lorn, he arranged a punitive expedition against Talorg Mac Congusa, a chief of the Northern Picts who had shown dissatisfaction with Angus in 731 A.D.

Talorg had once been punished by Brude, the son of Angus, and now was being seized by his own brother. Dungal, wounded in Dun Leithfinn, fled to Ireland while Talorg was delivered to Angus's men and was executed by drowning.

Talorg Mac Drostan, once chief of Athole and brother of King Nechtan, was now in Lorn fettered and imprisoned in Dunnoly, the fortress of the chief of Lorn, Muredach. It was a sign by which Muredach showed he was friendly to Angus.

In Argyle, Elphin Mac Eachach, ejected from Fortrenn, thirsted for revenge. In 736 A.D. he extended tenacious resistance to Angus who therefore wasted Argyle down to the end of Kintyre in order to annihilate the Gabhran clans and Elpin sympathizers who had directed against the Angus dynasty a series of evil intrigues. Angus then laid siege to Dunadd and occupied it and then, retracing his steps to Lorn, caught up with Dungal, his main aim. Angus fettered in chains Dungal and his brother Feradach, son of Selbach (Mac Ferchar Fada), former king of Dalriada of the Baedan House. Angus lost his son Brude in the campaign and Elpin, Angus's chief adversary, fled into hiding.

In the same year, after Angus had evacuated Dalriada, Talorgan Mac Fergus, the great-grandson of Ferchar Fada, raised a force among the clan of Lorn and planned to make a direct attack on the heart of Fortrenn, Angus's capital. They invaded from Argyle into Strathearn where there was located the stronghold of Dundurn. But Angus had left a sufficient garrison in his homeland while he kept his main army in Dalriada and Talorgan's army was turned to flight and was pursued through the glens and passes, losing many chiefs in the fighting.

223

Photograph (223) shows Dunnoly or Dunollie Fort (Dun Ollaimh) rebuilt in the Medieval Age. It was burnt down in 698 A.D. and 701 A.D., reconstructed and destroyed in 716 A.D., again reconstructed by Ollach Mac Briun in 724 A.D. and finally burnt down in 734 A.D.

Talorg Mac Drostan, brother of Nechtan whom Angus had left in Dunnoly in Lorn in 735 A.D., was captured just after he had been released along with his followers in 739 A.D. and he was executed by drowning.

The Picts recovered exclusive control of territories in the west and south of Lorn and Angus secured the exclusive right to appoint the king of Dalriada. A historian of the time relates that [50] Angus dealt Dalriada "smiting" (percussio) from which it did not recover for a long time, as a result of which the surviving Dalriadic nobles must have lost their positions and been forced either to leave their country or become vassals of the Picts. A series of matters initiated by Elpin had aggravated Angus into an antipathy to the Gabhran House. The chiefs in Lorn, who were kinsfolk of the House of Angus, were styled "kings" or "ri" of Dalriada, while those who inherited the tradition of Aedhan Mac Gabhran were styled "The False", "St Columba's nominee" or "high chiefs" (Ardfhlaith). Muredach Mac Ainbhceallach (737 – 45 A.D.) of Lorn, successor of Elpin, was the king of Dalriada, but when Aeda Find Mac Eachadh, Elpin's nephew from Kintyre, set himself up as successor to the throne he was instantly deposed to "high chief" by the Pictish kinsfolk of the Angus family.

In 740 A.D., just a year before breaking off his activities in Dalriada, Angus dispatched an expeditionary force to Northumbria. A description is seen in a fragment of real history written in the Legends of St Andrews, [51] and it says that on this expedition Angus camped at an ancient Roman camp called "Kartinan" (Caer Tinan) near the mouth of the Tyne and for some period of his operations wintered in the Merse in Berwickshire.

While Eadbert, the king of Northumbria, was in the field with his army, fighting against heavy odds, he was informed that Northumbria had been over-run by his Saxon neighbour Eathelbald (d.757 A.D.) and he had thus lost his own kingdom upon which he could fall back. It was a wise policy for both Eadbert and Angus to avoid taking a stand against the two big powers and they decided immediately to make terms and enter into alliance.

In 741 A.D. Dalriada made an attempt to overthrow the superiority of Angus but it ended in vain. When this attempt was made, Angus's adversary, Elpin, was with his army in Galloway (where there was located the seat of an Anglic bishopric at Whithorn) and he had participated in a conspiracy with Taudar Mac Bile, the king of the Strathclyde Britons (d.752 A.D.), to gain some part of the Brito-Pictish territories which had been until then under Eadbert. This attempt developed into a conflict between the allied forces of Angus and Eadbert and those of Elpin and Taudar. A battle was fought at Maes-y-dawac, though the locality is not certain, and there Elpin was assasinated. Though Angus lost his brother Talorg in the action, the allied force of Angus and Eadbert gained victory.

Eadbert repeated a series of punitive expeditions against the Strathclyde Britons and in 750 A.D. he added the plain of Kyle to his territory. However, he encountered disaster on his way back to

Northumbria from his expeditions to Dumbarton. The historian Green recounts, "Disaster befell Northumbria when in 756 A.D. King Eadbert's army was almost wholly destroyed on the march homewards from Dumbarton where he had been operating against the Britons of Strathclyde. After this there were fifty years of anarchy in Northumbria." [52]

Angus died in 761 A.D. His relics found a resting place near St Regles (or Regulus) or mother church, founded by St Canneeh of Achadh-Bo at Cill Righ Monaidh (or Kylrimont) in Fife, and thirty years after his death there was built a new church dedicated to St Andrew the Apostle (see p199).

There were many outstanding Pictish clerics in Pictland in the time of Angus, including both Pictish Celtic-Catholics and Roman Catholics. These included St Ronan who died in 737 A.D. but once presided over the muinntir (inhabitants) of Cinn Garadh (Kingarth) in the Isle of Bute, founded by St Catan towards the end of the sixth century; and St Tuatalan who died in 747 A.D. and had presided over the Roman Catholic muinntir of Cill Righ Monaidh. Churches bearing the name of St Ronan are in Islay; at Kilmaronock near Dumbarton; at Kilmaronaig in Muckairn; at Eoropie in Lewis; on the island of Rona; and on Iona where the old parish church is referred to as Teampull Ronaige. St Catan was a missionary who concentrated his attention principally on the western islands and adjoining coasts. The islands of Colonsay, Gigha, Islay, Luing and Lewis contain his churches, while Ardchattan in Lorn, which afterwards became one of the three Valliscaulian houses in Scotland, was also his church.

During the first eight years of the reign of Angus, Faibhe Mac Guaire, the successor of Maelrubha (or Ma-Ruibhe), presided over the muinntir in churches founded by Maelrubha in Abercrossan (or Applecross), Wester Ross, Banff, Moray, Ross, Sutherland and the Hebrides. Faibhe drowned at sea in 737 A.D. on his way with his mission to the church which Maelrubha had built somewhere in the outer islands. Maelrubha was a missionary who came from Bangor Mor and established a monastery at Applecross in 673 A.D. and exerted a widespread influence over eastern and northern Pictland.

In Easter Ross, "Fearn in Edderton" or the Abbey of Fearn (not far from the disused Fearn station), founded by St Ninian and once presided over by St Finbar, was on the active list. St Finbar or Finian (d. 578 A.D.) was a missionary who was trained at Candida Casa and, following in its founder's footsteps, conducted a wide-ranging mission. In the Black Isle, St Critan (or St Boniface), who was nominated by an edict of Nechtan Mac Derelei, exerted himself to popularize St Peter and Roman usage. In east Pictland St Comgan, a son of a king (Cellach Cluain) of Leinster, presided over the muinntir at Turriff, the seat of a Celtic monastery in Buchan, Aberdeenshire and his sister Kentigarna

224

Photograph (224) shows the ruins of a Valliscaulian priory founded in 1230 A.D, in Ardchattan, originally the site of St Catan's monastery.

lived in a cell on an islet in Loch Lomond and played an active role, while her son St Fillan (of Cluain Moesena) worked hard in Strathearn.

In 734 A.D. St Kentigarna died as a recluse on Inch Cailleach, or the Nun's Isle, in Loch Lomond, where the foundations of the old church dedicated to her still remain. Her son, St Fillan, after being abbot of a monastery on the Holy Loch, wandered about the West Highlands and built churches at Killin and Dundurn where he died. His original church at Dundurn remained until about 1500 A.D.; the ruined building now there took its place (see p244).

After Angus's death, control of the northern part of Dalriada was assigned until 785 A.D. to Domnall Mac Constantine, a vassal of the Angus clan, and Pictish sovereignty shifted to Angus's brother Brude Mac Fergus (761 – 63 A.D.) and then to Kenneth Mac Feredach or Ciniod Mac Wredech (763 – 75 A.D.). In 768 A.D. during his reign, Aeda Find Mac Eachadh (d.778 A.D.) (a half-Pict and nephew of Elpin who had once claimed the kingship of Dalriada and been deposed by the Pictish chiefs to "Ardfhlaith" of Kintyre) attempted to revive the kingdom of Dalriada and took the field against Kenneth. After Kenneth came Alpin Mac Fereda or Elpin Mac Wroid (775 – 80 A.D.), Drest (Drust) Mac Talorgen (780 – 83 A.D.) and Talorgen Mac Angus (783 – 85 A.D.). In the reign of Drest, a half-Pict and Ardfhlaith of Kintyre, Fergus Mac Aeda Find claimed the independence of Dalriada but died in 781 A.D. In 785 A.D. Domnall Mac Constantine, a vassal of the Angus family, died after controlling Dalriada for twenty-four years.

The exogamous matriarchy of the Picts, which had made the nation wealthy and mighty by matrilineal union with the Scots for a long time, began to reveal an aspect of self-destruction. The independence fervour of the Scots commenced to intensify quickly and the roar of disunity sounded stronger day by day between the two blood relatives. Fortrenn, or the House of Angus, the star nation of Pictland, once dominant, was now drawing near to its end.

Conall Mac Taidg (785 – 90 A.D.), a half-Pict who ascended the throne after Talorgen Mac Angus and held the post of joint-ruler of Dalriada with Conall Mac Caeim, claimed the crowns of both the Pictish nation and Dalriada. During his reign Conall was opposed by his successor Constantine, was dethroned and, after defeat in a war with Constantine from 789 A.D. to 790 A.D., was banished. Constantine Mac Fergus (790 – 820 A.D.) ascended the throne as king of Fortrenn and Dalriada, and his successor Angus II Mac Fergus reigned from 820 A.D. to 834 A.D. In the meantime, Caithness, Moray and Mar of the Northern Picts, being weakened by invasions and settlements of Vikings, seceded successively from the Pictish line of federation and formed Moravia or Moray, with Easter Ross, Sutherland and Moray as their territory.

There was no longer a "High King" in Pictland. The inrush of Vikings, which had already begun to be felt all over Pictland in the seventh century (as seen in the raid of Norsemen who slaughtered St Donnan and his fifty-two disciples on Easter Day, April 16th 617 A.D. in the Isle of Eigg), now had added impetus. These pagan Teutonic Vikings, who had already gained a foothold in the northern islands, invaded Iona, the sacred place of Dalriada, in 794 A.D. during the reign of Constantine Mac Fergus, and in 834 (?) A.D. they invaded Fortrenn, the heartland of Pictland. In face of this fatal inrush the Picts were forced to fight for their home and existence.

It was at that time that the father of Kenneth, Alpin Mac Eachach, took advantage of the preoccupied Picts to rebel against Angus II instead of joining up with the Picts. Alpin succeeded in defeating the hub of the Picts with large-scale slaughter at Easter, 834 A.D. and tried to add to his success but failed. He came into contact with the main army of the Fortrenn Picts in August of the same year and was captured and beheaded.

The reign shifted from Angus II to Aedh Mac Boanta (834-36 A.D.) and from Aedh to the joint-rulers Drust Mac Constantine (836-37 A.D.), Talorgan Mac Wthoil (836-37 A.D.) and Owen or Uven Mac Angus (836-39 A.D.). They were all kings of Dalriada and Fortrenn. In 839 A.D., during the reign of Owen, Norsemen invaded Fortrenn and there ensued some fatal struggles. The Norsemen were finally triumphant and Owen, his brother, and the former sovereign, Aedh Mac Boanta, and numberless vassals and men were dead. On the death of Owen Mac Angus, Ferat Mac Bargoit (839-41 A.D.) and Brude Mac Ferat (838-42 A.D.), the last king of Dalriada and of Pictland, succeeded to the throne as joint-rulers.

841 A.D. was the year of doom for the Picts of Fortrenn. While the

Pictish army, now quite diminished, was again forced to face a large army of Norsemen, they had to cope with the uprising of Kenneth Mac Alpin, son of Alpin Mac Eachach. The Pictish army was miserably destroyed. Though Kenneth's act was definitely a treachery, it was the usual way of the world in the war-torn civil war age for the strong to have control over the weak. Thus Kenneth obtained the Pictland of Fortrenn and it had all resulted from Fortrenn's failure to realize the dangerous potential of the family blood line of Aeda Find Mac Eachach in Kintyre, ever since the days of Angus I.

2. DALRIADA, BRITONS, ANGLES AND VIKINGS

It is time to enter Rex Pictorum or the United Realm of the Picts and Scots which was inaugurated by Kenneth Mac Alpin. However, it is necessary here to look back over the rise and fall of the Dalriadic Scots, together with those of the Britons, the Angles and the Vikings.

The Scots were colonists who came from Antrim, the coastland between Foyle and Fair Head in Northern Ireland, to the coast of Kintyre (the ancient name of which is "Epidum" in Latin) in 500 A.D. or 498 A.D. They were of the same tribe as the Scots who took active roles against the Roman army in Britain from the middle of the fourth century. They were Christianized *cineal* (or clan) tribes of some one hundred and fifty men and women led by Fergus and his brothers, Lorn and Angus, sons of Erc.

They were "the men of Britain" (or Dalriada) who were pushed out of Antrim by the pressure of their fellow-Scots, the O'Neils, and the Irish Picts who surrounded them. Their departure from Ireland was an inevitable exodus because of their lesser power.

At the end of this book is the pedigree of the Dalriadic kings (see pp269–270) which shows that the inheritance system of king was patriarchal, though the king or chief of the clan was not necessarily the eldest. Usually a patrimonial young male noble with no flaw in his character was chosen as the next king or chief of each clan during the former king's lifetime, the system known as "tanistry." The clan consisted of the patrilineal family members going back to the generation of great-grand-parents with lineal descendants, all under the control of the king or chief. In cases where the clan was too small, regulations of ten forms of union were permitted to the king or chief by archaic Celtic law, including marriage to a second wife, concubinage, and so on. Children were brought up under a fosterage system, boys until seventeen years old and girls until fourteen.

Clan members were required to be subject to their king or chief and had a liability for military and work services and tribute. It was a custom from the Iron Age that the king or chief should be subject to the high king, along with tribute. Fergus and his brothers, who had emigrated to Kintyre, were in the position of being subject to the high king of Pictland of Alba and to Nial, the high king of Ireland, with tribute, and this double allegiance had made the king of each generation urge the Dalriadic Scots to be independent from both high kings.

Fergus Mor Mac Erc died suddenly in the depths of Kintyre in 501 A.D. It was his third year (if they had emigrated in 498 A.D.) and his son Domongart succeeded him. He was equally enervated and died after serving only a short reign from 501 to 506 A.D. Domongart was followed by Comgal Mac Domongart (506 – 38 A.D.) and in 537 A.D. during his reign, Dalriada engaged in the Battle of Camelon as mercenaries of the Angles and, with Medraut, the rebel son of Loth, sped King Arthur to his death. Comgal died in the year following this battle and Gabhran Mac Domongart (538 – 60 A.D.) succeeded him.

In 547 A.D. Ida organized his fellow-pagans and founded an Anglian kingdom in Bernicia with the capital at Bamburgh in Northumbria. This Anglian kingdom expanded northwards towards the Firth of Forth but in 559 A.D. Ida died a tragic death in a battle with Owain, a descendant of Coel Hen, supposed father of St Kentigern and a hero of the Welsh Britons.

In the meantime, Gabhran of Dalriada also tried to expand his territories insidiously and slowly into the Pictland of Argyle and the western isles, causing offence to Brude Mac Maelcon (see p172). After him came Conail Mac Comgal (560-74 A.D.) as Brude's toiseach of Kintyre. In 563 A.D. St Columba (521-97 A.D.) entered Argyle with his mission and Conail dedicated the Isle of Iona to Columba with the sanction of Brude Mac Maelcon. In 574 A.D. Conail was slain in a battle at Delgon in Kintyre (although it is uncertain with whom it was fought) and his cousin Aedhan Mac Gabhran (574-606 A.D.) ascended the throne (see p172). He might also have been a toiseach of the Pictish high king Brude since he was dispatched to Orkney and to a part of southern Pictland. Anyway, he was a superb strategist among the kings of Dalriada.

In Northumbria, Hussa (564-74 A.D.), son of Ida, was on the throne and he repeated his expeditions to the north between the Tweed and Forth from 567 A.D. onwards. In his final expedition Hussa had to face four sturdy tribal kings of the Britons. They were Urien Map Cirmac, deified as a Celtic god of battle, father of Owain, whose territories extended to Annandale, Nithsdale, Clydesdale and Kyle; Rhydderch Map Tudgual or "Hael" (Liberal), a Christian king, and a descendant of the ancient Damnonii, whose territories extended to Ayr, Lanark, and Renfrew, including Strathclyde and Dumbarton; Guallauc (Hywel Map Laenauc, brother of St Gildas); and Morcant

Map Coledauc (or Morcant, grandson of Morcant Bulg) a Brito-Pictish chief. The allied force of the Britons successfully pushed back Hussa but Rhydderch, the Liberal, who was deified as the Celtic Mars or "Nudus", lost his two sons in this battle and there remains a tombstone which is presumed to have been dedicated to his sons. It has a Latin epithaph of six lines, now much weathered, and stands in the field of Yarrow 8 miles west of Selkirk (see photo 225).

The tribal kings of the Britons at this time were not always friendly and co-operative with one another. Some of the kings still adhered to Cymric paganism and tradition which they had inherited from their ancestors. Morcant Map Coledauc persecuted St Kentigern, and Gwenddolew, ruling the Solway region, encouraged the native bards to praise himself. They were anti-Christian and did not scruple to assist the Angles, bitterest foes of the Britons.

225

Photograph (225) is of The Yarrow Stone and the epitaph runs as follows: "HIC MEMORIAE ET(?) (???) LO INSIGNISIMI PRINCI PE(?) NVDI D(V)MNOGENI HICIACENT IN (T?) MULO DVO FILII LIBERALIS." Sir John Rhys (1840-1915), Welsh philologist, translates it as follows: "HERE NUDOS' PRINCELY OFFSPRING REST, DEAR TO FAME, IN BATTLE BRAVE, TWO SONS OF A BOUNTEOUS SIRE, DUMNONIANS, IN THEIR GRAVE."

In 573 A.D. a conflict between Christians and heathens evolved into a decisive battle. This was a battle between Rhydderch, with the assistance of Aedhan of Dalriada, and the pagan chief Gwenddolew and it was fought at Arthuret or Arderydd on the Esk, north of Carlisle. Rhydderch won a complete victory and the result confirmed his supremacy as king and ensured the possibility of peaceful development for the struggling Church of Strathclyde.

St Kentigern (518 – 603 A.D.), the Apostle to the Strathclyde Britons and patron saint of Glasgow, whose nickname was "Munghu" meaning Mwyn (Dear)-cu (dog) in Brythonic, was called back to Glasgow by request of Rhydderch in the same year of his victory. He was a saint who had built a monastery on the site of St Ninian's church on the River Molendinar in 553 A.D, but he had been driven out from

Glasgow by the persecution of Morcant Map Coledauc, and while taking refuge in Wales (circa 553 A.D.), a small church, St Asaph or "Llanelwy" on the river Elwy ("driving one"), was dedicated to him.

It was approximately at this time that St Myran (or Meadhan) founded the antecedent of Paisley Abbey on the River Cart, Renfrewshire. He came from Bangor to Paisley (< basilica, "church" in Latin) along with his colleague St Toman and planted a monastic community there, which in the reign of David I was transformed into or superseded by a priory of the Cluniac order, subordinated to Wenlock. From Paisley, St Myran's activities radiated northward and southward through Strathclyde.

The establishment of the Church of Strathclyde came about with unexpected ease in Glasgow, but in Northumbria a sturdy king Deodric (580 – 87 A.D.), whose nickname was "Fire-spear", another son of Ida, ascended the throne and commenced expeditions to the north. Urien and his son opposed him. The expedition led them as far as the island of "Medcaut", one of the Farne group, a short distance south-east of Tweedmouth. Either on the island or in returning from it, Urien was slain by his former ally Morcant Map Coledauc. Nennius writes that Morcant struck him through envy and because of the distinction Urien had won in the battle throwing back the Angles. [53]

As for Dalriada, Aedhan was dispatched to Orkney in 580 A.D. by order of Brude. In 583 A.D. he crossed Drumalban and, entering Clackmannan via Stirling, engaged in a battle with the Saxons and gained victory. In 590 A.D., when Pictland was under the reign of Gartnaidh Mac Domneth, he again invaded southern Pictland and fought with the Pictish Maetae who had occupied the lands just north of the Antonine Wall. In 596 A.D. he once again crossed Drumalban but was severely driven back by Gartnaidh Mac Domneth, losing his three sons, Arthur, Eachach Fion and Bran.

In Northumbria Aethelfrith (see p168), the grandson of Ida and a mortal foe to Aedhan, ascended the throne and commenced to accomplish what his uncles Hussa and Deodric could not carry out. He ravaged the territories on the borders of the Strathclyde Britons and secured those of the Brito-Pictish or Niduari Picts as recorded by Bede in his *Life of St Cuthbert*. He subjugated his fellow Angles of Deira and reigned from 593 A.D. to 617 A.D. as the king of both Bernicia and Deira, the great Northumbrian kingdom. He fixed the northern border of the Bernician kingdom at the Firth of Forth and, furthermore, extended it to the borders of West Lothian and Stirlingshire which then belonged to the Picts of Mannan, intending to isolate the Strathclyde Britons by cutting them off from the Picts to the north and the Scots to the west.

His activities brought Aedhan into the field for it was a source of concern for Aedhan that the south-eastern side of Drumalban adjoined the territory of the Angles. He planned to transport his men from Kintyre to the northern bank of the Solway Firth, taking them on board the fleet he had held in Kintyre, and try to lure out Aethelfrith and his men, the main force of whom was in Northumbria. Though it might have been an indication of his territorial ambition to the south, his true intention was to strike at Aethelfrith.

It was in 600 A.D., according to Irish annalists, and 603 A.D., according to the Anglo-Saxon Chronicle, when Aedhan and his men, Brito-Pictish and probably Britons, entered the Borders and reached the site of the Battle of Degsastan (or Dawstane Rig in Riddesdale) near the Kingside Hill Stone Circle (see p67), 6 miles south-south-east of Gifford in East Lothian. There Aedhan, a military leader by then seventy-one years old, met the allied force of Aethelfrith and pagan Lowland Scots who had settled there about the end of the Roman period. According to historians it seems to have been an appalling battle, though the scale of mobilized armies and casualties on both sides is uncertain, and Aedhan's troops were routed and the Angles secured the territories on the south side of the Firth of Forth. Aethelfrith lost his brother Theobald while Aedhan lost his third son, Domongart. After this crushing defeat, Aedhan fled back from the field with Mael-umae, son of Baedan Mac Muredach.

[54] W.J. Watson writes: "On the issue of this battle depended the fate of two districts or provinces, Urien's province of Rheged and the province of Lothian (of Strathclyde ?), which had been in alliance with Urien. If Aedhan had been victorious, the result might well have been the political fusion of Urien's province and even Lothian with Dalriada at that time". Though the result was to be reversed about four hundred and fifty years later at Carham, Aedhan had lost an important battle. He died in 606 A.D. at the age of seventy-four.

In 613 A.D. Aethelfrith moved his force to Chester (or Leagacaester) and defeated the Welsh Britons there, thus making the Strathclyde Britons stand alone, but he fell in a battle with his English neighbours in East Anglia in 617 A.D. Eadwine of Deira ascended the throne as king of Northumbria and reigned until 633 A.D.

In Dalriada Eochadh Buidhe Mac Aedhan (606 – 22 A.D.) succeeded to the hereditary throne and in 617 A.D. Oswald and Oswiu, princes of Bernicia, exiled from Northumbria on Eadwine's accession, entered Iona (see p174). In Dalriada, after the death of this Eochadh, there was a series of domestic conflicts between the two families of Aedhan's sons, Eochadh Buidhe and Ferchar Mac Conaig (Mac Aedhan). Claimants to the kingship appeared from the two houses and contended with each other. This continued until 676 A.D. when the Baedan of Lorn participated in this strife.

Ferchar Mac Conaig (622 – 38 A.D.) held the throne on the death of Eochadh Buidhe Mac Aedhan in 622 A.D., but in 629 A.D. Conadh

Cerr Mac Eochadh Buidhe entered into joint-ruling with Ferchar. He died after being on the throne for only three months and Domnal Brec (629 – 42 A.D.) replaced him. Domnal Brec and Ferchar Mac Conaig had been old enemies of each other, having already met at Cindelgthen on the shore near Loch Fyne in 621 A.D. just one year before Eochadh Buidhe died.

In the meantime in Northumbria, Eadwine, the successor of Aethelfrith, fell in battle at Haetfield in Yorkshire in 633 A.D. He was defeated there by the strangely allied army of Caedwalla, the Christian king of Gwynedd (North Wales), and Penda, the pagan king of Mercia. Osric of Deira, Eadwine's son, succeeded to the throne and reigned for two years until he was killed by Caedwalla in 634 A.D. The kingship of Northumbria was shifted to Oswald of Bernicia (605 – 42 A.D.) who had returned from Iona and he reigned over the Northumbrian kingdom from 634 A.D. to 642 A.D. In the year of his accession Oswald defeated Caedwalla, the murderer of Oswric, near Hexham, and in the same year he killed him somewhere near Hadrian's Wall.

He was now St Oswald and engaged in missionary works, inviting St Aedhan from Iona to Lindisfarne, a holy place which he had founded. At this time Strathclyde was ruled over by Gureit who died in 658 A.D., and Dalriada, befriended by Oswald, was at peace, but Oswald was defeated by Penda and killed in Shropshire in 642 A.D. In Dalriada Ferchar Mac Conaig died in 638 A.D. and Domnal Brec Mac Eochadh was slain in a battle in Strathcarron (near Stirling) by Hoan or Eugein, a king of the Strathclyde Britons, in 642 A.D. In Northumbria the last king of Deira, Oswine (642 – 51 A.D.), succeeded Oswald in 642 A.D. and died in 651 A.D. Oswiu, brother of Oswald and king of Bernicia, succeeded Oswine and reigned over Northumbria until 670 A.D. He defeated and slew Penda, who had allied with the Welsh Britons, and in 655 A.D. secured supremacy over all Mercia, the South and East Angles and the East Saxons.

Oswiu exercised sovereign control over the native Britons and the immigrant Irish Picts who were at that time in Galloway and gradually Dumfries and Galloway came to be in the possession of Northumbria. His military and strategic moves extended to a narrow strip of Pictish territory running from the neighbourhood of Eten (or Edinburgh) to the fords of the Forth near Stirling where Egfrid, his son, marched to enter Nechtansmere in May 685 A.D. in preparation for the Battle of Nechtansmere. Already in 657 A.D. Oswiu had laid claim to the allegiance of the Picts on the death of his nephew, Talorgan Mac Enfred, using as justification the fact that he and Talorgan were uncle and nephew.

In Dalriada, from 642 A.D. to 648 A.D., two kings of two factions, Duncan Mac Conaig (642 – 48 A.D.), brother of Ferchar Mac Conaig, and Conail Crandamna Mac Eochadh Buidhe (642 – 48 A.D.) ruled jointly until they were displaced by Domnall Donn Mac Crandamna (648 – 60 A.D.). Duncan Mac Conaig, brother of Ferchar Mac Conaig, was slain in 654 A.D. in fighting against the Picts at Srathra Ethairt, the locality of which is not certain, and Conail Crandamna died in 660 A.D. Domnall Donn, who had displaced Duncan and Conail, was himself displaced in 660 A.D. by his brother Mailduin Mac Crandamna (660–76 A.D.) and died in 696 A.D.

Now the family line of Eochadh Buidhe Mac Aedhan held a dominant position over that of Ferchar Mac Conaig Mac Aedhan in the rivalry to obtain kingship but an influential development occurred. This was the intervention of the Baedan of Lorn (Oban). They were the descendants of Loarn Mor, the Great Fox, the brother of Fergus Mor Mac Erc. From then on the competition was conducted between the descendants of Eochadh Buidhe and the Baedan of Lorn. Ferchar Fada Mac Feradaich of the Baedan usurped the throne from Mailduin Mac Crandamna in 676 A.D. and reigned until 696 A.D., although in 683 A.D. he suffered from an expedition by the Pictish high king Brude Mac Bile and in the same year he was also engaged in the siege of Dunadd in Argyle which was at that time in the possession of the Strathclyde Britons.

In 694 A.D. Eochadh Rianamhail, grandson of Domnal Brec of the Aedhan, ascended the throne as joint-ruler with Ferchar Fada, and died in 696 A.D. Ferchar Fada died in the following year and his son Ainbhcealla Mac Ferchar succeeded his father. He reigned for two years, but his kingship was usurped by his brother Selbach Mac Ferchar Fada who burned Ainbhcealla's fort at Dunnoly. Selbach reigned from 698 A.D. to 723 A.D., but he was an unsuitable king to rule over a tribe. He again burned Dunnoly in 701 A.D. and slaughtered the men of the Chathbath, a rival branch within the Lorn. In 704 A.D. he made an expedition to Dumbarton and was defeated at a place called "Valle Limnae" (or Vale of Leven). The year 707 A.D. was marked by Selbach's slaughter of Brec, the grandson of King Duncan Mac Conaig. In 711 A.D. Selbach turned the tables on the Britons by defeating them at Loch Arklet and in the following year he attacked the Gabhran in rivalry and, seizing Dunaverty, the principal stronghold of Dalriada in south Kintyre, burned it down. In 714 A.D. Selbach rebuilt the fort of Dunnoly only for it to be destroyed by his daughter Aileen.

In 717 A.D. Selbach won a victory in an encounter with the Britons at Clach na Braetan at the head of Loch Lomond and in 723 A.D. he abdicated his throne in favour of his son, Dungal Mac Selbach, later to be a freebooter as already mentioned (see p180), and put an end to his secular life. Dungal reigned until 726 A.D. and Ewen Mac Ferchar succeeded him until 742 A.D.

Now was the time of the invasion and settlement of the Vikings. The martyrdom of St Donnan and his disciples on the Isle of Eigg in

617 A.D. was an earlier example of victimization by the Vikings but it was mainly after the middle of the eighth century that their invasions and settlements began to take on a more drastic and fierce aspect and from the ninth century their assaults grew more serious at an accelerating pace. What was the source of the power and energy of the Vikings ? It had at least partly come from navigation-assisting winds which swept over the northern sea of the Atlantic Ocean (Haaf Atadal), at times as quickly as lightning; Lapland steel for sword making; and the primordial forest for shipbuilding.

In 722 A.D. St Maelrubha of Applecross (or Abercrossan) was martyred during an attack of Vikings at Gaharagh in Strathnaver in Sutherland. It is reported that they threw his body into the wood and in the hall of his church they drank a toast and so the place retains the name of "Skail" (in Old Norse a "hall").

At this time in the 8th century, the whole of Orkney and Shetland and the isles surrounding the mainland were under the control of Norse freebooters and their power extended to southern Scotland.

In 776 A.D. the new Anglo-Roman bishopric established in Candida Casa in Whithorn was disorganised for a time by the confusion brought about by the invasion of Vikings.

On July 7th in 793 A.D. the Lindisfarne priory in Northumbria was harried. Simeon of Durham records, "The invaders reached Lindisfarne, burned the settlement and killed many priests and monks." People were coerced into either leaving themselves to the cruelties of the Vikings or moving to the northerly outposts of the kingdom, the nuclei of which were located at Selkirk, Borrowstoun (Burf's town) Rig and Borrowsdale (Burh's dale) or in their territory in Dumfries and Galloway.

In 794 A.D. the Vikings invaded Iona and again in 806 A.D. They burned the church and houses and butchered sixty-eight clerics and in 822 A.D. the Irish-Pictish ecclesiastical centre of Bangor Mor near Dublin, which had fostered the Church of Pictland, was attacked and the settlements plundered. The bones of St Comgall (see Note 44), the founder of the community, were scattered from the churches, the first manifestation that the religious centre of the Picts had begun to adopt Roman usage.

In 825 A.D. the Vikings invaded Iona again, and in 829 A.D. St Diarmat, the abbot, decided to avoid running the risk of remaining any longer and carried away the reliquary and relics of St Columba to Ceanannus Mor (Great Head Fort) or Kells in the rural district 40 miles north-west of Dublin, the famous home of the Book of Kells and the site of the monastery which St Columba founded in 555 A.D. and which was dissolved in the 16th century.

In 838 A.D. the churches and lands of the Picts in Ulster were wasted and from then on Bangor became a deserted place for a decade while the Vikings continued to extend their invasion and devastation. In 866 A. D., Haldane (or Halfdane Halegg), one of the sons of Harald Harfagri (see p198), subdued the Northumbrian capital York and made his followers settle in the surrounding countryside.

Disaster inevitably caused harm to Lindisfarne as well and a group of monks and priests, who took with them their precious holy relics (the body of St Cuthbert, the skull of King Oswald, some of St Aidhan's bones and the Lindisfarne Gospels), left the island to seek a safer refuge. They tried to cross to Ireland but failed, driven back by storm, and they found temporary refuge at Whithorn where a Northumbrian monastery was still in existence.

Two types of historical tombstone remain in Whithorn, the site of Candida Casa in earlier times, an Anglic bishopric from the seventh century and where a great many Vikings invaded and settled in later times. One is a tombstone carved some time between the seventh and ninth centuries and dedicated to the Northumbrians, ordinarily called the "Northumbrian type," with a cross, an angular head and an Anglic runic epitaph. The other is a tombstone dedicated to the Gallovians with a cross and a round head, usually known as the "Whithorn type". Galloway is the birthplace of " the Gallovians" or a variety of Norwegianized Gauls arising from the stabilized settlement of Vikings.

226

Photographs (226) and (227) are of the tombstones of the Northumbrian type and the Whithorn type respectively.

Photograph (228) shows the ruins of Lindisfarne Priory destroyed by the vandalism of Vikings. Lindisfarne was a priory founded in the middle of the seventh century by St Oswald and it was attacked in 793, 869 and 871 A.D. The island remained uninhabited for more than two centuries until 1082 A.D. when a cell of Benedictine monks was granted the See of Lindisfarne and renamed it "the Holy Island."

227

Photographs (229) and (230) show copies of the Lindisfarne Gospels indicating a page with the large initial "Q" (St Luke) and the beginning of St Matthew's Gospel. The originals were written in honour of St Cuthbert by Eadfrith (Bishop of Lindisfarne 698-721 A.D.). They were removed by

228

229

230

monks in 875 A.D. and were once lost at sea but miraculously recovered on the beach near Whithorn.

Photograph (231) shows Ruthwell Cross (or Cross at the Holy Well), a testimony to Northumbrian influence, enshrined in Ruthwell Parish Church some 5 miles west of Annan.

231

The cross was sculptured in the early 8th century by a master mason from Northumbria and the model for it is said to be from the Eastern Mediterranean district. This cross, having been buried in the ground in the Viking Age, fortunately escaped total destruction. It is some 5 metres in height and on the front side of its pole, from top to bottom, there are elaborate carved panels depicting St John the Baptist holding a lamb with an Anglian runic text, and a panel of Christ in Majesty with the text "Jesus Christ, the Judge of Equity" around it. Also depicted are the two hermit saints, Paul and Anthony, breaking bread in the desert, along with the flight into Egypt of Mary and Child riding on an ass.

On its other side are, similarly from top to bottom, Mary Magdalene washing the feet of Christ, the Healing of the blind (with an incomplete text around it), the Annunciation, and the scene of the Crucifixion. At the head of the cross is the sculpture of an eagle; the symbol of the Ascension on one side; and on the other side a sculpture of St John the Evangelist and his emblem, the eagle. On the flanks of the pole are sculptures of vine scrolls or flourishes and birds with the runic text of "The Dream of the Rood." [55]

3. REX PICTORUM, THE KINGDOM OF ALBAN AND ITS CONFLICTS WITH VIKINGS, ANGLES, AND SAXONS, AND THE ESTABLISHMENT OF THE UNITED KINGDOM OF SCOTLAND

Kenneth Mac Alpin had justification for his claim on Pictish supremacy in Fortrenn. On the female side, which usually determined the eligibility of a candidate, he was descended from the royal house of Fortrenn and his great grand-uncle Elpin Mac Eachach had actually been sovereign of Pictland until his ejection by Angus I Mac Fergus, which gave the family of Eachach rights of their own which they had persistently tried to re-assert. What made him seek to impose Dalriada onto Pictland at the expense of the native Picts? Was it to get rid of a subordination to the Picts or was it revenge for his dark days when he lived in obscurity as a member of the Gabhran family?

He moved to Forteviot after he had stained his motherland with his bloody treacherous sword, placed there the hereditary Coronation Stone, carried from Dunstaffnage Fort in Lorn, and in 843 A.D. ascended the throne as chief of Rex Pictorum or the United Realm of the Scots and Picts. Though the pedigrees of this dynasty and of the following Kingdom of Alban are listed at the end of this book as supplementary data, Kenneth, taking account of the Pictish preference for matrilineal descent, restructured the traditional inheritance way of "tanistry" to a system whereby successive kings were chosen from different stems of the royal houses, though it was basically patrilineal.

The following year he organized expeditions and invaded the territories of the Angles for the first time since Aedhan's defeat in the

Battle of Degsastan and burned Dunbar and Melrose in Bernicia which had already submitted to the Saxons in 829 A.D. under the reign of Egbert. Dunkeld was a holy place where there was a Christian settlement in the 570's A.D. In 850 A.D. Kenneth moved there the relics and reliquary of St Columba to a new church which had been founded in 815 A.D. by monks who had escaped slaughter by Vikings, making there the ecclesiastical capital of the United Realm of Scots and Picts.

During his reign, though the date is not certain, Dunkeld was once invaded by Danish Vikings but Kenneth defeated them between Dunkeld and Clunie. He died in 859 A.D. and his brother Donald I Mac Alpin (859 – 63 A.D.) succeeded him according to the new inheritance method Kenneth had devised but Donald died on April 13th after reigning for four years and Kenneth's elder son Constantine I Mac Kenneth (863 – 77 A.D.) succeeded him as chief of different stems of the royal house.

In 866 A.D. Olaf the Fair, Viking king of Dublin, and his son Olaf Thorstein the Red, invaded Caithness, Sutherland and Ross and occupied the greater part of these territories which had once belonged to the Northern Picts, while Haldane, son of Harald Harfagri, subdued the Northumbrian capital, York.

In 869 A.D. Olaf the Fair and his men landed in Fortrenn and ravaged there. Constantine I fought a defensive battle against them in vain and a host of Pictish captives were carried off as pledges for tribute. In 870 A.D. Olaf and Ivar and their men invaded Strathclyde by putting their two hundred ships in a row. They besieged "Dumbarton Rock," the capital of the Strathclyde Britons. After cutting off the water-supply to the garrison in the fort for four months

232

Photograph (232) shows "Dumbarton Rock" (The Dun of the British), the oppidum of the Strathclyde Britons and earlier of the Damnonii.

they captured it and, with it as their base, they ravaged Strathclyde, Galloway and finally Bernicia. They killed a Saxon king and, making a host of Angles, Britons and Picts captives, returned to Dublin in the following year.

In 872 A.D. Harald Harfagri, son of Halfden the Swarthy (860 – 930 A.D.), became the sole king of Norway. He carried out an expedition against the western Vikings who had established their stations in Orkney, drove them from their haunts, subdued Shetland, Orkney, the Hebrides and the Isle of Man, and gave Orkney as an earldom of Norway to Rognwald, Earl of More. With this as a turning point the invasions of the Vikings to the mainland of Scotland rapidly began to take on a fiercer aspect and the place-names of coastal areas and circumferential isles began to be influenced by those of Old Norse as seen in words ending in -ay, -ey (isle, islet); -borough (fort, town); -quoy (cattle enclosure); -skail (hut, hall); -bister, -by, -setter, -sts, -ston, -ster (farm, hamlet); -voe, -wall, -wick (bay, inlet, creek); and so on.

In 874 A.D. Thorstein the Red over-ran Caithness, Sutherland, Ross and Moray. In 875 A.D. Sigurd the Mighty, who had received the earldom of Orkney from his brother Rognwald, formed an alliance with Thorstein the Red and they invaded the northern mainland and subdued Caithness and Sutherland as far as the district along the River Oykel and its estuary. As a result of an arrangement with Constantine I, whose authority over the northern Picts was probably little more than nominal, Thorstein became ruler of that region but he was shortly afterwards killed by the treachery of the people of Alban and this grouping was broken up for a time.

In 877 A.D. Constantine's reign was terminated by his death in a fierce battle with the Danes. A strong force driven out of Ireland by a competing body of Norwegians made an unlooked-for decent upon Fife. The armies met at Dollar and Constantine was defeated. After being pursued throughout Fife he again met the Danes at Inverdovet. There he was slain together with a multitude of Scots, including many religious refugees from Ireland who had settled there when Kenneth Mac Alpin ascended the throne. Tradition associates this battle with the neighbourhood of Balcombie Bay on the coast of Fife and the cave to which Constantine is said to have been dragged as a prisoner and then beheaded is still there. [56]

In the year following Constantine I's death there was another invasion of Danish Vikings to the Scottish coast. This event caused the shrine of St Columba and his relics in Dunkeld to be moved back again to Kells in Ireland.

Constantine I was succeeded by his brother Aedh, the last of Kenneth's sons. Of him, as of many kings in those hazy days, much is unknown. However, his death is recorded in the year following his enthronement. He fought a battle with St Cyric Map Dungal, a Briton, near Cyric's homeland at St Fillans at the lower end of Loch Earn and though the cause of the conflict is not certain, Aedh met with a tragic end. Cyric was a saint who contributed to free the Scottish Church from Pictish servitude and was a benefactor of St Andrews and, in addition, was said to have had a close relationship with the Northern Picts.

Nevertheless, he usurped the throne. If his relationship with the Northern Picts were a fact, the cause of the conflict could have been the existence of a standing rivalry between the Northern and Southern Picts. He might have been seeking an opportunity to enthrone Eocha, son of Kenneth's daughter and Cu, the king of the Britons, because he himself was a Briton, or he himself might have wanted the position of sovereign. In any event, Constantine I and Aedh died and Cyric placed Eocha, their cousin, on the throne, giving himself the position of king de facto as tutor of Eocha (878 – 89 A.D.). Herewith, the inheritance system Kenneth Mac Alpin had devised was to return for a time to the old Pictish way of inheritance (see p171).

In 889 A.D. Harald Harfagri took the Western Isles definitely into the possession of his country. In 893 A.D. Haldane, son of Harald Harfagri, was slain by Einar, the successor of Sigurd the Mighty. In Rex Pictorum, Eocha died and the throne passed to Donald II Mac Constantine (889 – 900 A.D.), chief of the Constantine house, with Cyric as tutor. However, Cyric died in 896 A.D. at Dundurn, the same place where he had slain Aedh in 878 A.D. Rex Pictorum, henceforth, proceeded to be called "the Kingdom of Alban" with its royal seat at Scone, the hereditary stone for the inauguration ceremony of the Dalriadic king having been moved there from Forteviot, and the king being called "the king of Alban." "Alban" is a Gaelic word originally meaning "Pictavia", and later "Scotland," but to the Scots it meant "Ireland," associating with their homeland.

From then on the kingship of Alban alternated between the two royal houses of the Constantine and the Aedh, as Kenneth had established, until the reign of Constantine III when the lineage of the Aedh family was discontinued. However, in 900 A.D. Danes from Ireland with Sitric, son of Imhair, as their leader, again appeared off the Scottish east coast and caused utter confusion. Donald II met them at Dunottar or Dun Fortrenn and was miserably jugulated to death in the fight there. The construction of round towers in Ireland, the number of which is over eighty, coincides with the period of plundering raids of Vikings. The type of round signal tower or bell-tower as left in Brechin and in Abernethy is a historical monument from which reports of the Norsemen's raids were dispatched in later centuries though, judging from the fact that they were always erected on church sites, they probably also served as refuges for the clergy and holy relics.

Donald II was succeeded by Constantine II Mac Aedh (900 – 43 A.D.), "the Swift Foot", and in 903 A.D. Dunkeld and its neighbourhood were plundered by Danish Vikings with their leader Ivar (presumably the grandson of Ivar who attacked Dumbarton with Olaf the Fair in 870 A.D.), but in the following year Constantine II, slaying Ivar and crushing his force to pieces at the Battle of Lucanty near Perth, secured a brilliant victory over them.

In 906 A.D. Constantine II convened an awe-inspiring assembly for the discussion of matters related to the Church and religion at Moot (or Boot) Hill in Scone. Constantine II and a presbyter attended but no Roman legate was invited, due to the fact that the Celtic Church was not yet controlled by the imperial city. Reformation of the laws and discipline of the faith, the rights of the Churches and the doctrine of the Gospel were discussed in light of the status quo in which the zeal of the Columban Church had waned. From this time on the Pictish and the Scottish Churches were united and placed in equality and supremacy was transferred from Abernethy, which had been the seat since 865 A.D., to St Andrews in Fife.

Photograph (233) shows the Scottish round tower erected in the 11th century in Brechin. Its height is 26 metres, its external diameter 4.5 metres and its inner one 2.5 metres at its top.

Photograph (234) shows a similar tower in Abernethy. Its height is 22 metres, its external diameter 4.5 metres and inner one 2.5 metres. It is made of the same blocks of stone used to build St Regulus (or St

233   234

Regles) which became a bishop's seat in 908 A.D. under the reign of Constantine II.

Photograph (235) shows "Moot Hill" (meaning "lump of rock") in Scone. This is the site where the hereditary stone for the inauguration ceremony of Dalriadic kings, the "Stone of Destiny," was finally placed, having been transferred from Forteviot via Dunstaffnage in Argyle, until it was taken away to England by Edward I in 1296 A.D. This hill has the other name of "Boot Hill" because the noble attendants at the inauguration ceremony of new kings, carrying the soil of their fief in their boots, contributed it to this hill and paid homage to the new king.

235

In 908 A.D. Ronald Mac Aedh, brother of Constantine II, succeeded to the throne of the Strathclyde Britons and planned the union of Strathclyde and Alban, but in 912 A.D. Strathclyde suffered from a large-scale invasion by a great number of Danish pirates led by Regnwald or Reginald, chief of the race of Ivar, who arrived from Ireland with the famed chiefs Ottir the Jarl and Oswl Gragaban. Though they were soon put to flight, Dunblane and its neighbourhood were ravaged and Ronald's plan was left unfulfilled. In 918 A.D. Constantine II fought with Danish Vikings of the same name by request of Eldred, the ruler of the Northumbrian Angles. The Vikings were in formidably large masses and the site of the encounter was Tyne Moor near Corbridge. Eldred was slain and Constantine II and his men were driven back at great sacrifice. Regnwald secured Northumbria and this result brought about the threat that the whole region from the Firth of Forth to the Humber might be a Scandinavian kingdom.

This caused Constantine II to recall the old example of Angus Mac Fergus who came to terms with Eadbert and entered into an alliance in 740 A.D. Constantine II promised Regnwald to marry his daughter to Olaf Cuaran, son of Sitriuc, brother of Regnwald and successor to the leadership of the Danish Vikings, and allied himself with Regnwald who was to die in 921 A.D. Constantine thus helped the Danish Vikings to retain their position in Northumbria. He intended to let them confront the Saxon dynasty in Northumberland which had been dominant since receiving the submission of Mercia and Northumberland in 829 A.D. under the reign of Egbert (802 – 839 A.D.).

In 924 A.D. there befell an unclear event, the Commendation of Constantine II to the Saxon king, as the Anglo-Saxon Chronicle relates in the passage of 924 A.D.: "In this year was Eadward king chosen to be father and lord of the Scots king (Constantine II) and of the Scots, and of Regnold (Regnwald) king, and of all Northumbrians, and eke of the Strath Clyde Wealas king, and of all Strath Clyde Wealas." [57] However, this Commendation, supposedly presented by Constantine II in 924 A. D. at Bakewell to Eadward (870 – 924 A.D.), the Saxon king and son of Alfred the Great, was a historical event of doubtful authenticity, as seen in the fact that Regnwald, the Norse king of Danish Northumbria, had already died and "gone to Odin's" in 921 A.D.

Anyhow, the new epoch, which could not evade coping with the Saxon dynasty, had come to the Alban kingdom, together with the problem of the Vikings. In 924 A.D. Eadward died and Aethelstan (924 – 40 A.D.) ascended the throne of the Saxon kingdom. In the following year 925 A.D. Aethelstan married his sister to Sitriuc, brother of Regnwald, and in 926 A.D. received the homage of the king of Alban, Strathclyde, Wales and the solitary chief of Northumbria, Sitriuc. In the same year he drove out Sitriuc from Northumbria and Sitriuc died in Ireland.

Northumbria was now under the possession of Aethelstan. Guthferth, brother of Sitriuc, came to Alban from Dublin and tried hard to recapture Northumbria but failed. In 933 A.D. Olaf Cuaran, the eldest son of Sitriuc, came to Alban for the same purpose and after a while he married the daughter of Constantine II as promised. This alliance offended Aethelstan as a matter of course and caused him to set out on destructive invasions by sea and land to the eastern coasts of the Alban kingdom up to Caithness.

In 937 A.D., as a reprisal, Olaf Cuaran and Constantine II, his father-in-law, appeared at the mouth of the Humber with a fleet of battle-ships and transports consisting of 615 ships; the Danes of Dublin led by Olaf, son of Godfrey; the Scots under Constantine II; and the Britons of Strathclyde who gathered and marched across England from northwest to southeast, attempting to regain Northumbria from the grasp of the Wessex king.

On the battlefield of Brunanburh, though the locality is not certain, Aethelstan clashed with the allied forces of the Scots, the Danes and the Strathclyde Britons, 61,000 strong, and the battle was a catastrophe with both sides making a great many sacrifices before it came to an end. Among the dead of the allied forces were Geleachan, the king of the Western Isles, and a prince or Mormaer of Moray. Constantine II lost one of his sons and Aethelstan two of his brothers. Constantine II and his surviving followers retreated to Alban, the Britons to Strathclyde and the Danes escaped on board ship to Ireland.

Just after this disastrous battle, another Olaf, the son of Sitriuc, opened his attack against Northumbria which was ruled by the former Norwegian king Eric, the Bloody Axe, who had replaced Sitriuc to whom Aethelstan married his sister in 925 A.D. and whose homage he enforced in the following year and drove out from Northumbria for reason of disaccord.

Eric was one of the sons of Harald Harfagri and the king of Norway (930 – 34 A.D.) but, having murdered several of his brothers to secure the throne, became unpopular and after being defeated and banished in 934 A.D. by his half-brother Haakon (a king of Norway 935 – 61 A.D.), fled to England and became the ruler of Northumbria after Haldane's death.

Olaf repeated his raids until 940 A.D. when Aethelstan died and his successor and half-brother Edmund (940 – 46 A.D.), who had fought at Brunanburh with Aethelstan, made truce with him. The contents of the armistice agreement stated that five Danish boroughs were to be protected from raids by Norwegian kings in Northumbria but there was no substantial concession to Olaf.

In 942 A.D. Constantine II, resigning the crown after his reign of forty-two years to Malcolm I (942 – 54 A.D.), son of Donald II of the Constantine house, retired from the secular life to Cill Righ Monaidh (St Andrews) on the brink of the waves.

With the power of Northumbria reduced, and tension in the south easing, Malcolm I carried out a campaign to the North to reduce the power of Cellach of Moray. But a temporary change of relationship between the kingdoms of Alban and Strathclyde had taken place, resulting from an intrigue which Edmund had devised to drive a wedge between the two kingdoms.

When Olaf carried out his campaigns to Northumbria, he had to pass through the domain of the Strathclyde Britons which at that time extended from the Clyde to Cumberland where a large number of refugees from the Strathclyde region had settled after the fall of Dumbarton to Olaf and Ivar in 870 A.D. Edmund, after over-running this area of Cumberland many, many times, declared that he would give it all up to Malcolm on condition that "Malcolm should be his co-operator (literally, ally and supporter, or fellow-worker) both on sea and land." [58]

In 946 A.D. the deceased Edmund was followed by Edred (946 – 55 A.D.), the youngest son of Edward the Elder, and the domain of Cumberland reverted to its former arrangement. In 949 A.D. Olaf made an expedition to Northumbria with the aid of the Scottish army and Constantine, former king and his father-in-law who was contentedly retired in his quiet retreat.

In *The Pictish Chronicle* it is written that it was Malcolm who made this expedition and it says that he wasted the Anglian territories as far as the River Tees and carried off a host of captives and flocks, and that he did it by instigation of Constantine. However, it is more likely that Constantine undertook the leadership in order to circumvent the obligation of Malcolm, as Scottish king, to the Saxon king.

Olaf seems to have regained Northumbria and for three years after this expedition he remained there and was baptized there. In Northumbria there then occurred an insurrection headed by Wulfstan, Archbishop of York, and Eric the Bloody Axe, the former Norwegian king. Edred took over Northumbria on Eric's death (954 A.D.) and granted limited autonomy to the Danes on the advice of Dunstan, a prelate and Edred's adviser, who sought to make the Danes an integral part of the nation and had once been expelled from Aethelstan's court. Ofaf was to be replaced by the previous leader, Eric, "The Bloody Axe," the ruler of Northumbria, but he himself decided to return to Ireland. He reigned as a renowned and powerful king of the Danes until 980 A.D. when his army was fatally defeated by the native Irish at Tara, after which he retired to Iona to spend his later years.

In 954 A.D. Malcolm was slain at Fettercairn in Kincardine (or Mearns) by the men of Mar, probably in revenge for the slaughter of Cellach of Moray. Indulf Mac Constantine II (954 – 62 A.D.), his successor, captured Dunedin or Edinburgh and *The Pictish Chronicle* tells us that the oppidum of Eden (Edinburgh) was evacuated by the Angles and surrendered to the Scots. This was the first definite step in the permanent extension of the kingdom of Alban between Forth and Tweed, but the acquisition of Cumberland remained to be resolved.

During Indulf's reign the coast of Buchan was the main site of Norse raids but Indulf resisted them stubbornly and successfully. However, after 962 A.D. there is no record of him in historical accounts and the cause of his death is not known.

The throne shifted from Indulf to Dubh Mac Malcolm I (962 – 67 A.D.) of the Constantine house. He reigned for five years but he was not able enough to hold the allegiance of his subjects. In consequence, Cuilean Mac Indulf, his eventual successor, attempted to oust him in 965 A.D. with the aid of Dunchad, lay-abbot of Dunkeld, and Dubhdubh, the governor of Athole. However, both of them were slain by Dubh at the Battle of Drumcrub in Strathearn attempting to realise Cuilean's scheme, but Dubh was expelled by Cuilean two years later and his death in the same year is recorded. Dubh was slain in his bedroom by two assassins and his body was hidden under the bridge of Kinross on July 10th, a day of solar eclipse. Cuilean (967 – 71 A.D.) reigned for four years until he (together with his brother Eoch) was also slain, in 971 A.D. in Lothian, by Britons in private revenge.

Kenneth II Mac Malcolm I (971 – 95 A.D.) succeeded Cuilean in 971 A.D. Straightway, he ravaged a wide range of the territories of the Britons in Lothian, probably in retaliation on behalf of his predecessor Cuilean Mac Indulf, though once he suffered a severe set-back at a marsh near Abercorn. It was not long after these events that Kenneth made an expedition to Northumbria which was by then the territory of the Saxons, harrying as far as the ancient territory of Deira. He completed the fortification of the fords of the River Forth and in the following year he made another expedition to Northumbria and carried off a son of the Saxon king Edgar (959 – 75 A.D.). In 977 A.D. he was engaged in "the Battle of Luncarty", though the date and precise locality are not clear. The realms of Moray, Ross, Sutherland and Caithness, north of the Spey, were at that time the pagan territory of the Earl of Orkney of Norway. Grelauga, daughter of Duncan, Celtic earl of Caithness or Duncansbay, had married Thorfinn (Hansakliuf), earl of Orkney and son of Einar (son of Rognwald) who had the other name of "Torf" (or Turf) because he had superintended "turf-cutting."

Now northern Mormaers were eager to avail themselves of every opportunity for securing their freedom from the Norsemen's sway. Kenneth II pondered how to resolve things, while regarding the realms as a dependency of Alban.

Towards the end of 980 A.D. a battle was fought between Liotir, one of the sons of Thorfinn, and Magbiot, a Scottish Mormaer in Liotir's earldom at Skida Moor in Caithness. It was a close fight which Liotir won but he was mortally wounded and Hlodver, his brother, who inherited the earldom, also died shortly after the battle, whereupon the earldom passed to his son Sigurd the Stout, a renowned strategist. While in Orkney as the chief of the earldom, he also governed Caithness, Sutherland and the territories as far south as the Spey. A Scottish army under Finlaic, Mormaer of Moray, fought vainly with him on the same battlefield on which Liotir had met his end.

Two Scottish earls, Hundi and Maelsnati, along with their men, invaded Duncansness in Caithness and slew Havard of Treswick, Sigurd's brother-in-law. Sigurd immediately crossed from Orkney, slaughtered them and slew Maelsnati before the main force had arrived. With the year of 987 A.D. as a turning point, Sigurd's energies began to be directed to the Hebrides. These were once possessions of Godfrey Mac Fergus, Ketill Flatnose, Olaf Cuaran and Maccus Mac Harald (son of Sitric Mac Imhair), but were now under Godfrey Mac Harald, although one year earlier Sigurd had encountered this Godfrey and defeated him.

At the year end of 986 A.D. Iona was plundered by the Danes on the eve of the Nativity and the abbot and fifteen clergy were slain. The western isles of the Inner and Outer Hebrides now turned into a centre of carnage. In 987 A.D. a battle was fought between Godfrey and the Danes of Dublin for possession of the Isle of Man and neighbouring isles. According to the Annals of Ulster, in the same year the Danes invaded the western coastlands of Alban on board three ships and hanged one hundred and forty coastal men.

Among Sigurd's courtiers there was a vassal called Kari Solmundson, a military leader of successive victories. He and the sons of Nial, a hero of Icelandic Vikings, made an expedition to the Isle of Man and, encountering Godfrey, King of Man, vanquished him. In the next summer of 988 A.D. they made a second expedition and harried the Hebrides. Thence they went to Kintyre and, fighting with landsmen, carried off plunder. Next they went down south to the Isle of Man and met Godfrey again, fought with him and slew his son Dungall.

In 997 A.D. Sigurd was converted to Christianity somewhat forcibly by Olaf Tryggveson, the first Christian king (995 – 1000 A.D.) of Norway who, baptized by a hermit in the Scilly Isles, was on his way back from England. Sigurd yielded to necessity, being given the alternative of whether he should choose to be a Christian and become a tributary to Norway or be executed. Olaf, on departing, carried off Sigurd's son Hundi as a hostage and pledge of fidelity. Kennenth II died in 995 A.D. after a reign of twenty-four years. *The Irish Chronicle* states that he was killed treacherously by his own people, while *The Scottish Chronicle* says that his death occurred at Fettercairn in Kincardine at the hands of a daughter of Cunchar, the Earl of Angus, whose only son had been executed some years before at Dunsinane as a result of some mistake by Kenneth II.

Constantine III Mac Cuilean (995 – 97 A.D.) of the Aedh house succeeded Kenneth II and he was the last representative of that house, having had no offspring. He was slain in action by his own people in 997 A.D. and the lineage of the Aedh became extinct. Kenneth III, the Grim, Mac Dubh (977 – 1005 A.D.) of the Constantine house, followed him. He obtained the land of Cumbria in 1000 A.D., routing the hosts of Saxons led by Aethelred II, the Unready (978 – 1016 A.D.), but the kingdom of Alban was now in dark and stormy days. Social disorder and civil war were daily occurrences and Kenneth was slain by Malcolm Mac Kenneth II in a battle in 1005 A.D. in Monzievaird, Strathearn, the outset of which was a dispute about the right of Kenneth to succeed Constantine III in 1005 A.D.

Having slain Kenneth III to usurp the throne, Malcolm killed Boedh Mac Kenneth III to install his grandson Duncan Mac Crinan (son of his daughter Bethoc) as his successor. He was a wicked man but he was also an able king who excelled in strategy and administrative ability. He was the last representative of the descendants of Kenneth Mac Alpin in the male line and he occupied the throne for thirty years. In 1006 A.D. under the reign of Athelred II, the Unready, he made an expedition to Bernicia to snatch it from English rule but while engaged in the siege of Durham he was encountered by Uchtred, son of the old Earl of Waltheof, and in a great battle he suffered a disastrous defeat with the loss of many of his vassals.

However, old historians pay tribute to the prowess of Malcolm in the conflict with the Vikings in 1006 A.D. when horde upon horde of plundering Danish Vikings entered the mouth of the Spey and made merciless havoc upon a defenceless country. Dugald Mitchell, the author of *A Popular History of the Highlands and Gaelic Scotland*, writes, quoting the passages of an old historian, as follows: [59] "Marshalling his forces, King Malcolm hurried forward for the relief of the northern provinces but in the first rush of battle he was badly wounded and his troops were driven back. Retreating into Mar, Malcolm recruited his forces and again joined battle at Murtlach (near Dufftown) and again the Scots were forced to retire. But Malcolm was not yet beaten and, rallying his men at a narrow pass, he awaited the onset of the Danes who attacked with great impetuosity. With the uttermost obstinacy the Scots resisted, slew the Danish leader and, taking up the offensive, rushed upon the invaders with great fury and turned defeat to victory."

Near the town end of Forres there is a memorial stone pillar 6.5 metres high called "Sueno's Stone" just below Cluny Hill where until recently there took place a Norsemen's "Clavie" (a midwinter fire-festival in which barrels enveloped in flames were trundled down from the hill-top). The stone is a sculptured explanation or epitaph which in popular belief recorded Malcolm's victory in this battle, though there is also another account which says that it is a record of the final defeat of the Danes in 1014 A.D. in which Swyne "Fork Beard" (d.1014), father of Cnut the Great (1016 – 35), died. The western side of the stone has a relief of a ring-headed cross and on the reverse side there has been carved a series of sculptures of the battle, divided into four panels with each panel divided into two tiers.

The top panel shows a line of figures, a leader and his guard travelling on horseback, and the second from the top shows foot soldiers and the scene of a single combat between warriors of each side. The third panel shows the scene of the beheading of captives with six headless corpses side by side. The next panel shows the rout of the defeated side and six horses on the left, away from the foot soldiers. Below it are something like a canopy and more headless bodies and at the bottom is the scene of a captured chief which represents the final defeat of the enemy.

236
Photograph (236) shows the reverse side of "Sueno's Stone."

In the spring following the battle with the Danish Vikings, who had entered the mouth of the Spey, there was another large-scale descent of Norsemen to the northern shores of the Tay, led by the Danish leader Camus, and the Scots were once more rallied. A bloody battle was fought at Barry near Monifieth in which the veterans of Denmark went down before the strong arm of the Scottish patriots. In the retreat the Danish leader was slain at a place called Camuston and the eastern shores of Scotland were freed from the sway of the invaders.

In the year 1008 A.D. Sigurd the Stout (Hlodverson) married a daughter of Malcolm. It was an alliance which Sigurd himself had proposed to Malcolm with the ambition that he could depict himself as a strong adversary among the chiefs of Moray. In 1014 A.D. Sigurd was slain at Cluantarch (Cluain Tarbh, "Pasture of Bulls") in the suburbs of Dublin by the Irish hero Brian or Broimhe Boru, and defeated in a bitter battle with the native Irish.

His son Thorfinn (1009-1064), five years old when Sigurd died, was to grow up, by an irony of fate, to be the mortal foe of Duncan who was the son of another daughter of Malcolm, Bethoc, and Crinan, a lay-abbot in Dunkeld. Thorfinn married Ingibiorg, daughter of Earl Finn Arnson, who later remarried with Malcolm Canmore Mac Duncan after she had been bereaved of Thorfinn in 1064 A.D. She was a political victim whose name immediately brings to mind the runic inscriptions concerning Ingibjorg on the wall of the Maes Howe Chambered Cairn, though it is uncertain whether or not this cairn was at that time in the possession of this house of Norwegian Vikings. The contents of the graffiti left on the wall of the grave seem to tell of her abandoned and disconsolate life, if the two Ingibjorgs were one and the same (see p21).

The Isle of Birsey off mainland Orkney was the headquarters and relaying station of the earldom of Orkney. This earldom was inherited through Rognwald by his brother Sigurd the Mighty; Einar, son of Rognwald; Thorfinn, son of Einar; Liotir and Hlodver, sons of Thorfinn; Sigurd the Stout; Sumarlidi, Brusi, Einar and Thorfinn the Mighty, sons of Sigurd; and finally by Earl John, son of Earl Harold Maddadason, who left no male issue and the lineage of the house became extinct on his death in 1231 King Alexander II created Magnus (son of Gilbride, Earl of Angus) Earl of Caithness and, separating Sutherland into another earldom, gave it to William, son of Hugh Freskyn.

With the death of Sigurd, the situation in the northern area of Scotland changed aspect. The sons by his first marriage, Sumarlidi, Brusi and Einar shared out Orkney among themselves. The partially colonized northern part of the mainland, a dependency of the Scottish Crown, was bestowed by Malcolm on his grandson Thorfinn. The southern part to the Spey, Moravia or Moray, and Ross, which were less affected by Norwegian influences, came under the native ruler Finlaic Mac Ruadhri (father of Macbeth or Maelbaethe) who had once fought against Sigurd in an earlier year. Thorfinn the Mighty, son of Sigurd the Stout, had as eventful a career as his father. He was made Earl of Caithness when he was only five years old and he later became earl of Orkney.

However, on the death of Malcolm, Kali Hundason of Norway held this territory and with the enthronement of Magnus Haraldson the Good (King of Norway 1035 – 47, and of Denmark 1042 – 47), son of Olaf Haraldson, the Holy (1016 – 28), this territory was given to Rognwald Brusason. Thorfinn was forced to spend many years campaigning against this rival claimant to the earldom, Rognwald Brusason, who was finally slain in battle in 1046 A.D. by Thorfinn. The earlier part of Thorfinn's career was taken up with campaigns against Ireland and later against Brusason. He also allied himself with Macbeth and gave his mind to the murder of Duncan I (the first king of the United Kingdom of Scotland).

Thorfinn seems to have felt guilty about the death of Rognwald Brusason and he went to Norway and then to Rome in order to obtain absolution from the Pope for his sins. On his return he built a cathedral on the Isle of Birsey and lived on this tidal island until his final day. During his rule the Norse in the northern isles formally became Christian.

In 1018 A.D. Malcolm made a last mighty expedition to the northern province of England, then under the reign of King Cnut the Great, the Danish ruler of England. This campaign was aided by Owen or Eoghainn the Bald, king of the Strathclyde Britons. Malcolm, Owen and their large allied army marched towards the Tweed, encountered the English army at Carham near Coldstream, and at the end of a great battle defeated them.

Dugald Mitchell, the author of *A Popular History of the Highlands and Gaelic Scotland*, writes, quoting the passage of Simeon of Durham, that [60] "previous to the battle a comet appeared for thirty nights and nearly the whole population from the River Tees to the Tweed died in the fight in which they engaged with a multitude of Scots at Carham."

And again Simeon writes that [61] "Eadulf Cudel the Earl yielded up to the Scots the whole of Lothian in satisfaction of their claim and for a solid peace and thus at last Tweed's silvery stream became the southern boundary of Scotland." However, it was not until 1031 A. D. that Malcolm added this new territory to his kingdom. *The Anglo-Saxon Chronicle* records in the passage of 1031 A. D. that King Cnut went to Rome and as soon as he came back he went to see the Scots King Malcolm and submitted to him and became his man, though only for a short time.

On the other hand, there were two Scottish nobles who submitted to Cnut, Maelbaethe and Iehmare. Maelbaethe, or Macbeth, was the son of Finlaic whose father was the chief of the semi-independent province of Moray or Moravia, slain in 1020 A.D. by his nephew, the son of his brother Maelbright. In 1034

237

Photograph (237) shows the Isle of Birsey comprising twenty-one hundred hectares: rectangular earth-mounds are the sites of the foundations of dwelling houses.

Malcolm II died and Duncan Mac Crinan, who had ascended the throne of the Strathclyde Britons on the death of Owen in 1018 A.D., succeeded Malcolm II in that year, and the new era of Scotland began as "The United Kingdom of Scotland." It was the product of cruel historical vicissitudes, full of anguish like the throes of creation.

238

Photograph (238) shows the site of the Bishop and Earl's Palace built by Thorfinn the Mighty in the settlement of Birsey.

239

Photograph (239) shows the site of the residential quarters which the former occupants, the Picts, used in earlier days.

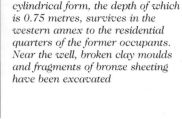

241

Photograph (241) shows a well associated with metalworking. Its cylindrical form, the depth of which is 0.75 metres, survives in the western annex to the residential quarters of the former occupants. Near the well, broken clay moulds and fragments of bronze sheeting have been excavated

240

Photograph (240) shows the cemetery near the palace. The graves of thick capstone are those of Norsemen and the thin ones of Picts. The stone standing in the centre of the cemetery is a cross slab but to whom it was dedicated is unknown. It has a simple cross on its rough surface like the cross slab at Creich (see p224).

Photograph (242) shows a Pictish Symbol Stone, a replica. The real one is in the National Museum of Antiquities of Scotland in Edinburgh. It stands 1.5 metres high and on the upper part are reliefs of a mirror and a crescent-form crown with an image of a V-shaped sign like a broken arrow. On the middle section are images of a sea-elephant and a large eagle resting on a rock. On the lower part is an image of three Pictish warriors marching in a line with spear and shield in hand. It is a testimony that the former occupants were Pictish.

242

CHAPTER VII

PICTISH SYMBOL STONES

Some scholars advocate that the Pictish were not totemists because they were not originally Aryans (who were known to have a belief in totemism) but the Picts were indeed totemists whose names derived from places and animals, birds, fish and plants, such as the Big Oxen of Raddary (Daimh mhora Radharaidh), the Bucks of Strathgarve (Buic Srath Ghairbh), the Kites of Loch Broom (Clamhanan Loch Bhraoin) and the Black Ravens of Loch Carron (Fithich Dhubha Loch Carronn). And this race, the Picts, had the custom of erecting a "totem pole" or "Pictish Symbol Stone" on which was inscribed a series of symbols and which seems to have displayed their totem, territory and sometimes their dealings.

Figure (27) shows motifs of fish, birds, and animals thought to be Pictish totems: bull, boar, wolf, stag, hind, horse, cat, sea-elephant, snake, eagle, salmon and so on.

Figure (28) shows the principal motifs commonly seen on most of the symbol stones. They are a crescent crown mark (which presumably shows "chieftaincy") with a V-shaped sign like a broken arrow (which might denote "honour" or a rank of nobility, or a sextant, an instrument for a s t r o n o m i c a l observation); a mark of a pair of rings or cauldrons linked with lines (which might

Figure 27

213

Figure 28

denote relation of marriage or rivalry in war) with or without a reversed Z-shaped sign (like a twice-broken arrow) which also might denote a rank of nobility or a degree of honour; and a rectangular sign like a tuning fork (which might denote a fort or something similar) with a reversed Z-shaped sign. Motifs of a cauldron, a hammer and a tongs sometimes appear, though they seem to be signs of an iron work-shop; and a mirror and comb or torque probably denoted a matriarch and the donor of the stone.

It is regrettable that what these motifs could tell us is not comprehensible. However, Pictish Symbol Stones can be classified into three groups. The stones of class (I) are single-faced symbol stones from pagan days, commonly inscribed on standing stones of the Bronze Age or on the surface of natural stone like the Knocnagael Stone (see pp175-6). Symbols consist of a crown mark; a mark of a pair of rings; a rectangular sign with or without a V-shaped sign and a reversed Z-shaped sign; a totem mark; and a mark of the donor, a mirror and comb.

Stones classified as class (II) are those carved after Christianization. The stones themselves are mainly processed slabs and a ring-headed Pictish cross is inscribed on one side with the signs of animals and abstract motifs; and on the other side are narratives of historical events like those of Sueno's Stone (see p207), together with a series of motifs and signs.

Stones classified as class (III) are types of gravestones, works of art, stone frames on which are carved a bullfight or animals on parade, and stones on which mighty animals like the bull, wolf and boar are carved. They seem to have been used for prayer or as a talisman like the Bull Stone excavated in the well of Burghead Promontory Fort (see pp117-8). All of these stones, irrespective of their category, are unevenly distributed where Pictish people had once settled.

243

244

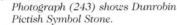
Photograph (243) shows Dunrobin
Pictish Symbol Stone.

Photograph (244) shows the "Eagle
Stone."

1. STONES OF CLASS (I)

Stones of Class (I) are not customarily found in museums whereas
stones of Class (II) and (III) are usually there enshrined. Class (I)
stones remain outside exposed to the weather, probably because they
are stones of pagan days. The site of erection seems to be the original
place, for it can hardly be supposed that any clan would erect its own
stone in the territory of another clan.

Dunrobin Pictish Symbol Stone stands in the precincts of Dunrobin
Castle in Sutherland. It is a "totem pole" of a tribe of the Cat of
Caithness, which now means the "Cape of the Cat". On the surface of
this standing stone from the Bronze Age, some 2 metres high, are
inscribed a symbol like a tuning fork near the top, a crescent crown-
like symbol with a V-shaped sign in the middle and a motif of a torque
at the bottom. A torque is a kind of personal ornament like a necklace
made of precious metal which noble women of ancient Gaul and Britain
used. It is suggestive of blood ties between Picts and Celts.

The stone commonly called the "Eagle Stone," standing on a
hillside in Strathpeffer in Ross-shire, is some 1 metre high, carved at
the end of the seventh century, and it has a crown mark without a V-
shaped sign on top of the stone and a motif of a bird at the bottom.
Strathpeffer is along the main road leading from Dingwall to Loch

245

246

Photograph (245) shows Edderton
Pictish Symbol Stone.

Photograph (246) shows Clach Ard
Pictish Symbol Stone.

Carron, the base of the Black Ravens of Loch Carron and full of place-
names related to a "raven," like "Raven Rock" (about 2 miles north-
west, a viewpoint or a watchtower, 262 metres above sea level) and
"the River Bran." The bird might not be an eagle but a raven. Was it
the totem of the Black Ravens of Loch Carron?

Edderton Pictish Symbol Stone is at the end of Edderton village to
the north of Tain. The stone is a standing stone from the Bronze Age
and is some 3 metres high. There are motifs of a salmon or some other
fish on top, and two cauldrons linked together with lines lengthwise
beneath it. To one of the lines is appended a motif of something like a
rectangle and a reversed Z-shaped sign, a mirror and comb but no sign
of who erected it.

Clach Ard Pictish Symbol Stone in Tote in the Isle of Skye is 1.3
metres high and 0.5 metres wide. It is probably a standing stone of the
Bronze Age. There are symbols of two crown marks with a V-shaped
sign driven in on top, the lower one of which is connected in the
centre of the stone to two cauldrons linked by lines lengthwise with a
reversed Z-shaped sign. The motif of a mirror and comb is at the
bottom but no totem symbol.

The symbol stone in Broomend of Crichei Ceremonial Centre,
south of Inverurie, Aberdeenshire (see pp44-5), has a motif of a sea-
elephant on top and beneath it a crown-like motif with a V-shaped sign

but it has no sign of a donor at the bottom.

Brandzbutt Pictish Symbol Stone situated 1 mile north-west of Inverurie bears motifs presumed to have been inscribed in the sixth or seventh century. These comprise the motifs of a crown mark with a V-shaped sign on top and, beneath it, a motif of a snake traversed with a reversed Z-shaped sign. On the left flank of the stone is a series of ogham letters, lengthwise, which have been deciphered as "IRATADDOA-REENS" or St Ethernanus.

Picardy Pictish Symbol Stone in Insch, Garioch, is a standing stone from the Bronze Age. It is some 2 metres high and carries the

247

Photograph (247) shows the Pictish Symbol Stone in Broomend of Crichei Ceremonial Centre.

motifs of two cauldrons linked by lines and traversed with a reversed Z-shaped sign on top, a motif of a snake with a reversed Z-shaped sign beneath it and a motif of a mirror and comb at the bottom.

Aberlemno Pictish Symbol Stone, situated midway between Nechtansmere and Brechin, is a standing stone with a cup-mark at the

248

Photograph (248) shows Brandzbutt Pictish Symbol Stone.

249   250

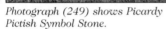

Photograph (249) shows Picardy   *Photograph (250) shows Aberlemno*
Pictish Symbol Stone.   *Pictish Symbol Stone.*

bottom. There are motifs of a snake on top, two cauldrons linked with lines and traversed with a reversed Z-shaped sign in the middle and a mirror and comb at the bottom.

Abernethy Pictish Symbol Stone in Fife is attached to the wall of Abernethy Round Tower. It might be the signboard of a blacksmith for it has a series of sculptures of an anvil, a hammer, something like a tuning fork, and a crown mark with a V-shaped sign. A smith was ranked among the nobility and their share of land, called "Smith's Mound," was dispersed throughout Pictland.

2. THE INTRODUCTION OF CHRISTIANITY

Adamnan recounts in his *Life of Columba (Vita Sancti Columbae)*, "On one occasion, while residing among the Pagan Pictish, the great missionary heard of a famous well which "foolish" men had worshipped as a God. It had evidently been tabooed for the belief was general that an individual who touched the water would become "leprous or purblind." The saint approached the well fearlessly, much to the delight of the Druids whom he had often "vanquished" and confounded, for they believed that he would suffer severely if he touched the baneful water. But Columba first blessed the water, then drank of it and washed his hands and feet. The demons departed forever from the well and in aftertimes many diseases amongst the people were cured by the water of this same well because the saint had blessed it." [62]

The propagation of Christianity in Scotland began, historically speaking, with that of St Ninian who set up "Candida Casa" in Whithorn in the late 4th century and it flourished from the 6th to the 8th century. St Catan of Kingarth (see p183), St Bridgid of Kildare (453 – 526 A.D.), St Myran of Paisley (see pp189, 221), St Odhran (or Oran) of Latterage (d.548 A.D.), St Comgall of Bangor (d.600 A.D., see p172), St Columba of Iona (see pp172, 220-22), St Cormac, ex-abbot of Durrow (see p172), St Finan (or Fhionain) the Infirm, St Moluag of Lismore (d.592 A.D., see pp172, 240), St Barochan of Barchan (see p222), St Ciaran (d.549 A.D.), abbot of Cluain Mac Nois (see p221), St Finbar of Moville (d.579 A.D., see p183), St Blaan of Dunblane (see p174), St Comgan (see p183), St Kentigarna (daughter of Cellach Cluain), the "Lady of Grace," or the saint of Loch Lomond (see pp183-4), St Fillan, son of St Kentigarna (see pp184, 244), St Donnan of Eigg (d.617 A.D., see pp174, 192), St Ethernan of the Isle of May, Fife, St Ernoc of Kilmarnock (d.635 A.D.), St Maelrubha (or Ma-Ruibhe) of Applecross (d.722 A.D., see pp183, 193, 210, 240), and so on, all came across from Ireland successively to the Western area of Scotland and began their missionary work.

However, in those days Scotland was still in the Iron Age. The social structure was still under the sway of the old world of paganism, as was the religion. The tribal structure had not been designed to support a church on the Roman principle and the Church was necessarily required to be monasteric.

The ordinary way of propagation was to found a "cell" and assimilate with the surrounding populace. This resulted in the foundation of many cells as shown in the large numbers of place-names combining "Kil" or Gaelic "Cill" with the missionary's name, such as Kilchattan (Cill Chattan), Kilkerran (Cill Chiarain), Kilfinnan (Cill Fhianan), Kilmarnag (Cill ma (my) Ernon), and so on.

Their technique was to superimpose the "mistletoe" of Christianity to live as a parasite on the "oak" of Druidism by implanting a new monastery in the old oak grove (the old Druidic holy land) as shown in the case of the Monastery of Durrow, the Monastery of the Oak field (Dair Magh); Kildare, the Monastery of the Oak Grove; Old Deer where there was the Monastery of St Drostan, the Old Oak-wood; and the Monastery of Derry, the Monastery of the Oak Grove, where St Columba spent his young days as a trainee monk. The attitude of their propagation was "dualism", and thus they could pass through all of Scotland unharmed. Ian Finlay, former professor of

Antiquities of the Royal Scottish Academy, writes in a passage in his book *Columba*, explaining the state of conversion to Christianity in Ireland, [63] "True enough, after Patrick much of the country lapsed into apostasy; but by the time Columba came much ground seems to have been recovered. That reliquaries and other sacred objects take a curiously equivocal form long after Columba's lifetime would imply that the people still wanted the best of both worlds, pagan and Christian, and that in some sort of fashion the church went along with them, if only to keep its hold on them."

Many of the earliest Christian monasteries were in pagan "woods" and the new Christianity in those days co-existed side by side with rituals and festivals for the pagan deities. Miracles and medical cures by herbs and spring-water, similar to traditional Chinese medicinal practice which had originated in remote antiquity, took place there in the name and in honour of both the new God and the old gods and goddesses.

Columba's final utterance went thus: [64] "These, my last words, I commend to you, O my sons, that ye have mutual and unfeigned charity among yourselves, with peace; and if, according to the holy Fathers, ye shall observe this God, the comforter of the good, he will help you; and not only will the necessaries of the present life be sufficiently supplied by Him, but the rewards of the good things of Eternity, prepared for those who keep His Divine commandments, shall also be bestowed."

251

Photograph (251) shows the site of Chapel St Finian near the beach of Corwall Port, Mochrum in Wigtown. St Finian or Finbar (shortened into Barr), was the founder of the famous Irish monastery at Moville near the head of Strangford Lough in County Down. His other chapel, Cill Bharra, is near Northbay in the Isle of Barra and his most northerly station was at Dornoch (see p183). St Finian was the tutor of St Columba.

252

*Photograph (252) shows the site of Chapel St Ciaran,
abbot of Cluain Mac Nois, near Loch Gorm in Islay.*

253

*Photograph (253) shows Paisley Abbey on the River
Cart in later days. The original was a cell founded by St
Myran (see p189)*

St Columba died in 597 A.D. as a complete saint, leaving his last
words to his brethren in the Isle of Iona. However, he was born in
pagan days when every firstling, every first-born, could be claimed by
the church or the Druidic temple as a tithe according to the practice
of old Brehon Laws. Though it is not known whether Columba was a
first-born son or not, he was given to Cruithnechan, a presbyter, to
foster, and if his parents had not been Christian he would have been
destined to be a high druid or an "ollam fili", a chief poet, an
honoured vocation devoted to serving the highest interests of the
tribe. He was one of the greatest Christian saints who matured in the
"oak grove" when Christianity was still a strange and untried faith.

254

255

"That man is little to be envied, whose patriotism would not gain force upon the plain of Marathon, or whose piety would not grow warm among the ruins of Iona!" is the eulogy which Dr Johnson, who did not like Scotland, paid on October 20th 1773 to St Columba's achievement. It is on the plaque set in the stone fence along the roadside near the priory.

Photograph (254) shows a cross dedicated to St Barchan (or Barochan), an Irish Pict who came to Barochan, 6 miles west of Paisley, in the middle of the 6th century to evangelize the muinntir there. The stone, 3.5 metres high, had once stood with its bottom section buried 1 metre in the earth near Mill of Barochan (where there was once a Roman fort) but now stands in the precincts of Paisley Abbey. It is much weathered but its principal motif is interlace. The front panel of the shaft is divided into three parts and though the meaning of the narrative is uncertain, from top to bottom there are chiselled a mounted warrior with a spear in his hand facing a figure holding a horn; a small human figure attended by two men, one of whom has something in his hand; and a pair of beasts facing each other. On the reverse side there are carved human figures with cloaks and others having spears and horns. The style of sculpture of the stone is very similar to that of the Pictish Symbol Stones, but it is called the "Strathclyde series of sculptured stones." Also in this area there have been excavated many hogback tombstones which have been classified under Pictish Symbol Stones Class III although some scholars have thought that they originated with the Norsemen, the successors of the Picts (see p235).

Photograph (255) shows Torr Abb's (or Abbot's Mound) or the site of St Columba's cell in the Isle of Iona, originally the seat of the Druids. Before St Columba and his mission arrived, inhabitants had lived in the small hill-fort on Dun Bhuirg on the west coast of the island.

The Benedictine Cathedral and Abbey of the Isle of Iona now stand on the site where in 563 A.D. St Columba and twelve missionaries built a monastery with a rampart and ditch, 150 metres from north to south and 330 metres east to west. The monastery was near the centre of the south-eastern side and his cell was somewhere near the centre of this site. It was devastated by Vikings in 794, 806, 822 and 825 A.D. (see p193) and in 806 sixty-eight clerics were butchered in Martyrs' Bay near it. In 1093 A.D. the Norwegian king Magnus Barefoot (1093-1103), son of Olaf III, gained control over the isle and Viking devastation calmed down, but it did not come under Scottish control until 1266 under the reign of Alexander III.

In 1151 the old monastery was demolished and the work of restoration was begun. However, in 1203 the cludees were replaced by Benedictines and the work of founding a new monastery and nunnery (near the ferry port) was advanced by the Benedictines with the aid of Reginald Somerled and MacLean and their descendants. The decision of the Scottish parliament to dissolve the monasteries in 1561 resulted in many items, crosses and sculptured stone of the monastery, being heaved into the sea. Monastic life on the isle died and the monastery itself began to fall into ruin. Restoration work has been in progress since 1910, but it was only after 1899, when the Duke of Argyle presented the monastery to the Church of Scotland, that the reconstruction of the cathedral, made of Romanesque and early Gothic elements, could begin to make progress.

The chapel on the right-hand side is St Oran's Chapel of which it was said that St Margaret, Malcolm's wife and sister of Edgar Aetheling, was too generous with her help in its reconstruction. Beyond it is the Relig Odhran (The Burial Ground of St Oran) where there were buried forty-eight Scottish kings, including Gabhran Domongart, Duncan I and Macbeth; and four Irish and eight Norwegian kings.

256

Photograph (256) shows the Benedictine Cathedral and Abbey of the Isle of Iona.

3. THE STONES OF CLASS (II)

The Pictish Symbol Stones of Class (II) are monuments showing the drift of Christianization in eastern Scotland which had been under Pictish control for a long time and was converted to the Roman Church just after the beginning of the 8th century. The stones influenced by Northumbrian masonry have fine and profound engravings while these not so influenced are simple and artless.

Most of the stones of this class are now installed in museums nearest to where they originally stood or were excavated. Among museums in which they are installed are Dunrobin Castle Museum in Sutherland, Groam House Museum in the Black Isle, and Meigle Museum and St Vigean's Museum in Tayside, but some still stand outdoors.

In Farr Parish Church 0.5 miles north of Bettyhill in Sutherland is a cross slab which stands in the graveyard and is known as Farr Cross Slab. It is a single-faced symbol stone so weathered that its carvings need to be observed under the effect of sunshine. It is 2.3 metres high, standing with its base buried directly in the ground without a pedestal. The main motif is a ring-headed cross consisting of panels of key, braided cord and curved linear designs. The central boss of the cross consists of a spiral design and at the base is a pair of birds with crossed necks. Though now much obscured by lichen, it is a stone by which the earliest Christians once showed zeal for their faith.

At Creich 3 miles east of Bonar Bridge on the Kyle of Sutherland is the Creich Cross Slab which was dedicated to St Devenic. The stone is single-faced and some 2 metres high, retaining only the outline of a large cross which probably means that the coarse-grained stone was too hard to carve in fine relief. A contemporay of St Columba and St Machar of Aberdeen, St Devenic was the patron saint of Lower Banchory (Bangor), a centre of the Irish-Pictish ecclesiastical community. He settled in Sutherland while St Machar went to Caithness.

In olden times, most parts of Scotland were covered by forests and mires and presumably the earlier the time, the more this was the case. Among the wild creatures regarded with awe seem to have been the wolf, bear, boar, snake and so on, and numerous motifs of these creatures appear on these Pictish Symbol Stones Class II, together with the bull, horse and dog which lived together with people daily. Those of the snake are markedly numerous while an imaginary creature like a sea-elephant is less often engraved on the stones.

Shandwick (Seanndabhach) Cross Slab is a fine large Pictish symbol stone which was erected in the late 8th or early 9th century A.D. and has the other name of Clach a' Charridh, or The Rock of the Monument. It stands 2.7 metres high on a hill overlooking the little fishing village of Shandwick. The shaft and arms of the ring-head cross consist of a series of small prominent bosses with unidentifiable reliefs in the upper part of the arm. Below the arms are reliefs of a pair of angels with wings, animal-figures seemingly of a bull and a boar, and ribbon-like entangled snakes along the shaft. At the base below the cross are four large rings with braid patterns inside.

The other side of the stone is divided into five panels. At the top is a motif of a crown mark with two rings containing three fine comma-shaped spiral designs at each end, and below it is a motif of a huge Pictish beast symbol, a gigantic sea-elephant or whale butchering and compressing smaller animals. Below this beast symbol there is a panel of motifs consisting of warriors in costume on horseback, a groom holding a horse, a man with a drinking horn in his hand, men on horseback hunting a stag with a dog, two foot soldiers fighting each other with shields and drawn swords, boars, foxes, an eagle, a warrior or hunter on horseback with a dog, two wolves confronting each other, a woodpecker and a man shooting a stag with a crossbow. Below it is a panel consisting of a total of fifty-two fine comma-shaped heraldic designs of three sizes. The panel at the bottom is divided into two: the one on the right is a relief of square mesh work and the other on the left consists of two rings with braid work, within which there are ribbon-like symbols.

257

Photograph (257) shows Farr Cross Slab.

Though the legend has grown around the stone that the cross slab there, together with two other slabs at Nigg and Hilton nearby, was erected to mark the graves of three Norwegian princes who were wrecked on a reef off Shandwick Bay, the hill where Clach a' Charridh was erected was once the site of a Druidic fort like Navity in Cromarty in the Black Isle, the ancient "nemeton" where it had been believed the last judgment was to be held. Outside the churchyard of St Regulus in Cromarty there was an inscribed gravestone sacred to the memory of Alexander Wood, a stammerer who, having quarrelled with

258

Photograph (258) shows Creich Cross Slab.

his neighbour, hoped to reach Navity on the last day and have enough time to tell the Lord his story before his enemy, whose grave is inside the churchyard, could arrive on the scene.

At Nigg nearby there was also another Druidic holy place where there was once "The Well of the Black Swords of Erin, facing the Sun in the Druid's port," [65] though its precise locality is now not certain. The Pictish symbol stone in Nigg (or Nigg Cross Slab) is now enshrined in Nigg Old Parish Church. The top of the stone takes the form of a pediment with motifs of St Paul and St Anthony in the desert, two animals and the raven which used to supply St Anthony with a loaf of bread, as recounted in *The Lives of the Saints*. The animals may be the lions which helped St Anthony when he buried St Paul.

The cross itself consists of a key-pattern at the base and on the arm and the upper part of the shaft an interlaced pattern with a mesh-like

259

*Photographs (259) and (260) show both the front
and reverse sides of Shandwick Cross Slab.*

pattern at the centre. The interlaced threadlike bodies seem to be patterned shapes of pairs of snakes. This stone was once damaged but then repaired. The part immediately above the arms is blank but there remain two bosses above the blank part. On the central two panels on either side of the cross shaft below the arm there are bosses covered with mesh-like interlace and surrounded by the bodies of snakes.

The other side is all carved in relief with the top and both flanks framed by a wider margin. At the top is a symbol of a huge eagle resting on a rock, and to the left is a warrior with a spear

260

and shield in hand facing two beasts. In the left of the centre is a motif of a heavily-woolled sheep and below it a harp. To the right is a human figure rending the jaws of a lion. At the bottom are motifs of a man

261   *262*

Photographs (261) and (262) show both the front and reverse sides of Nigg Cross Slab.

holding something like a pair of cymbals and a hunter on horseback
hunting a deer or similar animal.

263   264

*Photographs (263) and (264) show the front and reverse sides of Maiden
Stone Cross Slab.*

In the former territory of the Southern Picts are Maiden Stone
Cross Slab erected in the 9th century in Garrioch 5 miles north-west
of Inverurie; two Aberlemno Cross Slabs erected in the 9th century
midway between Angus and Forfar; Glamis Cross Slab in the garden of
the manse opposite the church, erected in the late 7th or early 8th
century; St Orland Cross Slab erected near Glamis in the 9th century;
Fowlis Wester Cross Slab, erected between the late 8th and early 9th
century in the village centre near Crieff; and Dunfallandy Cross Slab
erected in the 8th century near Pitlochry.

Maiden Stone Cross Slab is thus entitled after the legend of the
daughter of a native chief of Balquhain who died in the course of her
elopement with her lover. It is a pink-coloured granite slab some 2.5
metres high. The arms and shaft of a fine ring-headed cross are carved
in low relief of key-pattern, surrounded by a low relief of interlace of
thread. Above the cross are motifs of two fish monsters surrounding a
human figure with outstretched arms, and at the base of the cross is
a huge disc with spiral work surrounded by key-pattern and knotwork
with something resembling a motif of entangled snakes within. The
reverse side is divided into four panels and at the top is a motif of a

small animal and a huge Pictish beast like a centaur. Below it are motifs of a rectangle traversed with a reversed Z-shaped sign, a sea-elephant or whale, and a mirror and double-sided comb.

265

266

Photographs (265) and (266) show the front and reverse sides of Aberlemno Cross Slab (1).

One of the two Aberlemno Cross Slabs stands near the Aberlemno Pictish Symbol Stone (see pp217-18), though its initial locality is not certain; the other is within the precincts of the parish church. The former one, or Aberlemno Cross Slab (1), is some 3 metres high and the ring-headed cross is carved in high relief with four bosses as if of inlaid jewels within the ring which is of interlace work in low relief. Just under the ring are motifs of entangled snakes in high relief. The cross shaft consists of panels of knotwork in low relief and a sculptured angel is placed on either side of the shaft just under motifs of snakes. Under these motifs are carved spiral work on the right-hand side and interlace work on the left-hand side. At the bottom, on either side of the shaft, is a pair of animals fighting each other.

The top of the reverse side is dominated by a large symbol of a crown notched by V-shaped signs and a pair of cauldrons which both have seven carved bosses within them. They are linked by lines and traversed with a reversed Z-shaped sign, and under these motifs is a narrative panel of a battle scene or an expedition. There are warriors, on horseback, and foot soldiers, horses and hounds, and at the bottom are motifs of a centaur and a human figure rending the jaws of a lion, along with motifs of a sheep and a harp.

267   268

Photographs (267) and (268) show the front and reverse sides of Aberlemno Cross Slab (2).

Aberlemno Cross Slab (2), in front of the parish church, is some 2 metres high with a pedimental head. The cross is carved in high relief and the centre of the ring is spiral work, surrounded by four hollow rings with surrounding outer lines. Both ends of the arms have mesh-work; part of the shaft just above and under the centre of the ring is of knotwork; and there is a motif of an animal in low relief on either side of the top of the shaft. The lower part of the shaft is interlace work flanked by panels of abstract designs of elongated dragons on the left and of two snakes and two horses, male and female, head to head, on the right.

The reverse side is a narrative in low relief of a battle, perhaps the Battle of Nechtansmere in 685 A.D. conducted by Brude Mac Bile. At the top is a motif of a tuning fork (or a fort with a gate) with a flower design traversed with a reversed Z-shaped sign and it is flanked by a motif of a cauldron with handles. In the centre there is carved a series of motifs of warriors on horseback with swords and shields, foot-soldiers with swords and spears, and so on.

Glamis Cross Slab is 2.7 metres in height with a pedimental head. The cross is filled with designs similar to those of Aberlemno Cross Slab (2), except for the absence of a ring linking the arms. There are two motifs of a centaur and a dog on both right and left sides of the top of the shaft, and under the arms is a motif of a doe's head linking a cauldron with two handles on the right side along the shaft. On the

Photographs (269) and (270) show the front and reverse sides of Glamis Cross Slab in the garden of the manse, opposite Glamis Parish Church.

left side of the shaft are flanked motifs of a pair of men fighting with axes and a cauldron from which a pair of legs protrude. It might be linked with the historically narrated Pictish tradition of execution by drowning.

On the other side are carved three Pictish symbols: a snake, a fish, and a mirror on a rough and unprocessed surface. It might be an indicator of a family site and its simplicity brings to mind the Stone of the Hill of Hostage (Knocnagael) (see pp175-6) in Inverness which was presumably a camp for captives.

St Orland Cross Slab, dedicated to an unknown saint, is in a field of Cossans Farm some 3 miles north-north-east of Glamis. It is 2.4 metres high, the cross is ring-headed and its workmanship is very similar to that of Aberlemno Cross Slab (1) with the carving on both sides in high relief. The reverse side consists of five panels and there are symbols, from top to bottom, of a crown mark notched by a V-shaped sign, two cauldron marks traversed with a reversed Z-shaped sign, several horsemen and hounds, a boat with six voyagers on board, and a bird (probably a bran) being attacked by a monstrous beast. The last two panels are probably a narrative of the legendary voyage (565-73 A.D.) of St Brendan (or Bran, 484-577 A.D.) to the promised land of saints in the Western Islands, written by St Finian or Barr whose chapel was on Barra (see p220), and the beast is a sea-monster which St Bran and his five companions encountered during their voyage,

271

272

Photographs (271) and (272) show the front and reverse sides of St Orland Cross Slab.

273

Photographs (273) and (274) show the front and reverse sides of Fowlis Wester Cross Slab.

according to the tale. St Barr was contemporary with St Bran, the patron saint of Irish mariners, and the chapel dedicated to St Bran was also on Barra.

Fowlis Wester Cross Slab is a magnificent 3 metres high tapering stone, though now much weathered. The cross resembles that of St Orland Cross Slab in its workmanship except that it has no ring but it has eight bosses in the centre of the cross. Faint interlace decoration fills the shaft and key-pattern work the arms. The reverse side consists of six panels and at the top are two cauldron marks traversed with a reversed Z-shaped sign and a crown mark notched by a V-

274

shaped sign. Below them is a motif of a man on horseback with a groom. Below it are two horsemen, one of whom has a hawk or an eagle on his arm, and a motif showing a man leading a cow with a bell around its neck, attended by six bearded men, and below that is a crown mark with a V-shaped sign and a beast eating a man.

Dunfallandy Cross Slab is a stone which was transferred from a disused chapel at Killiecrankie. It now stands on a knoll near Pitlochry and is some 2.7 metres high. At the centre of the cross head is a square panel with knotwork inside it, and the shaft consists of two square panels with five bosses and spiral work inside. The arms have two square panels with three bosses and key-pattern inside. The lower part consists of interlace and mesh-work. At the top right above the arm is a carving of a wolf attacking a baby in a cradle, with a dog at the top left. Under the right arm are carved four panels: two identical angels, a long-necked animal and entangled snakes from top to

275

Photograph (275) shows the reverse side of Dunfallandy Cross Slab. It is difficult to take a photograph of the front side because it faces out from a steep precipice!

bottom. Under the left arm are another four panels: two panels of a wolf, a panel of a stag and one of a sea-elephant. The reverse side consists of three panels with the bodies of two facing fish-tailed, animal-headed monsters as its entire framework. At the top are motifs of two cauldrons linked by lines, a crown notched with a V-shaped sign, an angel, a sea-elephant, and under them, a motif of two saints conversing, one on each side of a table. At the centre are motifs of a man on horseback, a crown mark notched with a V-shaped sign, a sea-elephant, and at the bottom are motifs concerning a blacksmith-hammer, tongs and an anvil.

4. THE STONES OF CLASS (III)

The stones of this Class are all kept in the museum of each district. In the ancient world, mighty and fearful animals with tusks, fangs and horns were presumably all gods or goddesses and their sculptured figures are guardian deities or charms against evil.

Photograph (276) shows a stone piece on which is displayed a sculpture of a boar. It was excavated in Kingsmills in Inverness, the location of King Duncan's Well which marks the king's first burial place. It is owned by Inverness Museum, Archaeological Room.

276

Photograph (277) shows a stone piece bearing a sculpture of a wolf, excavated in Ardross, Easter Ross and owned by Inverness Museum, Archaeological Room.

Photograph (278) shows a recumbent grave-stone showing the patterning of the backbone of a boar, owned by Meigle Museum. In ancient British graves a boar's tusk was placed as a symbol of immortality or a sign of the cross, but the ultimate origin for this grave-stone is said to be Scandinavia where the Pictish settled and most of the stones were carved in the 10th century. If the stones of this type had been introduced through the settlement of Norsemen, these stones must be excepted from the classification of Pictish Symbol Stones.

Photograph (279) shows a stone frame where a triton is carved in the centre and a bear and a dog at the end of either side. It is owned by Meigle Museum.

Photograph (280) shows a stone piece on which are carved bouts of bullfighting. This is also owned by Meigle Museum.

The bull was a god of fertility as with Mithras's Bull, and stones bearing its image were probably dedicated to the Earth-Mother Goddess, the Celtic Genius Loci, wishing for the fertility of their offspring, domestic animals and crops. As to the "bull stone," please refer to photograph (157) of the bull stone of Burghead Well (see p117).

277

278

279

280

Day, which was until recent years observed in some parts of the Highlands with extraordinary ceremonies. . . Like the other public worship of the Druids, the Beltane feast seems to have been performed on hills or eminences. They thought it degrading to him whose temple is the universe to suppose that he would dwell in any house made with hands. Their sacrifices were therefore offered in the open air, frequently upon the tops of hills, where they were presented with the grandest views of nature. And according to tradition, such was the manner of celebrating this festival in the Highlands within the last hundred years.

But since the decline of "superstition", it has been celebrated by the people of each hamlet on some hill or rising ground around which their cattle were pasturing. Thither the young folks repaired in the morning and cut a trench, on the summit of which a seat of turf was formed for the company. And in the middle was placed a pile of wood or other fuel which of old they kindled with "tein-eigin" - i.e. forced fire. Although for many years past they have been contented with common fire, yet we shall now describe the process, because it will hereafter appear that recourse is still had to "tein-eigin" in extraordinary emergencies.

The night before, all the fires in the country were carefully extinguished, and next morning the materials for exciting this sacred fire were prepared. The most primitive method seems to be that which was used in the islands of Skye, Mull and Tiree. A well-seasoned plank of oak was procured, in the middle of which a hole was bored. A wimble of the same timber was then applied, the end of which they fitted to the hole..."

Another bonfire was observed on the eve of Samhuinn or Hallowe'en (Celtic New Year's Eve) which was connected with the return of herds from pasture and the renewal of land tenure.

Both were very important bonfires to mark the commencement of the two main seasons of the Celtic year. The sun, after climbing higher day by day or describing a downward curve in the sky, stops and thenceforth retraces its steps. The days of Beltane and Hallowe'en once seemed to have marked the two solstices of the year, and why the bonfire of Hallowe'en was burned in the eve seems due to the fact that the next day of Hallowe'en was a missing day.

In Japanese mythology it is a memorable eve when Amaterasu (Heaven-Shining Great Deity), the sun goddess, retreats into the Cave Rock (or Amano-Iwato) and eternal darkness, due to the extinction of the sun (suggesting the winter solstice), begins to prevail, and all the deities, meeting and building up a big bonfire outside the Cave, perform a convivial phallus dance to entice the sun goddess out from the Cave (suggesting the resurrection of the sun) with the help of the persuader Amano-Uzume, the loud-voiced goddess. These bonfire rites of Beltane and Hallowe'en, though originally pagan, co-existed side by side with Christian rites for a long period of time as national festivals, together with similar rites of Norsemen which were added in later times.

Water, as well as fire, was a basic necessity of life, and many wells and springs in Scotland still retain a degree of ancient sanctity, but it seems to have been something mysterious and spirit-haunted to the ancients. Many early Christian saints, who came from Ireland and propagated Christianity in Scotland, specified water of a certain river, loch, spring or well as water of virtue for medical cure and consecrated it as Aqua Vitae, just as St Columba performed in Inverness when he visited Brude Mac Maelcon in 565 A.D. or as many other saints did in the springs and wells of their monasteries or in the streams of annats (see Note 41). They had not abandoned the belief that water, endowed with magical virtue by the Earth-Mother Goddess in the depths of the earth, was blessed with a miraculous efficacy, a belief that their ancestors in Gaul had cherished in their minds. They imparted to the water of a certain well or spring a Christian significance and substituted their own name for that of the old pagan deity or rededicated it to the Blessed Virgin Mary instead of their ancestral pagan Earth-Mother Goddess, as seen in the cases of Tobermory and also Motherwell, the site of which remains in Ladywell Road in the town of Motherwell (Well of the Mother of God) south-east of Glasgow.

Among the famous healing and wishing wells consecrated by the early Christian saints are, or have been, St Fergus's Cave and Well in Glamis; St Columba's Well near Cramond, Firth of Forth and his well in the parish of Caerlaverock, Wigton; St Mary's Well (Tobar Mhoire) at the north end of Mull from which Tobermory takes its name and which is on high ground about 1 mile to the west of the town centre; St Fergus's Well in Rath of Eire in Strathearn; and Tobar na h-Annaide at Kilbride on Loch Salpin. However, while this cult of a wishing or healing well - which originated in the cult of the Earth-Mother Goddess in Druidism - took root as a Christian cult, it survived vividly as an original pagan practice in the name of a Christian saint.

In the wishing well cult people implore or implored the water of the Earth-Mother Goddess for their well-being, the fertility of offspring, domestic animals and crops, and for exorcism.

Though the ceremony now takes place before the dawn of the first Sunday of May, it used to be performed before the bonfire of Beltane at a well now known as a "Clutie Well," or "Rag Well."

The other, the healing well cult, though now nearly lapsed, took place in a river or loch to heal the sick and mentally handicapped and was in existence until about the end of the Victorian Age.

As to the manners of a visit to a wishing well, F. M. MacNeil, the author of *The Local Festivals of Scotland*, writes, quoting the example of a Clutie Well in Culloden, as follows: [67] "The path leading down to the well is thronged with people who make for a glade of trees with the encircling stone of the well in their midst. The ritual remains virtually unchanged. Before drinking the crystal-clear water, each pilgrim has to observe certain rites. He must first walk thrice sunwise round the well. Before drinking he must silver the water - that is, he throws in a silver coin. He cups his hands and drinks, at the same time formulating his wish. And finally he ties a rag or a fragment of his clothing to the branch of an overhanging tree in strict silence and out of sight of the well in the absence of the sun. By this last act he casts off all his ills and cares."

Among similar facilities are St Corbet's Well in Stirlingshire; the Clutie Well in Munlochy; Hainuck's Well and Charles' Well in the north of the village of Avoch in the Black Isle; and there were once three wells in the parish of Culsalmond near Ythan Wells, i.e. St Mary's Well on the farm of Colpie; St Michael's Well at Gateside; and another one at the foot of the Culsalmond bank, a little to the west of The Lady's Causeway.

The Clutie Well in Munlochy at the innermost depth of Munlochy Bay (at the entrance of which are the haunted crags and the cave of Craigiehowe) is a natural spring of sweet water and people still visit it as a wishing well, but it was originally the holy well of St Curitan or St Boniface: Hill o' Hirdie or "Cnoc Cille Churdaidh" nearby proves it. The water which drips from the roof at the entrance of the cave of Craigiehowe (see p265) once had a legend that it was a water of efficacy for deafness, though it presumably depended mostly on the initial condition of the patient, and it is said that it was the proper formality for the handicapped person to lie down and let the drops fall first into one ear and then into the other. St Corbet's Well at the summit of the Touch Hills, Stirlingshire, was a similar well which was believed to possess an efficacy for youth and long life.

As to the healing well cult, famous examples were St Fillan's Well in Muthil, which drew annually two hundred patients, and the Holy Well on Eilean Marui in Loch Maree, associated with the name of St Maelrubha (or Ma-Ruibhe) of Applecross, which had, in addition, a legend connected with the Druidical rite of bull-slaughter. The water of these wells was of a miraculous efficacy for healing the lunatic, just as with the water of St Helena's Well and St Bennet's Well in Cromarty in the Black Isle which St Moluag, "The Hundred Monasteries," seems to have presided over before the days of St Curitan (or St Boniface). In St Fillan's Well it is said that in cases of treatment of mental disorder patients were, for effect, thrown from a high rock nearby down into the well ("a shock therapy") and then locked up for the night in the chapel in the wood of witch elm which was gaily knotted with rags.

In the case of the Holy Well on Eilean Marui (the Isle of Maree), the customary practice was that the patient was taken out on a boat which was rowed around the islet three times clockwise. With hands and feet bound, the patient was thrown overboard on each round and ducked into the loch. Only those who endured and survived this violent baptism were permitted to drink the water of the Holy Well, and when the treatment had effect the patient used to drive a nail or coin into the ancient Holy Tree of Father God nearby.

In 1877 Queen Victoria (1837-1901) added her donation to it but the old oak, which had been embedded with a large quantity of nails and coins for centuries, died during World War I, while the well, which took charge of the unity of body and soul with the Holy Tree, fell into disfavour after a man had washed a mad dog in the water.

In Scotland there survived until the 17th century a mysterious rite which seems to have been similar to the Mithras's bull-slaughter. Plinius (Secundus, Gaius, the Elder, 23-79 A.D.), a Roman naturalist, has left us the only and precious detailed account of the rite of the Continental Druids who, opposing Roman conquest, seemed to have been wiped out at an earlier time as a result of Rome's victory.

He writes: [68] "This was determined by observing the growth of mistletoe on an oak tree, a circumstance of rare occurrence. The time chosen for the subsequent rite was the sixth day of the moon and preparations were made for a feast and the sacrifice of two white bulls. A Druid in a white robe climbed the tree and with a golden sickle cut a branch of mistletoe which was caught as it fell on a white cloak. The bulls were then sacrificed ... The ritual necessity of gathering the plant, left-handed while fasting, barefoot and with the right hand through the left sleeve of a white tunic, were performances of private magic rather than corporate ceremonial."

The 6th day of the moon was presumably an important or holy day in the Druidical world. After the day of "Furze" (the vernal equinox), the 6th day of the month of "Fearn" (or Alder, the month of Resurrection, Mar.18 – Apr.15) presumably corresponds to Easter in Christianity in later days, the next day being a missing day. A similar rite had taken place on the isle of Maree.

Ian Finlay, the author of *Columba*, referring to an instance of bull-slaughter for the choosing and consecration of the king, conducted at the Feast of Tara in Ireland by the Druids in the sixth century (contemporary with St Columba), writes, [69] "Here at Tara the rite of the Bull-Dream took place. A bull was slaughtered and a druid fed on its flesh and broth and when he fell insensible, spells were chanted over him and on waking he was able to point to the rightful successor to the kingship." Though succumbing eventually to Christianity's advance, Druids in Scotland and Ireland maintained their practices longer than the Continental Druids.

287

Photograph (287) shows the Brow Well, once a healing well, near Caerlaverock Castle, south-west of Dumfries, which Robert Burns (1759-96), the famous Scottish poet, is said to have often visited to cure his chronic rheumatism, his last visit being early in June just before his death.

286

Photograph (286) shows "Scotland Well" or "Fons Scotiae" to which the Scottish king Robert Bruce (1306-29), who defeated the large army led by Edward II at Bannockburn in 1314 and regained the independence of Scotland, is said to have often visited to cure his chronic disease of scrofula. It is a well for both wishing and healing.

288

Photograph (288) shows St Fillan's Chapel near Dundurn Fort. The holy well in the vicinity was the source of a host of stories concerning miraculous cures.

289

Photograph (289) shows the Water of Loch Fyne, one of those said to constitute Aqua Vitae or The Water of Life (am Buadhach or of the Virtue). "Fyne" derives from the same root word as the Latin "Vinea" (or Wine). It flows near Inveraray, Gleann Fine (Glen Fyne) and falls into Loch Fine, at the foot of which was the church site of Kilmorich (St the Mightie) with a clachan (churchyard) near it.

290

Photograph (290) shows the Water of Virtue near Cill Chuimein (Fort Augustus), once the site of Cill Chuimein and now of a Benedictine Abbey. James Fraser, Minister of Wardlaw, relates that by reason of virtue derived from the bell of Cill Chuimein "the water, or as the vulgar call it the wine, of Loch Ness is medicinal, and beasts were carried to it or the water of the lake brought to them to drink, which I have often seen." [70]

CHAPTER IX

THE OUTLOOK OF DIRECTION AND COLOUR

The most cardinal point of direction in ancient society was east (ear or the "front"); north was left (tuath) as it is left of the front; south "right" (deas); and west was "behind" (iar) as it is opposite the front. The pointer of Ursa Major (or the Great Bear) goes round to the east in spring, the south in summer, the west in autumn and the north in winter. Knowledge and use of this probably goes back to ancient times when early farmers measured the passing of the seasons of the year by observing certain heavenly bodies. Thus, making a round clockwise as the pointer of Ursa Major does was considered natural and auspicious and "right" was good-omened, while to go around counterclockwise was considered ill-omened, even if it were the turning of an unthinking sea-gull. And the eternal tour of the sun and of the pointer of Ursa Major had been naturally a revelation to ancient agriculturists of a belief in the immortality of all creation.

In the old days warriors drove their chariots around an opponent's fortress three times "by the left" as a sign of declaration of war; fishermen setting out from anchorage used to take the trouble of turning the boat "by the right," even though turning "by the left" could be more speedily effected; housewives stirred pots in which food was being cooked "by the right." "Omens" were drawn from birds wheeling either "by the right" or "by the left." Whatever it might be, turning by the left was presumably an important taboo to be avoided in ancient society. [71]

The bronze statue of Boadicea (d. 62 A.D.), the Britonic chief of the Iceni, standing at the foot of Westminster Bridge in London as if facing the Parliament building, is an example demonstrating how the ancient Celtic warrior declared war. She led a revolt against a devious and cunning Roman government but was defeated by Paulinus Suetonius, the Roman governor, and finally took poison. She wears a

247

Thus to this Ben Nevis, presumably by reason of its being near the Cove of the Black Goddess, there clings a legend that it is the habitation of Beira or Cailleach Bheur, "a daughter of Jack Frost". She has one eye on the flat of her forehead like a Cyclops, her face is blue-black and her hair like frost-encrusted leafless twigs. She was imagined to be an evil-natured goddess whose duty was to prevent the grass growing and keep the world desolate and vexed by tempest, an abomination to farmers and fishermen, and in her wandering she appeared riding on dark storm clouds referred to as black boars or wolves. Hence the taboos associated with such creatures, so that all the streams which had their sources at Inbhir Lochaidh (or Fort William) or in its vicinity were called "Abhainn Lochaidh" or River Lochy or Lochay (the River of the Black Goddess).

Rivers called "Lochy" are three: one has its source near Fort William and flows into Loch Lochy; the next River Lochy has its source near Tyndrum and, running through Glen Lochy and joining with the River Orchy, finally flows into Loch Awe; and another River Lochay runs through Glen Lochay from west to east and into Loch Tay.

The Gaelic ending "-aidh" represents "goddess", and it is a manifestation of Celtic animism that they deified rivers and lochs. The nomenclature is quite similar to that of the Gauls giving "-ona" to the names of their rivers like Matrona (Mother Goddess), Nemetona (Wood Goddess), Divona (Fountain Goddess), and Ritona (Ford Goddess). The Celts were fond of finding a soul in the water of rivers and lochs and creating a deity or a monster in association with its colour, sound and characteristic phenomenon.

To the south-west of Inverness is Loch Ness where the water of the River Lochy flows in through the Caledonian Canal after collecting the waters of Loch Lochy and Loch Oich. A never-freezing loch devoid of islands, Loch Ness's total length is 23 miles with a width of from a mile to a mile-and-a-half and a depth of 226 metres at its deepest. Its enormous depth has given it a dark and murky appearance through discolouration by peat and it is supposedly the den of "Nessy". The name "Ness" derives from "ned-ta", now obsolete, or "neidiad" in Old P-Celtic to mean "roaring one" or "rushing one." However, it is also thought to be the Anglicised diminutive of "nathair" in Gaelic and Old Irish, "neidyr" in Old P-Celtic and "natrix" in Latin, all meaning "water-snake."

Stories about large serpents are not unusual in Scotland. There is, for example, the story that a huge serpent destroyed a whole fleet of shipping, or the one which tells that when a bed made in the earth by one of these huge serpents was pointed out, the size of the monster could not have been less than fifty feet long with a chest like a puncheon. [75]

The problem is the original reason for the name "Ness" but it was Adamnan (625 – 704 A.D.) who wrote about the Monster "Nessy" for the first time. He was the tenth abbot of Iona and bibliographer of St Columba, though if what Adamnan described is the same creature as that rumoured in recent years, Nessy will be over fourteen hundred years old!

According to Adamnan, the earliest witnesses of Nessy were St Columba and his disciples who were on their way to King Brude Mac Maelcon in Inverness in 565 A.D. He writes that St Columba witnessed the burial of a man after the monster had caught him in its mouth but had not devoured him. The saint was undeterred by this and wished to cross the water but, unfortunately, his boat was on the far side of the loch and so he, rather intelligently, ordered one of his companions, Lunge Mocumin, to swim over for it. This was done and when the monster duly appeared in pursuit, the saint rebuked it. [76]

295

Photograph (295) shows the water of Loch Lochy, or Loch of the Black Goddess.

Ian Finlay, the author of *Columba*, writes that [77] the aquatic monster story is inevitable in any collection of Celtic legends because most streams and lakes were credited with denizens of this sort, and James Watson, the author of *A History of the Celtic Place-names in Scotland*, writes that such instances of our own time help us to realize, or at least to imagine more or less dimly, the state of matters in early times and its effects on the people. It is not too much to say that a feeling of divinity pervades and colours the whole system of our ancient stream nomenclatures. [78]

The principal rivers in Scotland, the Dee, the Don, the Doon, the Tay, the Forth, the Clyde and the Tweed, have names derived from a good deity or benevolence. The River Dee (90 miles) which flows

301

Photograph (301) shows Loch Morar.

302

Photograph (302) shows Loch Sgamhain, the "white horses" of which never cease to be raised up by the wind blowing through Glen Carron.

Chapter XI

The Other World and the Outlook on Reincarnation of the Celtic People

A Druidic belief which struck the classical authors of Greece and Rome was the concept of immortality amongst the Celtic peoples. Posidonius, the Greek Stoic philosopher of the early first century B.C., and the Roman Julius Caesar both remarked upon the outlook on the afterlife of the Celts and their faith that the souls of men are immortal and their souls live on in an after-life, passing to other bodies after a definite number of years. Strabo (?63 B.C. – ? 24 A.D.), a Greek geographer, in line with other authorities, comprehending this belief as a form of Druidical doctrine, remarks on it as a faith in which men's souls and the universe are indestructible, although at times fire and water may prevail. Mela Pomponius, a Latin geographer of the first century A.D., mentions it as the best-known dogma of the Druids where souls are eternal and there is another life in the infernal regions. He says that the Celts beatified the act of death and this is the explanation for their seemingly pointless bravery in war which Caesar also mentions. [83]

In a land situated in a northern cold region, where food is hard to yield without the assistance of gods and goddesses, where people are forced to acknowledge poverty and the stern realities of life, it is easy to encourage people's resignation to their fate, denial of and escape from this world, and desire for a new world, that is, the "other world." The Celtic belief in transmigration is extraordinarily primitive and animistic: an innate soul is believed to pass into not only natural phenomena but also things animate and inanimate. The Pictish, who had repeated racial mixture with the Celts from the beginning of the Iron Age, are held to have had a faith similar to the Celts who were devotees of this belief in the immortality and the animistic transmigration of the soul.

Procopius, the Byzantine historian (b.527 A.D.), roughly contemporary with St Columba, writes of the Northern Gauls' belief in the "Happy Isle" to which the souls of the dead were carried: [84] "There are jewels and gold in abundance, and honey and wine. The trees bear fruits and blossoms and green leaves all the year round. There are fine swords and rich robes, steeds and hounds, countless herds, maidens without number, and above all, there is neither decline nor death nor decay."

This is the equivalent of the Britons' "Lyonesse", the Caledonians' "Schiehallion", and the Gaelic "Tir nan Og", where the life of a day is said to be equal to that of one hundred years on earth. It also corresponds to Paradise or the Celestial World of the six reincarnation cycles in Buddhism, [85] and to the Arthurians' Avallon or Avilion which is, in Tennyson's words, an island-valley,

> "Where falls not hail, or rain, or any snow,
> Nor ever wind blows loudly; but it lies
> Deep-meadowed, happy, fair with orchard lawns,
> And bowery hollows crowned with summer sea."

However, this cauldron of rebirth in the time of the Druidical Age is actually under the earth on slightly elevated mounds or knolls. It is often found together with a yew tree, as the name "Tom na h-Iubhraich" (the Knoll of the Yew Tree) shows, though nowadays, through a long period of cult practice, it is a synonym for a Christian cemetery or graveyard, far removed from the original. The yew is a tree symbolizing the winter solstice, the last day of the last month of the year or "Doomsday" when all creation stops its activities, represented by "i" the initial letter of "Iodh" (yew) in the Druidic Alphabet (see pp46-7).

In the cemetery of Fortingall Parish Church near Schiehallion there survives a yew-tree over three thousand years old and it shows that this cauldron of rebirth originated in the Druidical Age in the Iron Age.

A cemetery or a knoll is also a "Womb of Earth" and the yew-tree is the Father of Earth which the dead need for their rebirth as with the stone phallus in the days of the Neolithic and Bronze Ages.

As Tom na h-Iubhraich is a place to which the souls of the dead are transferred by ship, its approach is often close to the water's edge of a stream or a well. The site of King Duncan's Well in Kingsmills in Inverness is the place where, it is supposed, though with no convincing proof, the body of King Duncan was purified and buried somewhere nearby. His body was afterwards transferred to St Oran's graveyard (Relig Odhran) in the Isle of Iona (see p223) which is located off the coast to the south-west of Inverness.

Schiehallion is located near Loch Tummel or Teimheil (Loch of Darkness) at the western end of the ancient Caledonian territory, and the Well of the Dead (or Tobar nam Marbh) was also necessarily associated with ancient battlefields.

303

*Photograph (303) shows Schiehallion or the Sith of the
Caledonians. "Sith" means the dwelling of fairies or
supernatural beings. As in Wales "Snowdon" is "The
Tomb" (Yr Wyddfa <Gwyddfa), so "Sith" served as a
Tomb for the Caledonians.*

304

*Photograph (304) shows Tom na h-Iubhraich in Inverness, to which is
attached a verse showing envy of Thomas the Rhymer's personal relation with
the Queen of Fairyland:*

> *"Nar thigidh sluagh Tom na h-Iubhraich.*
> *Co dh' rireadh air tus ach Tomas ?"*

> *"When the folk of Tomnahurich come forth.*
> *Who will be first but Thomas ?" [86]*

Tom na h-Iubraich has the other meaning of "The Knoll of the Stately Lady."

305

Photographs (305) and (306) show Fortingall Parish Church (near which there was Dun Geal, Finn MacCool's citadel), and the yew-tree, the age of which is over three thousand years.

306

307

Photograph (307) shows the Well of the Dead in Culloden Battlefield where sleep nearly five thousand clansmen of thirty-three Highland clans who were killed in action with the Hanoverians in the dawn of April 16th 1746.

How did reincarnation take place and what was the mode of
community of Tom na h-Iubraich? In Celtic society, men and women -
especially many heroes and heroines - were named from their
association with animals, fish and birds. Cu Chulainn was "The Hound
of Culann", Oisin "Little Deer", Oscar "Deer-Love," MacCon "Son of
Wolfdog", Bran "Crow," and so on. Some heroes had a close affinity
with a particular species of animal, bird or fish so that they were not
permitted to kill or eat their flesh. This is totemism. Cu Chulainn was
forbidden to eat dog, and Conaire to kill birds which were dear to him
because of his father. Finn was forbidden to eat salmon and, tasting of
the salmon of knowledge as a youth, was eventually slain by a fishing-
gaff.

In the case of Diamid it was a pig or a boar that he was forbidden
to kill. Finn's dogs began to fight and Diamid's foster-brother, seeking
refuge between the knees of Diamid's father, was crushed to death.
The father of the foster-brother transformed the corpse into a crop-
eared pig and put a spell over it to give it the same life-span as Diamid.
The latter met it by chance in a boar hunt in which he killed this pig
and was himself mortally wounded by it.

The Celts were animists and totemists who loved and respected
certain animals as their ancestors. In his *Book of Taliesin* written in
the sixth century, Taliesin, who was a Welsh bard and panegyrist of
Urbgen or Urien Map Cirmac (see p187), the Welsh hero, left many
passages of poems connected with Celtic reincarnation, together with
a series of songs praising Urien for his victories. The manuscript is
from the thirteenth century and he writes,

> "I have been teacher to all Christendom,
> I shall be on the surface of the earth until Doom,
> And it is not known what my body is, whether flesh or
> fish." [87]

He claims, in other poems about the pilgrimage of his own soul,
that he had witnessed the Fall of Lucifer, the Flood, and the Birth and
Crucifixion of Christ, while in other poems he says he was created by
Gwydion, [88] but he was in the Court of Don [89] before Gwydion
was born! In poems beginning with "I have been ..." he says he had
been at times inanimate objects such as stock, axe, chisel, sword,
shield, harp-string, raindrop and foam, while he had been at other
times man, animal, bird, fish and plant life, such as bull, stallion, dog,
cock, salmon, snake, eagle, and grain. [90]

Celtic reincarnation is grand and magnificent. The spirit wanders,
comes now here, now there and occupies whatever frame it pleases. It
passes from beasts, fish, birds and inanimate objects to other bodies
at will and it never perishes, though it seems that the cause and effect

of the reincarnation are due to conduct in the former life and to choice. If it were an essence of Celtic belief, the set-up of the community of Tom na h-Iubhraich must be thought to be the very world where those from a past creation undergo a kaleidoscopic reincarnation.

In folktales the residents of Tom na h-Iubhraich are as a rule about four feet high and usually wear a green or grey attire with red-peaked caps. There are silver spangles on the gown of a woman of high rank while a lonely fairy "Gunna" wears only a small fox's skin and the great majority of the fairy folk have golden hair and blue eyes. Knoll fairies are mainly female and behave like the Nereids in Greek legend which moved about in whirlwinds. The "Banshee" always washes, at a ford, the death-clothes of one about to die, singing a melancholy song, while "Bodachan Sabhaill" or "The Little Old Man of the Barn" is a household brownie which helps elderly folk by threshing corn during the night. This is the sum of the residents of Tom na h-Iubhraich. However, each of them is a transformation of someone or something in a former life, together with the swords, shields, hounds, trees, axes and so on which there existed.

Thomas the Rhymer was a legendary man who lived with the Queen of Fairyland in Tom na h-Iubhraich in Eildon Mid Hill (Yr Ucheltwyn, high or noble hillock in P-Celtic) and was granted the powers of a Druidic seer by the Queen. It is the way of the mythological world that, if anyone or anything has once entered Tom na h-Iubhraich, he or it cannot leave until the promised day, except in the case of a man or creature of extra-special talents such as Thomas. Thus Thomas came out one day and, meeting two Strathspey fiddlers who were performing in the streets of Inverness, decided to invite them to Tom na h-Iubhraich, intending to provide music for the ball. The fiddlers made merry in a brilliantly-lit hall below it, but next morning when they awoke they came to realize that they had stayed there for a hundred years, not a single night.

With the peculiarity that one hundred years in the secular world is equal to one single day in Fairyland, most of the legends and folklore of this kind follow a similar and customary plot, just as seen in Rip Van Winkle's experience in *The Sketch Book of Geoffrey Crayon* by W. Irving (1783-1859). However, belief in the after-life was suddenly enhanced with the publication in 1775 of the *Poems of Ossian* by J. MacPherson (1736-96) in which was narrated the story that Ossian, an Irish warrior and bard, the son of Finn MacCool and Saidh whose totem was a doe, was bewitched by the Sea Goddess Niamh and went across to Tir nan Og with her. The enhancement of the belief was also encouraged by the staging of "Tannhauser" in 1845 by W. R. Wagner (1813-83) and "Orfeo ed Euridice" in 1762 by C. W. Gluck (1714-87) in which Orpheus, a master-hand of the harp and founder of "Orphism," a Greek cult of the immortality and transmigration of the soul, mourns the death of his wife Euridice and tries to go to the Shades to take her back.

In Scotland there is another kind of world for the after-life. It is mostly located in caves by the sea-shore and is for sea-warriors incarnated into the form of giants. There is a cave called "Fingall's Cave" in the Isle of Staffa, to the north of the isle of Iona, which bewitched and compelled F. Mendelssohn (1809-47) to complete his "Hebrides Overture" or "Fingall's Cave" in 1830, though there is also an amusing explanation that what bewitched him was not the melodious echo-sounding of the waves in the cave but the call of haggis living there! [91] The original Gaelic name of the cave is *An Uamh Bhinn*, or Melodious Cave. However, it has the name of "Fingall's Cave" because it is imagined that the Fingall, the clan of Finn MacCool, father of Ossian, and Gaelicized Norsemen, are sleeping there as metamorphosed giants, having not yet completed their rebirth.

The world for the after-life is, then, Tom na h-Iubhraich, likening a cave to a womb for the next world, and similar ones are Smith Rock in Skye, the locality of which is not certain; Cragiehowe Cave near the Cloutie Well in Munlochy in the Black Isle; Drooping Cave in Cromarty; and so on. Dunvegan Castle, the seat of Clan MacLeod in Skye, was originally similar, as Dr Johnson writes that [92] the house was accessible only from the water until the last owner opened an entrance by stairs upon the land.

These caves have similar legends with similar plots [93] and this is just one story, the legend of the cave of Craigiehowe in the Black Isle. Someone, finding the key of the rock-door of the cave, opens the door and enters the cave. He notices that a horn is suspended from the roof and gigantic warriors and hounds lie on the floor. He blows a blast on the horn and the sleepers shake themselves and try to rise on their elbows, opening their eyes. The invader blows a second blast and they rise to their feet. Greatly terrified by the appearance of giants, he tries to turn and escape and then the giants call out in anguish, "Dhuine dhon a dholaich, 's miosa dh' fhag na fhuair," or "Evil", or "Grief-causing man, you have left us worse than you found us." In the legend it requires someone to blow a horn or wooden crier three times to make the sleepers rise up alive and well as they formerly were.

308

Photograph (308) shows the Eildon Hills. On top of the North Hill (the right one) is an oppidum of the Selgovae in the Iron Age and on the south-west flank of the top of Mid Hill is a Bronze Age cairn 15 metres in diameter. To the foot of this hill adheres the legend of Thomas the Rhymer and the Queen of Tom na h-Iubhraich.

THE GENEALOGY OF THE PICTISH HIGH KINGS

The names are those which A. B. Scott records in pp 212-22, 229, 329 and 437 in his book *The Pictish Nation, Its People and Its Church* (PIN) as quotations from M.M. REEVES (1856-91).

The figures in parentheses show the years that each high king was on the throne.

The names with an * are those taken from the St. Andrews MS. The others all derive from The Irish Annals.

Talorg Keother (*? 396-413 A.D.)
Drust Mac Erp (413-53)
Talorg Mac Aniel (453-56)
Nechtan Mac Erp (456-80)
Drust Gernot (* 480-510)
Galan Arilith (* 510-22)
Drust Mac Gyrom (522-32)
Drust Mac Udrost (522-27, co-sovereign with Drust Mac Gyrom)
Gartnaidh Mac Gyrom (532-39)
Celtan Mac Gyrom (539-40)
Talorg Mac Muircholaidh (540-51)
Talorg Mac Munaidh (551-52)
Galan or Cenalph (552-53)
Brude Mac Maelcon (553-84)
Gartnaidh Mac Domneth (584-99)
Nechtan Mac Canonn (599-621)
Ciniath Mac Luthrenn (621-31)
Gartnaidh Mac Wid (631-35)
Brude Mac Wid (635-41)
Talorg Mac Wid (641-53)
Talorgan Mac Enfred (653-57)
Gartnaidh Mac Donnel (657-63)
Drust Mac Donnel (663-72)
Brude Mac Bile (672-93)
Taran Mac Entifidich (693-97)
Brude Mac Derelei (697-706)
Nechtan Mac Derelei (706-29)
Angus I Mac Fergus (729-61)
Brude Mac Fergus (761-63)
Kenneth Mac Feredach, or Ciniod Mac Wredech (763-75)
Alpin Mac Fereda, or Elpin Mac Wroid (775-80)
Drest Mac Talorgen (780-83)
Talorgen Mac Angus (783-85)

Conall Mac Taidg (785-90) ⎫
Conall Mac Caeim (785-90) ⎬ Joint High Kings
Constantine I Mac Fergus (790-820)
Angus II Mac Fergus (820-34)
Aedh Mac Boanta (834-36)
Drust Mac Constantine (836-37) ⎫
Talorgan Mac Wthoil   (836-37) ⎬ Joint High Kings
Owen, or Uven Mac Angus (836-39, co-sovereign with Talorgan Mac
    Wthoil until 837)
Ferat Mac Bargoit (839-41)
Brude Mac Ferat (839-42, co-sovereign with Ferat Mac Bargoit until
    841)

THE GENEALOGY OF THE DALRIADIC KINGS

The letters in parentheses show the family branch. FF means the Fergus Family, FG the Gabhran of the Fergus, FC the Comgal of the Fergus, LB the Baedan of the Lorn. The figures in parentheses show the years that each king was on the throne.

Additional notes.

Fergus Mac Erc (498 or 500-501 A.D.) (FF)
Domongart Mac Fergus (501-6) (FF)
Comgal Mac Domongart (506-38) (FC)
Gabhran Mac Domongart (538-60) (FG)
Conail Mac Comgal (560-74) (FC)
Aedhan Mac Gabhran (574-606) (FG)
Eochadh Buidhe Mac Aedhan (606-22)(FG)
Ferchar Mac Conaig (Mac Aedhan) (622-38)(FG)
Conadh Cerr Mac Eochadh Buidhe (629 #1)(FG)
Domnal Brec Mac Eochadh Buidhe (629-42 #2)(FG)
Duncan Mac Conaig (642-48 #3)(FG)
Conail Crandamna Mac Eochadh Buidhe (642-48 #4) (FG)
Domnall Donn Mac Crandamna (648-60)(FG)
Mailduin Mac Crandamna (660-76)(FG)
Ferchar Fada Mac Feradaich (676-97)(LB)
Eochadh Rianamhail, grandson of Domnal Brec (694-96 #5)(FG)
Ainbhceallach Mac Ferchar Fada (697-98)(LB)
Selbach Mac Ferchar Fada (698-723)(LB)
Dungal Mac Selbach (723-26)(LB)
Ewen Mac Ferchar Fada (726-42)(LB)
Eochaidh Mac Eachach (726-33 #6)(FG)
Elpin Mac Eachach (733-37 #7)(FG)
Muredach Mac Ainbhceallach (737-45 #8)(LB)
Ewen Mac Muredach (745-48)(LB)
Aeda Find Mac Eachadh (748-78)(FG)
Fergus Mac Aeda Find (778-81)(FG)
Selbach Mac Ewen (781-95)(LB)
Eachach Mac Aeda Find (795-825)(FG)
Dungal Mac Selbach (825-32)(LB)
Alpin Mac Eachach (832-34)(FG)
Kenneth Mac Alpin (834-43#9)(FG)

#1. Conadh Cerr was co-sovereign with Ferchar Mac Conaig for a few months in the year of 629 A.D.

#2. Domnal Brec was on the throne with Ferchar until 638 A.D. after Conadh Cerr died.

#3. Duncan Mac Conaig served as co-sovereign with Domnal Brec from 638 A.D., when Ferchar died, to 642 A.D. when Domnal Brec died.

#4. Conail Crandamna was on the throne with Duncan Mac Conaig after the death of Domnal Brec.

#5. Eochadh Rianamhail served as co-sovereign with Ferchar Fada until 696 A.D. when he himself died.

#6. Eochaidh Mac Eachach was on the throne with Ewen Mac Ferchar Fada from 726 A.D. to 733 A.D.

#7. Elpin Mac Eachach was on the throne with Ewen Mac Ferchar Fada from 733 A.D. to 737 A.D.

#8. Muredach Mac Ainbhceallach was on the throne with Ewen Mac Ferchar Fada until 742 A.D. when Ewen died.

#9. From 843 to 859 A.D. Kenneth reigned as King of the United Realm of Picts and Scots, Rex Pictorum (see pp196-7).

THE GENEALOGY OF THE KENNETH MAC ALPIN DYNASTY (REX PICTORUM)

Kenneth Mac Alpin (843-59 A.D.)
Donald I (859-63)
Constantine I Mac Kenneth (863-77)
Aedh (877-78)
Eocha (878-89). Cyric (878-896) was probably the virtual ruler as nominal tutor.
Donald II Mac Constantine (889-900). Cyric served as tutor until 896.

THE GENEALOGY OF THE ALBAN KINGDOM

The letter in parentheses indicates the family branch each king came from. (C) means the Constantine family; (A) the Aedh family.

Donald Mac Constantine I (889-900 A.D.)(C)
Constantine II Mac Aedh (900-43)(A)
Malcolm I Mac Donald (943-54)(C)
Indulf Mac Constantine II (954-62)(A)
Dubh Mac Malcolm (962-67)(C)
Cuilean Mac Indulf (967-71)(A)
Kenneth II Mac Malcolm I (971-95)(C)
Constantine III Mac Cuilean (995-97) (A), the last king of the Aedh.
Kenneth III, the Grim, Mac Dubh (997-1005)(C)
Malcolm II Mac Kenneth II (1005-34)(C)

In 1034 Duncan Mac Crinan (1034-40) ascended the throne and the United Kingdom of Scotland was effected. On his death in 1040 A.D. Maelbaethe or Macbeth, the son of Finlaic, succeeded him.

REFERENCE BOOKS

Abbreviated capitals are used to indicate the source of quotation to which notes refer.

AMA: McLellan, R. : Ancient Monuments of Arran. Her Majesty's Stationery Office, Edinburgh, 1977.

ARG: The Royal Commission on the Ancient and Historical Monuments of Scotland, Argyll, Vol 5. Islay, Jura, Colonsay & Oronsay, 1984.

ASC: Savage, A. : The Anglo-Saxon Chronicles, translated and collated by A. Savage. London, Macmillan, 1982.

ASD: Rosworth & Toller : An Anglo-Saxon Dictionary. Oxford University, 1980.

BFC: Hole, C. : British Folk Customs. Hutchinson & Co. Ltd., 1976.

BFG: Caesar, Julius : The Battle for Gaul, translated by A. B. Wiseman. London, Chatto & Windus, 1980.

BLI: Marshall, E. : The Black Isle. Ross-shire Printing and Publishing Co. Ltd.

BOH: Menzies, J. : The Book of the Highlands, published for the Inverness Board of Advertising. J. Menzies & Co. Ltd., Glasgow, 1936.

CAT: MacDonald, M. : Crinan and Tayvallich. Printed by Oban Times Ltd., 1986.

CCS: Simson, W. D. : The Celtic Church in Scotland. Aberdeen University Press, 1935.

CEH: Rees, A. & B. : Celtic Heritage. Thames & Hudson, London, 1978.

CHS: Points, G. A. : A Concise Guide to Historic Shetland. Shetland Tourist Organisation, 1984.

COL: Finlay, I. : Columba. Victor Gollancz Ltd., London, 1979.

CPS: Watson, W. J. : The History of the Celtic Place-Names of Scotland. William Blackwood & Sons Ltd., 1926.

DKB: Dunkeld & Birnam. A pamphlet published by Dunkeld and Birnam Tourist Association, Perth.

DRD: Piggot, S. : The Druids. Penguin Books, 1968.

DSI: Vries, A.D. : Dictionary of Symbols and Imagery. North-Holland Publishing Co. Ltd., 1974.

EAG: Shepherd, I. & Ralston, I. : Early Grampian. A guide to the Archaeology. Grampian Regional Council, 1985.

ECC: Stevenson, J. B. : The Clyde Estuary and Central Region, Exploring Scotland's Heritage. Her Majesty's Stationery Office, Edinburgh, 1986.

EDG: Stell, G. : Dumfries & Galloway. Exploring Scotland's Heritage. Her Majesty's Stationery Office, Edinburgh, 1986.

EGR: Shepherd, I. A. G. : Grampian, Exploring Scotland's Heritage. Her Majesty's Stationery Office, Edinburgh, 1986.

EIS: Magnusson, M. : Echoes in Stone. Ancient Monuments Division, Scottish Development Department, 1983.

FTH: Smith, G. I. : Folk Tales of the Highlands. Lang Syne Publishers Ltd., 1977.

GLB: Frazer, J. G. : The Golden Bough. The MacMillan Press Ltd., 1990.

GPS: Ferchem, R. : Guide to Prehistoric Scotland. B.T. Batsford Ltd., 1977.

GRB: Green, M. J. : The Gods of Roman Britain. Shire Archaeology Publication Ltd., Buckinghamshire, 1983.

HAG: MacLean, G. : The Haggis. Gartocham, Famedram Publishers Ltd., 1986.

HGS: Mitchell, D. : A Popular History of the Highlands and Gaelic Scotland. Alexander Gardner, Paisley, 1900.

HIK: MacDonald, M. : Historic Kintyre. Printed by Oban Times Ltd., 1986.

HMN: Grimble, I. : Highland Man. Highlands and Islands Development Board, 1980.

HOD: McDowall, W. : A History of the Burgh of Dumfries. Penwell Ltd., Cornwall, 1986.

HPC: MacKay, A. : A History of the Province of Cat. Peter Reid & Co Ltd., Wick, 1914.

HSC: Lang, A. : A History of Scotland. William Blackwood and Sons, Edinburgh and London, MDCCCC (1900).

HSD: Mackie, J. D. : A History of Scotland. Penguin Books, 1964.

IEM: Cavendish, R. : An Illustrated Encyclopaedia of Mythology. Crescent Books, New York, 1984.

IOA: Iona Abbey. A Pamphlet Typeset & Printed in the University of Strathclyde.

IOI: Gore, C. : The Isle of Iona. Finlay Ross Ltd., 1976.

IRE: Ranelach, J. : Ireland. An Illustrated History. Collins, London, 1981.

ISL: Newton, N. S. : Islay. Davis & Charles, London, 1988.

JWI: Johnson, S. A. : A Journey to the Western Islands of Scotland. Oxford University Press, 1984.

KIS: Holiday in Kinross-shire. A Pamphlet published by the Tourist Office, Kinross Service Area.

LRS: Lochs and Rivers of Scotland. Huntingdon, Cambridgeshire, Colourmaster Publication, 1975.

MFS: Jobes, G. : Dictionary of Mythology, Folklore and Symbols. Scarecrow Press Inc., New York, 1962.

OAS: Laing, L. : Orkney and Shetland. An Archaeological Guide. David and Charles, London, 1974.

PGD: McAlpine, N : A Pronouncing Gaelic Dictionary. John Grant, Edinburgh, 1898.

NOTES

Ref. No.   p.

Preface

1   vi   The genealogy of the Canmore Dynasty continues as follows:
Malcolm III (1057-1093), son of Duncan; Donald Bane (1093-1094) son of Duncan; Duncan II (1094), son of Thorfinn the Mighty and Ingibjorg (the first wife of Malcolm III); Donald Bane re-enthroned (1094-1097); Edgar (1097-1107 (?)) son of Malcolm III and Margaret, the second wife of Malcolm III, who was the grand-daughter of Edward Ironside and a sister of Edward Athel; Alexander I (1107(?)-1124), son of Malcolm III and Margaret; David I (1124-1153), son of Malcolm III and Margaret; Malcolm IV (1153-1165), son of Malcolm III and Margaret; Malcolm IV (1153-1165), son of David's son, Henry; William I (William the Lion) (1165-1214), son of David's son Henry; Alexander II (1214-1249), son of William I; Alexander III (1249-1286), son of Alexander II.

I.   Chambered Cairns, Antiquities of the Neolithic Age

2   2   Since its origination there have been twenty-five emperors.

3   3   Cf.   WHG, p 213.

4   10   Cf.   GLB, xxxviii.

5   21   Cf.   HMN, p 90.

II.   Monuments in the Bronze Age

6   40   Cf.   CPS, p 261.

7   46   Cf.   BFG, VI, 18.

8   47   Cf.   MFS, Part I, p76.

9   47   Cf.   GLB, Lxii, 6.

wine of the burn of the Annat, its taste was of honey to drink it.)

42	171	Cf.	CPS, p 275.
43	172	Cf.	PIN p 8. Cantyre with its colony of Gaidheals or Scots was at that time within the lordship of Mac Maelcon because in 560 A.D. this sovereign had expelled many of the encroaching Gaidheals from South Argyll, had shut up the remnants in Cantyre and, after slaying their righ or king Gabhran in battle, had left the new chief with the title of a mere tributary, a "toiseach" or military magistrate.
44	172		A saint who came from Ireland to visit Dalriada and Pictland and in 563 A.D., along with St Cannech Achodh Bo, sponsored St Columba on the occasion of his famous interview with King Brude Mac Maelchon at Inverness.- CCS p 78.
45	172		CPS, p 166. Cormac Ua Liathain, abbot of Durrow, styled "Cormac Leir," (or Industrious or Devout).
46	172	Cf.	OAS, p 113.
47	174		CPS, p 337. Mol-Luag and Curitan of Rosemarkie are both commemorated between the Dee and the Spey as well as in Ross and Inverness-shire.
48	176	Cf.	PIN, pp 322-25.
49	178	Cf.	CCS, p 112.
50	182	Cf.	CPS, pp 171-72.
51	182		PIN, p 415. The legend in the Colbertine MS. In the amplified legend of the Harleian MS., this is explained as " ad ostium fluminis Tyne" (near Tynemouth).
52	183	Cf.	CPS, p 172.
53	189	Cf.	PIN, p 177.
54	190	Cf.	CPS, p 156.
55	196		Old English lyric, the earliest dream poem and one of the finest religious poems in the runic script preceding the English language. The complete version became known with the

discovery of the 10th century *Vercelli Book* in northern Italy in 1822.

56	198	Cf.	HGS, p 148.
57	202	Cf.	HSC, p 45.
58	203	Cf.	HSC, p 48.
59	207	Cf.	HGS, p 164.
60	210	Cf.	HGS, p 167.
61	210	Cf.	HGS, p 167.

VII. Pictish Symbol Stones

62	219	Cf.	BOH, p 89.
63	220	Cf.	COL, p 20.
64	220	Cf.	COL, p 183.
65	226		In Gaelic it is called "Tobar a' Chlaidheimh duibh an Eirinn, 's i air aghaid na greine an port an Druidh" or "Well of the black sword of Erin, facing the sun in the Druid's port."

VIII. Paganism surviving in Scotland

66	237	Cf.	GLB, pp 617-18, The Beltane Fires.
67	239	Cf.	SIB, pp 113-14.
68	241	Cf.	DRD, pp 98-99. The Druids in Classical and Vernacular Texts.
69	241	Cf.	COL, p 57.
70	245	Cf.	CPS, p 436

IX. The Outlook of Direction and Colour

71	247	Cf.	BOH, p 94.
72	248	Cf.	IRE, p 22
73	250	Cf.	SCS, p 32. Superstitious Customs at Fodderty.

X. Monstrous Beings in Lochs and Rivers

74	251	Cf.	Inverness Gaelic Society Transactions, vol. xxxvi, p 463.
75	252	Cf.	PGD, p 189
76	253	Cf.	LRS, p 9.
77	253	Cf.	COL, p 128.

78	253	Cf.	CPS, pp 426-27.
79	255	Cf.	CPS, p 426.
80	255	Cf.	CPS, p 426.
81	255	Cf.	CPS, p 427.
82	256	Cf.	CPS, pp 427, 463. Peallaidh may be from pelldae, formed from pell (a hide), with reference to the shaggy coat of hair with which the uruisg was covered.

XI.   The Other World and the Outlook on Reincarnation of the Celtic people

83	259	Cf.	DRD, p 102. The Belief in Immortality.
84	259	Cf.	Col. pp 28-29.
85	260		"Buddhism," the most influencial religion of eastern and central Asia, was founded by Gautama Buddha in India in the fifth century B.C. and introduced into Japan through China and Korea in the sixth century A.D. Its ideal lies in the attainment of nirvana.
86	261		A verse by Mac Codrum, a Uist bard. He reads "Tom" as Thomas the Rhymer and "Iubhraich" as a stately lady and makes fun of Thomas regarding the belongings of the Queen of Fairyland.
87	263	Cf.	CEH, p 230.
88	263		In Cymric mythology, son of Don, brother of Amaethon, Gilvaethwy and Govannon.
89	263		A Britonic sky goddess, mother of one of the families of the gods of heaven, life and light, who were in constant conflict with the tribe of Llyr, those of the sea, darkness and death.
90	263	Cf.	CEH, p 230.
91	265		HAG, p 3. One group of "research" workers has put forward the theory that the sounds heard by Mendelssohn on his visit to Fingal's Cave were made by the last remaining aquatic haggis and not the waves of the sea!
92	265	Cf.	JWI, p 61.
93	265	Cf.	STM, p 105.

GLOSSARY OF TERMS

alignment: an arrangement of one or more ancient rows of standing stones.

amphora: an ancient Greek or Roman two-handled narrow-necked jar for oil, wine, etc.

annular: ring-shaped; of or forming a ring.

artiodactyla(e): an even-toed ungulate or placental mammal having hooves with an even number, such as pigs, boars, etc.

azimuth: the angular distance usually measured clockwise from the south point of the horizon in astronomy.

ballista(e): an ancient catapult for hurling stones.

basal: pertaining to or situated at the base.

broch: a circular dry-stone tower large enough to serve as a fortified home. They date from the Iron Age and are found especially in the north and the islands of Scotland.

Candida Casa: (in Latin) a shining or glittering white hut, cottage or cabin.

cineal: offspring; clan.

cinerary: pertaining to ashes; for containing ashes of the dead.

cist: a tomb consisting of a stone chest covered with stone slabs.

cludee: in the early Christian Church, a monk who practised great self-denial and austerities and abstained from worldly comforts and pleasures, especially for religious reasons.

corbel: a bracket, usually of stone or brick.

corbelling: the laying of a stone or brick so that it forms a corbel.

counterscarp: the outer side of the ditch of a fort.

crannog: an ancient Celtic man-made dwelling in a lake or bog, dating from the late Bronze Age to the 16th century A.D.

cromlech: a circle of prehistoric standing stones; no longer technical usage, it means a megalithic chambered tomb or dolmen (see dolmen).

cruciform: shaped like a cross; a geometrical curve, shaped like a cross, that has four similar branches asymptotic to a mutually perpendicular pair of lines.

dolmen: (In British archaeology) a Neolithic stone formation, consisting of a horizontal stone supported by several vertical stones and thought to be a tomb.

dun: (Gaelic) a fort, fortress, a castle or a fortification.

eponym: giving a name to something.

exogamy: the custom or act of marrying a person belonging to another tribe, clan or similar social unit.

hegemony: ascendancy or domination of one power or state within a league, confederation, etc.

henge: a circular area, often containing a circle of stones or wooden posts, dating from the Neolithic and Bronze Ages, a back formation from STONEHENGE.

inhumation: depositing in the ground; burial.

jugulate: in the obsolete sense, to kill by cutting the throat of, < Latin jugulare.

megalith: a stone of great size, especially one forming part of a prehistoric monument.

menhir: a single standing stone, dating from the middle Bronze Age in the British Isles and from the late Neolithic Age in W. Europe.

mesolithic: intermediate between Palaeolithic (of the early Stone Age) and Neolithic (q.v.)

monolith: a large stone block.

neolithic: of the later or more advanced Stone Age.

oppidum: a town (in Latin); a fortified wood in Britain.

palisade: a strong fence made of stakes driven into the ground, especially for defence.

penannular: of or forming an almost complete ring.

perilith: one of a number of surrounding stones , a word compounded from "peri" (surrounding, encircling) and "lith" indicating a stone or rock.

peristalith: a stone circle.

puncheon: a large cask of variable capacity, usually between 70 and 120 gallons.

quatrefoil: a leaf such as that of certain clovers, composed of four leaflets.

quern: a stone hand mill for grinding corn.

scarcement: (Scot.) a ledge formed by the setting back of a wall, buttress, or bank.

souterrain: (in archaeology) an under-ground chamber or passage.

tanistry: a custom or system for choosing the heir apparent to a Celtic chieftain during the chief's lifetime. The chosen heir was usually the worthiest of his kin.

toiseach: a chief of a clan or tribe in Gaelic.

trapezoidal: of or forming a quadrilateral having a pair of parallel sides.

trefoil: (in architecture) an ornament in the form of three arcs, arranged in a circle.

tutelary: a person, deity or saint invested with the role of guardian or guardianship.

uruisg: (in Gaelic) a water sprite.

INDEX

Proper nouns (personal and place names) are listed in alphabetical order only for the convenience of cross-indexing.